RESEARCH IN SPECIAL EDUCATION

ABOUT THE AUTHORS

Phillip D. Rumrill, Jr., Ph.D., is an associate professor and Director of the Center for Disability Studies at Kent State University. Dr. Rumrill received his bachelor's and master's degrees from Keene State College in New Hampshire and his doctorate from the University of Arkansas. His professional work experience includes residential services for people with developmental disabilities, substance abuse counseling, and assistive technology training for college students with disabilities. Dr. Rumrill's research interests include the career development implications of disability, transition services for adolescents with disabilities, and disability issues in higher education. He has authored or co-authored more than 100 professional publications, including books entitled *Employment Issues and Multiple Sclerosis, Research in Rehabilitation Counseling, Emerging Issues in Rehabilitation Counseling,* and *Multiple Sclerosis.* Dr. Rumrill has received awards for his research and program development efforts from such organizations as the National TRIO Foundation, the National Association of Student Personnel Administrators, and the National Multiple Sclerosis Society.

Bryan G. Cook, Ph.D., is an assistant professor of Special Education at Kent State University in Ohio. Dr. Cook received his bachelor's, master's, and doctoral degrees from the University of California, Santa Barbara. His professional work experience includes teaching youths and adolescents with a variety of disabilities in educational and residential settings. Dr. Cook's research interests include policy issues regarding individual differences in education, as well as society at large. He has authored numerous journal articles in the fields of special education and disability studies, and he is a frequent presenter at national and international conferences. In 1999, Dr. Cook received an Initial Career Research Award from the United States Department of Education, Office of Special Education Programs. He also serves as Co-Editor of the Council for Exceptional Children's Division of Research newsletter, *Focus on Research.*

RESEARCH IN SPECIAL EDUCATION

Designs, Methods, and Applications

By

PHILLIP D. RUMRILL, Jr.

and

BRYAN G. COOK

Kent State University
Department of Educational Foundations & Special Services
Center for Disability Studies

Consulting Editor: James L. Bellini

Syracuse University
Department of Counseling and Human Services

Charles C Thomas
PUBLISHER • LTD.
SPRINGFIELD • ILLINOIS • U.S.A.

Published and Distributed Throughout the World by

CHARLES C THOMAS • PUBLISHER, LTD.
2600 South First Street
Springfield, Illinois 62794-9265

ISBN 0-398-07172-1 (cloth)
ISBN 0-398-07173-X (paper)

Library of Congress Catalog Card Number: 00-053666

With THOMAS BOOKS *careful attention is given to all details of manufacturing and design. It is the Publisher's desire to present books that are satisfactory as to their physical qualities and artistic possibilities and appropriate for their particular use.* THOMAS BOOKS *will be true to those laws of quality that assure a good name and good will.*

Printed in the United States of America
CR-R-3

Library of Congress Cataloging-in-Publication Data

Rumrill, Phillip D.
    Research in special education : designs, methods, and applications / by
Phillip D. Rumrill, Jr. and Bryan G. Cook ; consulting editor, James L. Bellini.
        p. cm.
    Includes bibliographical references and index.
    ISBN 0-398-07172-1 (cloth : alk. paper) -- ISBN 0-398-07173-X (pbk. : alk. paper)
    1. Special education--Research--United States--Handbooks, manuals, etc. 2.
Handicapped--Education--Research--United States--Handbooks, manuals, etc.
I. Cook, Bryan G. II. Bellini, James L. III. Title.

LC3981 .R85 2001
371.9'07'2073--dc21

                                                                    00-053666

For Douglas...... PDR

For Lysandra, Zoe, and Benjamin...... BGC

CONTRIBUTORS

JAMES L. BELLINI, PH.D.
Associate Professor & Coordinator
Rehabilitation Counseling Program
Syracuse University
Department of Counseling & Human Services
Syracuse, NY

SHAWN M. FITZGERALD, PH.D.
Assistant Professor
Kent State University
Department of Educational Foundations & Special Services
Kent, OH

MARY L. HENNESSEY, M.ED.
Vocational Specialist
VocWorks, Inc.
Dublin, OH

LYNN C. KOCH, PH.D.
Assistant Professor
Kent State University
Center for Disability Studies
Department of Educational Foundations and Special Services
Kent, OH

CONNIE J. MCREYNOLDS, PH.D.
Assistant Professor
Kent State University
Center for Disability Studies
Department of Educational Foundations and Special Services
Kent, OH

MELODY J. TANKERSLEY, PH.D.
Associate Professor & Coordinator
Special Education Program
Kent State University
Center for Disability Studies
Department of Educational Foundations and Special Services
Kent, OH

MEGEN E. WARE, M.ED.
State of Ohio
Bureau of Vocational Rehabilitation
Akron, OH

JAMES M. WEBB, PH.D.
Associate Professor
Kent State University
Department of Educational Foundations and Special Services
Kent, OH

PREFACE

This book was written as a text and resource guide for graduate-level students, practitioners, and teachers in the fields of special education, disability studies, early intervention, school psychology, and child and family services. The primary purpose of the book is to offer a broad-based examination of the role of scientific inquiry in contemporary special education. Our aim was to provide a comprehensive overview of the philosophical, ethical, methodological, and analytical fundamentals of social science and educational research—as well as to specify aspects of special education research that distinguish it from scientific inquiry in other fields of education and human services. Foremost among these distinctions are the research beneficiaries, i.e. children with disabilities, their parents, and special educators; the availability of federal funds for research and demonstration projects that seek to improve educational outcomes for children with disabilities; and the historical, philosophical, and legislative bases for the profession of special education.

The book is divided into ten chapters. Chapter 1 establishes the theoretical underpinnings of social scientific inquiry; provides a foundation in the philosophical, epistemological, and methodological considerations related to the design and execution of research in general and special education; and discusses the broad purposes of research in special education and disability studies. Chapter 2 addresses issues that are preparatory to designing and evaluating special education research, such as sources of research ideas, translating research ideas into research hypotheses, identifying variables, and sampling issues. Chapter 3 discusses key measurement and statistical concepts used in the quantitative research tradition, including reliability and validity of measurement instruments; the purposes of descriptive, inferential, and non-parametric statistics in analyzing numerical data; and selected methods of statistical analysis. Chapter 4 reviews ethical issues and guidelines for the design, implementation, and reporting of research in special education. Chapter 5 addresses key criteria for evaluating the quality of special education research, drawing valid inferences from results, and generalizing findings from the research sample to the target population.

Chapters 6, 7, and 8 review the wide range of quantitative, qualitative, and integrative approaches to conducting research in special education, and they feature examples of these designs that we drew from the contemporary educational and disability studies literature. Chapter 6 addresses intervention/stimulus, relationship, and descriptive studies in the quantitative paradigm. Chapter 7 discusses qualitative research methods as they apply to special education. Chapter 8 examines and categorizes a variety of synthetic literature reviews according to their purposes. Chapter 9 presents a published research article section by section; annotates the components and composition of a research report; and provides a protocol that students, practitioners, and educators can use to evaluate the technical soundness and scientific merits of published research articles. The final chapter of this text addresses future trends in special education research as they apply to a variety of stakeholders (e.g., administrators, policymakers, educators, researchers, children with disabilities, parents, funding agencies, consumer advocates).

Because this book was written as an introductory text for graduate students and practitioners in special education, we focus much of the information contained herein on the role of the reader as a "professional consumer" of research. In so doing, we not only orient the student or practitioner to the fundamentals of research design, we also introduce him or her to the professional literature in this dynamic field of inquiry. Like the companion text written by James Bellini and Phillip Rumrill, *Research in Rehabilitation Counseling* (Charles C Thomas Publishers, 1999), this book provides the "basics" that one would need to begin conducting a research investigation, but we would encourage that person to supplement this book with coursework in statistics and advanced research design before initiating an empirical study.

Phillip D. Rumrill, Jr.
Bryan G. Cook

ACKNOWLEDGMENTS

We would like to express our sincere gratitude to the people who made this project possible and successful. We begin by thanking our faculty mentors–Dr. Richard Roessler of the University of Arkansas and Dr. Mel Semmel of the University of California at Santa Barbara–who introduced us to research in disability studies and whose work continues to inspire our teaching, research, and writing. We also express our gratitude to the numerous friends and collaborators around the United States who have worked with us on research and writing projects: Dr. Michael Gerber of the University of California at Santa Barbara, Dr. James Bellini of Syracuse University, Ms. Cheryl Reed of the University of Arkansas, Dr. James Mullins of Towson University, Ms. Patricia Brown of the University of Arkansas, Dr. Lynn Koch of Kent State University, Dr. Connie McReynolds of Kent State University, Dr. Charles Palmer of Mississippi State University, Dr. Pamela Luft of Kent State University, Dr. Timothy Landrum of the University of Virginia, Dr. Melody Tankersley of Kent State University, Dr. Brian McMahon of Virginia Commonwealth University, Dr. Robert Fraser of the University of Washington, Dr. Shawn Fitzgerald of Kent State University, Ms. Mary Hennessey of Kent State University, Dr. Dimiter Dimitrov of Kent State University, and Dr. Paul Wehman of Virginia Commonwealth University.

We are indebted to Dr. James Webb of Kent State University for his expert contributions to the chapter on quantitative research designs, to Drs. Lynn Koch and Connie McReynolds of Kent State University for their contributions to the chapter on qualitative research, to Dr. Shawn Fitzgerald of Kent State University for his contributions to the chapter on measurement and statistics, to Dr. Melody Tankersley of Kent State University for her contributions to several chapters, to Dr. Barbara Schirmer of Kent State University for assisting us with the chapter on the future of special education research, to Ms. Megen Ware and Ms. Mary Hennessey of Kent State University for their contributions to several chapters, and to Consulting Editor Dr. James Bellini of Syracuse University for allowing us to draw from his co-authored companion text to this book, *Research in Rehabilitation Counseling* (Charles C

Thomas, 1999). For their editorial and clerical assistance, we thank Ms. Deborah Minton, Ms. Tamara Tabor, Ms. Kristi Shearer, and Mr. David Martin—all of Kent State University.

Last, but certainly not least, we extend our appreciation to Mr. Michael Payne Thomas of Charles C Thomas Publisher for the opportunity to undertake this project. We look forward to many more cooperative writing and publishing endeavors in the years to come.

CONTENTS

RESEARCH IN SPECIAL EDUCATION

Chapter 1

INTRODUCTION TO RESEARCH IN SPECIAL EDUCATION

BRYAN G. COOK

INTRODUCTION

T HE PURPOSE OF THIS CHAPTER is to establish practical and scientific bases for the special education research enterprise. We begin with an introduction to and overview of the field of special education. We then proceed with a discussion of the role that research plays in developing a profession's knowledge base, with special attention given to ways of knowing and the defining properties of scientific inquiry in an applied field such as special education. We conclude by synthesizing our discussions of the field of special education and general scientific principles into a summary examination of the current special education research scene—including the primary goals of special education research, its relevance to practice, and how research findings in our field are disseminated to and used by stakeholders in the education of children with disabilities.

THE PROFESSIONAL PRACTICE OF SPECIAL EDUCATION

Special education is a multifaceted and extensive service delivery system. The Twenty-first Annual Report to Congress (U.S. Department of Education, 2000) documents that, in the 1997 to 1998 school year, 5,598,668 American children with disabilities received special education services. Students in special education range from 0 to 21 years in age and are identified as having learning disabilities, speech and language impairments, behavior disorders, mental retardation, multiple disabilities, orthopedic disabilities, autism, traumatic brain injuries, visual impairments, hearing impairments, and deaf-blindness. Because the characteristics and needs of students with disabilities vary so dramatically, a vast number and array of professionals are needed to attempt to meet the needs of this large and diverse population. As of the 1996 to 1997 school year, 356,216 special education teachers (includes fully certified and uncertified teachers) and 412,270 other individuals—representing job titles including teacher aides, psychologists, speech pathologists, physical therapists, vocational education teachers, and interpreters—were employed in the delivery of special education services (U.S. Department of Education, 2000). Moreover, an almost infinite variety of policies, settings, (e.g., general education classes with and without special education support, resource rooms, separate special education classes in public schools, special schools, institutions, and hospitals), and service delivery techniques are used in hopes of attaining the most appropriate outcomes possible for students with disabilities.

Although large numbers of students with disabilities now attend American public schools, it is important to remember that a history of legislation and court decisions was necessary to provide children with disabilities, especially those with severe disabilities, access to these schools. Historically, the common belief that people with disabilities are not capable of learning kept them out of educational settings. Indeed, the common characteristic of the diverse group of children and youth served in special education is that they do not perform adequately given typical instruction in typical environments (Cook, Tankersley, Cook, & Landrum, 2000, p. 117). However, over the past decades it has been widely recognized that students with disabilities can learn and are entitled to an appropriate education (Hallahan & Kauffman, 2000). Thus, one of the central functions of special education involves the development, identification, and application of theories and services regarding how to best educate these most difficult-to-teach students. Or, as Hallahan and Kauffman (2000) stated, "the single most important goal of special education" is "finding and capitalizing on exceptional students' abilities" (p. 13).

Enacted to provide an appropriate education for students with disabilities, the Individuals with Disabilities Education Act (IDEA, originally the Education for All Handicapped Children Act) mandates that an educational team formulate an Individualized Education Plan (IEP) that stipulates the annual educational goals, objectives, services, and placement for each identified student with a disability. However, there is no guarantee that the individuals comprising a student's IEP team (e.g., general and special education teachers, specialists such as speech therapists, school administrators, and parents) will decide on goals, services, and placements that will produce optimal outcomes for the student about whom they are concerned. Further, IEPs serve only as a loose guide for day-to-day student-teacher interactions. Teachers are largely free to implement whatever instructional methods they see fit. Thus, the determination of what instruction that students, even the most difficult-to-teach students in special education, receive is largely made by teachers who are trying to do their best, but who often have not received sufficient relevant training and do not have enough time or resources to optimally meet the needs of their large and diverse classrooms of students. It is little wonder that interventions known to be effective are frequently not implemented, whereas some interventions that have been shown to be relatively ineffective are commonly used (Kauffman, 1999).

Reflective of the importance and necessity of developing, identifying, and applying effective educational policies and practices, the Council for Exceptional Children (CEC [the nation's largest advocacy group associated with exceptional students], 1997) lists among its Standards for Professional Practice that, "Professionals strive to identify and use instructional methods and curricula that are ... effective in meeting the individual needs of persons with exceptionalities" (¶1). However, it is seldom an easy process to determine what method is most likely to result in appropriate outcomes for students with disabilities. Indeed, if selecting appropriate and effective teaching methods for students with unique and often problematic learning needs were simple determinations, there would likely be little or no need for special education.

Research is one way—we argue that it is the most reliable and valid way—for determining the relative educational efficacy of a given procedure. In fact, special educators have used research, in one form or another, to determine which policies and practices are most effective since the inception of the field. For example, one of the critical and recurring issues in special education is attempting to determine what educational environment (i.e., inclusive or segregated) results in the best outcomes for students with disabilities. To address this issue, dating back to the 1920s, special education researchers have conducted a series of research studies (known as the efficacy studies) comparing the outcomes of students with disabilities who have been included in general education classes to those of students placed in segregated special education classes (see Semmel, Gottlieb, & Robinson, 1979, for a review of this research). As detailed in the sections and chapters that follow, we hope that this text will enable special education professionals to better use research as a means of bringing about improved outcomes and quality of life for students with disabilities.

WAYS OF KNOWING

Science, which involves making knowledge claims by testing (and confirming or disconfirming) stated hypotheses on the basis of collected data, is one way by which educators come to know what and how to best teach students with disabilities. Although science provides a relatively objective method for "knowing," it is not the preferred method of many policymakers and teachers for making decisions about what happens in special education classrooms. As Landrum and Tankersley (1999) metaphorically noted, many educators prefer "flying by the seat of their pants" (p. 325) to using research findings as the basis for pedagogical judgments. Three of the most prevalent methods that special educators use to make decisions regarding the effectiveness of educational techniques—personal experience, expert testimony, and science (see Landrum, Tankersley, & Cook, 1999)—are reviewed in the following subsections.

Personal Experience

Personal experience involves relying on one's previous experiences or the experiences of others in a similar situation to determine what one thinks or knows to be effective. For example, if a teacher perceives that using a whole language approach resulted in improved reading for one student with a learning disability (LD), she may decide to use whole language techniques for all students with LD whom she has in her class in subsequent years, because she believes that she knows that this method works for these students. Alternatively, if a teacher does not have relevant experience teaching reading to students with LD, she is likely to seek the advice of a fellow teacher in the building who she likes and trusts. If the consulting teacher relates that the whole language approach seemed to help the reading performance of a student with LD in her class last year, the advice-seeking teacher may decide to implement this approach on the basis of her new "knowledge" regarding its effectiveness.

Use of personal experience has many advantages for teachers. First, and most obviously, it is very easy to access this knowledge base. All one has to do is remember his or her past or ask someone else with relevant experience. Similarly, the information provided is likely to be perceived as "usable" (see Carnine, 1995, for a discussion of the accessibility, usability, and trustworthiness of educational information). That is, if teachers themselves or their colleagues have already successfully used a particular technique, it is likely that the information will be easily transferred into practice in their current or own classroom. Also, because the information derived from personal experience comes from sources typically perceived as reliable (i.e., their own memory or from a fellow teacher), it is likely that teachers consider the information to be trustworthy and believe that it will be effective.

However, using personal experience to determine what and how to teach frequently allows students to receive less than optimal instruction. For example, just because an intervention works with one student in one situation does not mean that it will work if implemented for other students in other contexts. Furthermore, individual teachers tend to be imperfect judges as to what really works. If a teacher strongly believes that a particular instructional method is going to work, agrees with the philosophy or theory behind the method, and has devoted a lot of time and energy to implementing the intervention, he or she is likely to evaluate the intervention as more effective than it actually has been. Indeed, popular beliefs derived from interpretations of personal experience and observation (e.g., belief that the earth is the center of the universe) have been disproved throughout history (Kauffman, 1999). Moreover, teachers, as well as other professionals, are generally resistant to change. Therefore, if a particular method is perceived as working "well enough," many teachers may not be willing to implement a different technique even if it is more effective. Simply put, basing our knowledge of what works and making instructional decisions on the basis of personal experience frequently results in the use of relatively ineffective teaching strategies.

Expert Testimony

Sometimes, educators believe that they know a particular instructional practice works because an expert has said or written that it does. The use of expert testimony, or authority, as a way of knowing has certain advantages. In the field of education (like most fields), we have no shortage of experts whose opinions are readily available. An astounding number of textbooks and professional journals are published on a wide variety of topics, and many experts have begun using the internet to disseminate their material. Teachers also attend professional conferences and in-service trainings at which experts present their ideas. Moreover, the college courses that all prospective teachers are required to take to gain licensure are taught by professors typically thought of as experts (especially by the professors themselves). Because the primary purpose of experts disseminating instructional information is for teachers to implement it, much of expert testimony is presented in usable formats that teachers can easily apply in their classroom planning and instructional practices. In addition, because of their status as experts and the training and credentials that most experts have, it is likely that many experts are trustworthy and will advocate for methods that are, in fact, effective more often than not.

However, it is becoming increasingly difficult to tell who is a bona fide and trustworthy expert. An individual who creates a website touting or selling instructional materials and techniques is not necessarily an expert advocating for a truly efficacious intervention. Indeed, special education's history is rife with examples of so-called experts recommending methods that have become popular and widely implemented, only to be proven ineffective when scientifically examined (see Hulme, 1995, for a review of nonstandard treatments used with people with disabilities such as auditory training, dolphin therapy, electric shock therapy, and facilitated communication). Oftentimes, individuals promoting techniques that are not supported by research, or that have even shown to be ineffective by research, hold doctorates and are publicized as leaders in their fields. By virtue of their titles, credentials, and reputations, these so-called experts may garner the trust of many teachers and parents. However, without systematic and objective evaluation of any procedure, we can never be sure that it is effective regardless of the support of those claiming to be experts.

Science

Science refers to "the methodologies of testing disconfirmable hypotheses and proofs through publicly verifiable data" (Kauffman, 1999, p. 265). Science has advanced knowledge and served as a common basis for diverse academic disciplines by using the scientific method in which theories ranging from the way the world works to the way children learn are tested by examining (i.e., observing, recording, and analyzing) observable phenomenon. Inherent in the notion of science is three norms: common ownership of information, cultivated disinterest, and organized skepticism (Bellini & Rumrill, 1999; Merton, 1968).

Common ownership of information means that no one person possesses, in the traditional sense, the data used to investigate hypotheses and theories. There are at least two purposes to common ownership of information. First, it is important that other scientists be able to authenticate or check the findings of any given investigation. Although falsification of data and results is rare, it does occasionally occur. More often, misleading results are due to honest mistakes made in entering and analyzing data. Common ownership of information allows others to verify that the findings of a study are appropriately derived from the data. Second, common ownership of information allows researchers to build on each other's work. Researchers may want to corroborate previous findings to strengthen the knowledge claims associated with the results of their research. In this case, because information about how the research was conducted and who participated in the research is publicly available, it is possible to replicate the study with similar (or different) participants in similar (or different) contexts. Indeed, a great deal of research focuses on expanding the findings of previous research. For example, if a particular intervention has been shown to work with elementary children, another researcher may wish to investigate whether the same intervention is also effective for students in middle or high school. Common ownership of information allows researchers to replicate specific aspects of previous work to investigate whether the implications of earlier findings might be applied to new contexts or populations of individuals. Common ownership of information is typically accomplished through the reporting of research approaches and findings. In the "Method" section of a research article, the author(s) report(s) detailed information on the participants, research design, procedures, and analysis involved in the study (see Chapter 9). Contact information for the primary author of research studies is also provided, so that readers with more in-depth questions about investigations can direct their queries to the author.

Cultivated disinterestedness means that researchers should not have a vested interest in the results of their investigations. If a researcher stands to gain in some way from showing that a certain intervention works, he or she might–consciously or unconsciously–bias aspects of the research, such as the selection of participants or the phrasing of questions directed to participants, thereby influencing the outcomes of the study. The goal of scientific research, to confirm or disconfirm hypotheses through empirical observations, can only be accomplished meaningfully if the investigator(s) conduct(s) the research in a disinterested and objective manner. If the norm of cultivated disinterestedness is not adhered to, the findings from an investigation may be a result of the investigator's biased methods rather than allowing the data to "speak for themselves." Common ownership of information allows the scientific community in a field to investigate whether gross violations of the norm of cultivated disinterestedness occur.

Finally, science involves *organized skepticism*, which means that individual scientists and the larger scientific community should be relatively skeptical when examining new knowledge claims and evaluating the findings and implications of research studies. This is not to say that scientists should never favor new or novel approaches. Instead, the norm of organized skepticism is intended to guard against uncritical acceptance of invalid ideas and methods. This critical approach is especially important in special education, because acceptance of invalid knowledge claims can adversely affect the education and lives of millions of children with disabilities. Common ownership of information should allow the scientific community to rigorously examine the methods used in any particular research study to determine whether the research was conducted without bias (as per the norm of cultivated disinterestedness). In that process, the scientific community skeptically assesses the interpretation of the researcher's findings to ensure that the stated implications of the research are warranted. The skepticism embodied in science is probably best exemplified in the incremental approach of scientists in the generation and expansion of new knowledge. Even when a single study that generates new knowledge claims has been cautiously and rigorously examined, the new claim to knowledge is viewed in the context of other existing findings. Evidence generated from a single study is not, by itself, acceptable as a valid knowledge claim. Acceptance of a new knowledge claim, e.g. that intervention X results in improved reading achievement for students with learning disabilities, by the scientific community requires an accumulation of findings over time. In this way, science does not allow knowledge to be determined by a single study, which is likely to involve some degree of error. Instead, science skeptically guards against putting one's faith in invalid ideas or methods by only accepting knowledge claims that have been supported by numerous investigations–which have, themselves, each been subjected to rigorous, skeptical examination.

The use of science as a way of knowing in special education has potential shortcomings that may help to explain why it is not universally used by practitioners for determining how to most effectively teach. Because of the skeptical nature of science, it is a very slow process that may not give teachers or policymakers immediate answers to their day-to-day problems. In addition, because knowledge claims are the product of an accumulation of research findings over time rather than the result of one particular study, different people can and do interpret the same literature base differently. Many practitioners become frustrated that competing interpretations of the research literature base sometimes occur, thereby resulting in confusion over whether a particular technique actually should be used. Critics of the scientific method have also begun to challenge the notion that researchers are, or can be, disinterested and objective. Indeed, in most research, investigators pose hypotheses or predictions regarding the outcomes of the study. Can someone who has publicly stated his or her beliefs about the results of an investigation be truly disinterested? Another issue is that most practitioners do not have the requisite knowledge of and facility with the principles of research design and analysis to meaningfully examine reports of research findings. Thus, research to many educators is simply another form of expert testimony. Moreover, science never guarantees that a particular method or intervention will be successful all of the time with all people. Science, as applied in special education, primarily involves providing us information on what works more often or more effectively than other techniques, but it cannot predict that any intervention will, without any doubt, be completely successful with any specific student or groups of students.

Despite these limitations, science provides the most reliable, objective, and meaningful manner to determine what works and what to use in special education. As Kauffman (1999) stated, "it [science] is a peerless tool for establishing common knowledge" (p. 266). Without science, special educators are left to make decisions about what practices and policies to implement through their own or others' experiences, the advice of so-called experts, or their own intuition. The use of "good" science, which adheres to the norms of common ownership of information, cultivated disinterestedness, and organized skepticism, is not perfect, but it does lead to a knowledge base that has been objectively verified and is less prone to producing invalid knowledge claims. The existence and use of such a knowledge base is a sign of a mature profession (Kauffman, 1999), one that enables special educators to provide the best possible education for children with disabilities.

RESEARCH AND SPECIAL EDUCATION

Special education is considered, along with other disciplines such as sociology and psychology, to be a social science. In contrast to the hard sciences, such as physics and chemistry, social sciences investigate people and their interactions with one another. One of the interesting and frustrating aspects of conducting and consuming research in the social sciences is that people's motivations for their behaviors are so complex and multifaceted that scientists cannot reasonably hope to fully predict all the behaviors of any individual or group of individuals. Nonetheless, scientific exploration has identified many empirically supported theories that explain a great deal of human behavior and can be used to improve the education of students with and without disabilities.

Research can be thought of as the process of applying science. Researchers in special education actively collect and analyze empirical data regarding how students respond to specific educational interventions, how performance is affected by grouping students in different ways, how students interact under certain conditions, how characteristics of teachers influence student experiences and outcomes, and other issues to expand the professional knowledge base and, in turn, improve practice. Indeed, CEC (1997) views scientific research and its contributions toward improving the instruction of students as so vital to the enterprise of special education that the following is listed among the professional responsibilities of special educators:

> Special education professionals initiate, support, and/or participate in research related to the education of persons with exceptionalities with the aim of improving the quality of educational services, increasing the accountability of programs, and generally benefiting persons with exceptionalities (¶1).

Scientific research has been used as a tool for investigating the efficacy of policies, procedures, and interventions in special education since the inception of the field. The roots of special education can be traced to a scientist, Jean Marc Gaspard Itard, who enacted the principles of scientific research in his attempts to educate the "Wild Boy of Aveyron" in France during the early 1800s (Lane, 1976). Although many questions in special education remain unanswered or partially answered after decades of focused research, researchers have provided direct guidance to special education teachers by showing that certain educational practices are more effective than others for students with disabilities (see Forness, Kavale, Blum, & Lloyd, 1997). Research has at least three related purposes in the field of special education: building the professional literature base, theory-building, and identifying effective practices (Bellini & Rumrill, 1999).

Building Professional Literature Base

The professional literature base of special education exists in an almost innumerable variety of journals, books, and other sources. The existence of a reliable and valid literature base is important so that every teacher does not have to personally investigate the efficacy of every technique that he or she comes across. Instead, by accessing the special education literature base, professionals are able to review previously completed research to determine whether a particular intervention is effective or which intervention is most effective in a given area or with a particular population of students. The importance of producing and accessing research within the context of a larger literature base, rather than focusing on an individual study, is that investigations typically replicate or in some way build on previous research to more thoroughly investigate a practice or policy. The formation of a literature base allows educators to form a more comprehensive perspective that places the findings of one study in the context of numerous related findings. Therefore, the person's practices become less prone to error than when only a single study is reviewed. Although different studies may have competing results, e.g. one study finds a particular intervention to be effective, whereas another study does not, the relative efficacy of a procedure or policy tends to become clearer over time once the professional literature base accumulates a number of high-quality research investigations.

The professional literature base in special education can be accessed through a variety of sources. Some textbooks are devoted to summarizing research in a particular area. For example, Swanson, Hoskyn, and Lee (1999) synthesized and analyzed research conducted on interventions for students with learning disabilities in *Interventions for Students with Learning Disabilities: A Meta-Analysis of Treatment Outcomes.* Research is also reported and synthesized in a variety of monographs and reports. For example, two divisions of CEC–the Division for Learning Disabilities and the Division for Research–have recently cosponsored the publication of a series of "Alerts" that synthesize the research literature on specific instructional techniques such as direct instruction and formative evaluation (see Espin, Shin, & Busch, 2000; Tarver, 1999). The most voluminous portion of the special education research literature base is contained in a variety of professional and academic journals. Although position papers, book reviews, and responses to previously published articles are often included, the reporting of original research is a primary purpose of most professional journals. The scope of journals may be specific to a particular disability, e.g. *Learning Disability Quarterly, Behavioral Disorders, Mental Retardation,* a range of related disabilities, e.g. *Focus on Autism and Other Developmental Disabilities, Journal of the Association for People with Severe Handicaps,* an age range, e.g. *Topics in Early Childhood Special Education, Journal of Early Intervention and Young Exceptional Children,* or teaching in special education, e.g. *Teacher Education and Special Education, Teaching Exceptional Children.* Other journals in our field include issues related to the entire spectrum of topics associated with special education e.g. *Exceptional Children, Exceptionality, Journal of Special Education, Remedial and Special Education.*

Theory Building

Theory building is a critical but often overlooked aspect of research in special education. Theories in the social sciences are ideas about how and why people behave, e.g. learn, perform on tests, interact, act out and feel as they do, which are based on conceptual logic and/or previous observations and research. Theory provides us with the purpose or rationale for conducting research. By cogently applying relevant theory to the issue being examined, researchers are able to generate logical predictions (i.e., hypotheses about what will happen in an investigation). In essence, research is implemented to test predictions that are based on theory. Theory, in turn, is used to explain the findings of a research investigation. If the results of the investigation are in accordance with the theory-based predictions, the theory is supported, and the researcher is able to explain why things happened as they did. In this case, teachers are then able to improve the learning of their students by applying the theory, which has been validated through research, in their own classrooms. Conversely, if research findings do not consistently support the theory, the researcher is forced to re-examine his or her theory and either abandon or refine it so that it corresponds with research findings. In this manner, "science incorporates a self-correcting mechanism in which theories that cannot be reconciled with empirical data are not accepted" (Mayer,

2000, p. 38). Theory provides the overarching rules by which scientists make sense of phenomena in the world around them, whereas research findings provide the specific examples on which these general rules are confirmed or disconfirmed. Without theory, then, it is difficult for practitioners and other educators to understand why a technique being researched worked or did not work, and thereby to apply the research findings to their own lives and classrooms. Because our field's understanding of theory guides how we train teachers and mandate policies, the role that scientific research plays in developing and refining theory is a critical one.

Identifying Effective Practices

To repeat a recurring theme of this chapter, a fundamental purpose of research in special education, in addition to building a professional literature base and theory, is to identify effective practices that enable educators to more effectively instruct students with disabilities. Individual research investigations begin to detect successful methods that become more definitively identified as effective practices through subsequent and related research that molds theory and strengthens a knowledge claim as part of the professional literature base. In addition, educators and professionals in "helping" fields such as special education adhere to what has been referred to as the "scientist-practitioner" model. In this model, special education teachers engage in scientific research in their own classrooms to determine what practices are most effective for them and their students. For their part, researchers must maintain a strong grounding in field practice so that empirical studies are relevant to the day-to-day experiences of teachers and the children with disabilities. This model will certainly advance the knowledge of individuals–as well as the field, if teachers publish or otherwise disseminate their findings–thereby improving the education delivered to students with disabilities (assuming that teachers have received the training to apply scientific principles in their classrooms). Unfortunately, some practitioners believe that they are engaging in valid scientific research when they are unsystematically reflecting on their personal experiences to form subjective opinions. In a similar manner, many researchers believe that they have a "handle" on classroom practices when they actually do not, which is likely to result in the generation of research that is not relevant to those delivering services to children with disabilities. In addition to the goal of providing special educators with the tools to understand and profit from critically reading the professional literature base, this text aims to provide teachers with some of the initial knowledge necessary to conduct sound scientific research in their own classrooms as scientist-practitioners. We will also endeavor to underscore the critical link between scientific inquiry and field practice, with the abiding hope that research in our field will become more practical while teaching practices become more strongly grounded in the scientific method.

CHALLENGES TO SCIENCE IN SPECIAL EDUCATION

In addition to the difficulties associated with using science to produce knowledge claims in the field of special education noted previously in this chapter (e.g., slow and incremental production of knowledge, need for training to meaningfully interpret findings, inability to perfectly predict behavior), special education researchers have recently faced new and serious challenges to the traditionally held assumption that science is the most valid way to determine what works. Often under the mantle of postmodernism, scholars in a variety of disciplines have recently posited that because we are all individuals who can never fully understand or live through another's experiences, it is impossible to conclude that one person's way of knowing is more valid than another person's. Such thinking has led some experts to advocate for a relativistic approach to educational research (see Eisner, 1997). Relativists contend that alternative approaches to conducting research, such as production of a work of art, should be given the same weight as scientific research. These ideas are being taken very seriously in some educational communities, and debates rage regarding, for example, whether doctoral dissertations in education can include films and interpretive dance. As we detail later in the book, scientific research should not be limited to traditional quantitative techniques or methods (methods should instead be guided by the purpose of the investigation and the types of questions posed). Yet, we strongly believe that scientific research, which tests hypotheses and theories through the empirical collection of data, produces knowledge claims that are more valid than does literary critique or other alternative forms of educational scholarship. By understanding and implementing the incremental and cautious, yet reliable and valid, process by which science produces and refines knowledge, special educators can avoid "the fatal leap into the abyss of relativism" in which "all that remains is a chorus of equally valid opinions" (Mayer, 2000, p. 39).

SUMMARY

This chapter provides a brief overview of science and its role in special education. In addition to science, the use of personal experience and expert testimony as ways of knowing is discussed. Through the use of precepts of science such as common ownership of information, cultivated disinterestedness, and organized skepticism, special education researchers have built a professional knowledge base, refined theory, and identified effective practices. It is our hope that, by reading the detailed discussions of special education research presented throughout the next nine chapters of this book, special educators (i.e., practitioners, administrators, teacher-trainers, and parents) will become more active and critical consumers (and, with additional training, producers) of research that will ultimately lead to improved educational opportunities and outcomes for children with disabilities.

Chapter 2

GETTING STARTED IN SPECIAL EDUCATION RESEARCH–VARIABLES, RESEARCH QUESTIONS, AND HYPOTHESES

JAMES L. BELLINI,
PHILLIP D. RUMRILL, JR.
MELODY J. TANKERSLEY

INTRODUCTION

RESEARCH IN THE SOCIAL SCIENCES, including education, is rooted in conceptual frameworks or theories; that is, every scientifically sound research investigation begins with an idea or hypothesis. Both qualitative and quantitative research methods are characterized by the careful collection and analysis of data. More than anything else, making careful observations to confirm or disconfirm a hypothesis is the essence of scientific investigation. However, between the identification of a fruitful idea for research and the collection and analysis of data are several crucial steps in the research process. This chapter will address issues that are preparatory to designing and evaluating special education research. We include sections on sources of ideas for research, identifying and operationalizing research questions, statistical hypotheses, types of variables, and sampling issues.

SOURCES OF RESEARCH IDEAS

Ideas for research can come from a number of different sources. Individual curiosity, personal interests, past and current teaching experiences, service work with school districts and community agencies, and ongoing contact with children and youth with disabilities may provide inspiration for a special education research project.

In an effort to understand certain phenomena, researchers propose concepts, models, and theories to synthesize ideas, variables, and processes in an orderly fashion. The overarching purpose of scientific inquiry is to explain how phenomena relate to each other, which is accomplished using a wide variety of research methods (Bellini & Rumrill, 1999). Theory is a particularly rich source of research ideas. Often, research is undertaken to test specific hypotheses suggested by theories or models. Moreover, there is an ongoing, reciprocal relationship between theory and research. Theory begins the process by suggesting possible fruitful avenues of research. The theory or model may specify the nature of the relationship among its concepts, elements, or processes, which can be tested directly, or the researcher may deduce other hypotheses from theory. Research is then implemented to test the predicted relationship among the elements of the theory or model. If the researcher's hypothesis is supported by the data analysis, the validity of the theory is upheld and thereby strengthened. If the hypothesis is not supported, proponents of the theory need to critically examine the propositions of the theory that did not hold up in the empirical test. This process may lead to revision of the theory, new hypotheses, and subsequent tests of these hypotheses.

Research efforts are often stimulated by the need to measure or operationalize various constructs. For example, special education researchers have long been interested in issues such as labeling, teacher attitudes toward children with disabilities, and peer acceptance—all of which have direct bearing on the way that educational services for children with disabilities are identified and implemented. At the level of the individual investigation, research is often precipitated by previous efforts in a given area. A substantial proportion of the published research in special education is directed to building on or expanding the results of previous studies. Therefore, it is vital for researchers to have a thorough knowledge of the literature in their area of research interest. This permits them to select a topic for research that is capable of yielding significant new knowledge and that builds on the previous efforts of others. In the discussion section of a research manuscript (see Chapter 9), the author will often include suggestions for future research efforts in the given area that are intended to build on the findings discussed in the paper, address ambiguities in the research findings, or illuminate areas not addressed directly in the paper. These suggestions provide valuable direction for subsequent researchers. In that regard, the hours spent reading the works of others (a habit that often begins in graduate school) constitute the best preparation for a researcher wishing to conduct a study of his or her own.

IDENTIFYING AND OPERATIONALIZING
RESEARCH QUESTIONS

Stated most simply, "research explores or examines the relationships among constructs" (Heppner, Kivlighan, & Wampold, 1992, p. 36). A construct is a concept that has no direct physical referent (e.g., intelligence, self-esteem, role, joy, sorrow). Because constructs refer to such characteristics as a person's mental state, capacities, or motivations that we cannot directly sense, we must infer their presence from behaviors and other consequences of their existence (Krathwohl, 1993). Most often, research questions in the social sciences express curiosity about the relationships between or among constructs (Bellini & Rumrill, 1999; Heppner, Kivlighan, & Wampold, 1992; 1999).

Research Questions

As previously discussed, researchers generate ideas for their investigations from a number of sources, including personal experience, casual observation, existing theory, and previous investigations of the phenomena of interest. Whatever the original idea that provides the impetus for research, it must be described concretely so that it can be tested. The research question is usually stated in broad, abstract terms (Bellini & Rumrill, 1999). Often, the broad research question that motivates the research is not stated explicitly in the research article, but it can usually be deduced from a careful reading of the title, the abstract, and the purpose statement that typically concludes the introductory section of a published article (see Chapter 9). The following is a sampling of research questions drawn from recent issues of special education journals:

A. What are the preferences of middle school students with disabilities for specific homework adaptations (Nelson, Epstein, Bursuck, Jayanthi, & Sawyer, 1998)?
B. What is the effect of self-determination on positive adult outcomes one year after leaving school (Wehmeyer & Schwartz, 1997)?
C. What is the effect of level of integration on cognitive and language development of preschool children with disabilities (Mills, Cole, Jenkins, & Dale, 1998)?
D. What is the relationship between prenatal drug exposure and subsequent identification of disability and special education placement (Sinclair, 1998)?
E. What are the effects of a preschool-based prevention program on the social behaviors of young children at risk for developing behavior disorders (Tankersley, Kamps, Mancina, & Weidinger, 1996)?

Drew (1980) identified three categories of research questions: descriptive, difference, and relationship questions. Descriptive questions ask what some phenomenon is like. Example A is a descriptive research question because the study sought to describe students' preferences for a variety of homework adaptations made by their general education teachers (Nelson et al., 1998). Difference questions ask if there are differences between groups of people as a function of one or more identified variables. Examples B and C are difference questions, although these may not be readily identifiable as such from the research question. Wehmeyer and Schwartz (1997) asked whether there was a difference in positive adult outcomes for students who had varying levels of self-determination as measured in high school, whereas Mills et al. (1998) asked whether there was a difference in cognitive and language skills when preschool children participated in different types of integration programming in their classrooms, i.e. special education only, integrated special education, or mainstreaming. Example E also addresses a question of difference. Tankersley et al. (1996) asked whether there was a difference in the social behaviors displayed by Head Start children at risk for behavior disorders who received a preschool-based intervention program compared with other at-risk Head Start children who did not receive the intervention. Relationship questions explore the degree to which two or more constructs are related or vary together. Example D is a relationship question in which Sinclair (1998) examined how prenatal drug exposure is related to a child's subsequent identification with an emotional and behavioral disorder and placement in a special education kindergarten program.

Operational Definitions

Each of the research questions cited previously represents the fundamental research idea that motivated the given study. However, considerable work is needed to translate these broad research ideas into empirical research projects that can be executed. The concepts inherent in the broad research question must be formulated into operational definitions. Operational definitions refer to defining constructs on the basis of the specific activities and operations used to measure them in the investigation (Heppner et al., 1992). Particular measurement instruments are often used to operationalize the constructs inherent in the broad research question. For a knowledge claim to have merit, the manner in which the broad research question is translated into the specific operations of the investigation must make sense to others in the research community.

Operational definitions link the general ideas and concepts that motivate the study to the specific, measurable events that constitute the empirical test of the research question (Heppner et al., 1992; Kazdin, 1998). It is an essential link in the chain of reasoning leading from formulating a research question to making a knowledge claim on the basis of the results of a study. A weak link between research questions and research operations will reduce the credibility of the knowledge claim no matter how exemplary the investigation may be along other important dimensions (Krathwohl, 1993). A second function of the operational definition is to permit replication of the research procedure by other researchers using similar and different samples (Cronbach, 1988).

In example A cited in the previous section on research questions, "preferences" were operationalized in the form of a 17-item survey instrument, the Student Preferences for Homework Adaptations Questionnaire, which was developed for the study and administered to the students in small and large groups (Nelson et al., 1998). Students could indicate the degree to which they would like a specific adaptation made for them on a scale ranging from *they would dislike it* to *they had a high preference for it.*

In example B, "self-determination" of participants was measured during their final high school year on a 72-item self-report scale, the Arc's Self-Determination Scale. The scale provided data relating to autonomy, self-regulation, psychological empowerment, and self realization, as well as an overall score for self-determination (Wehmeyer & Schwartz, 1997). The extent of students' self-determination was assessed in relation to their adult outcomes one year after they left school. "Adult outcomes," such as living arrangements, current and past employment situations, and postsecondary education status, were operationalized as parents' reports of their children's participation in each area as reported on a mailed questionnaire.

In example C, "level of integration" was operationalized as the extent to which children with disabilities were enrolled in classrooms with children without disabilities. Three levels of integration were defined on the basis of the classroom ratio of children with disabilities to children without disabilities: (a) special education only classrooms in which 14 children with disabilities and no children without disabilities were enrolled; (b) integrated classrooms in which three children without disabilities and 11 children with disabilities were enrolled; and (c) mainstreamed classrooms in which nine children without disabilities and five children with disabilities were enrolled (Mills et al., 1998). Cognitive and language development of the children with disabilities was operationalized through two measures, the McCarthy Scales of Children's Abilities and the Preschool Language Assessment Instrument. Both measures were given to the children with disabilities before to placement in one of the three levels of integrated classrooms (i.e., pretest) and again approximately six months later (i.e., posttest).

In example E, social behaviors were operationalized as the frequency and/or duration of several behaviors that were measured through direct observation in the preschool setting. The researchers observed children dur-ing free play, small and large group activities, and recess. The researchers then made a record of specific social behaviors: (a) interactions with peers, (b) compliance with teacher directions, (c) aggression toward self or others, (d) destruction of equipment or materials, (e) grabbing objects from others, (f) being out of an assigned area, and (g) making negative verbal statements. Each social behavior was defined in observable, measurable terms so that researchers would know when the behavior was happening and not hap-pening. For example, grabbing was defined as "any attempt to take an object from a peer or adult without consent. This also includes taking an object from a designated area without permission" (p. 175). Social behaviors, then, were operationalized to encompass the number of times or the amount of time children were engaged in each specific response of interest.

Although the previous examples represent quantitative research studies, it is important to note that the operationalization of variables is not exclusive-ly limited to quantitative investigations. Qualitative studies also translate key abstract concepts into specific research operations for the purpose of gener-ating knowledge. For example, Wiener and Sunohara (1998) used a qualita-tive method (analysis of telephone interviews) to investigate parents' percep-tions of the quality of friendships of their children with learning disabilities. Clearly, how "friendship" was defined in the context of the methods the researchers used to identify children's friends was key to the credibility and usefulness of the study findings. Friendship was operationalized through chil-dren's nominations of whom they viewed as their friends and parents' lists of their children's close friends. Four to six weeks after receiving these nomi-nations, the researchers asked the parents to describe their children's rela-tionships with each child nominated as a friend.

Limitations of Operational Definitions

Operational definitions of constructs are essential to virtually every scien-tific investigation, and they serve to link the abstract conceptual foundation of a study to its concrete procedures. However, there are several limitations of operational definitions to keep in mind (Bellini & Rumrill, 1999; Kazdin, 1998):

1. An operational definition may be incomplete, may greatly simplify, or may bear little resemblance to the abstract construct of interest. For exam-ple, an important special education concept such as inclusion may be oper-ationalized for the purpose of an investigation as teachers' self-reported level of inclusiveness in their classrooms (respondents' perceptions of inclusion

may be affected by mood or recent events, or they may not accurately reflect the facts), the proportion of children with disabilities in general education classrooms (a measure of quantity rather than quality of inclusion, such as "the level of inclusion" used in the Mills et al., 1998 study described in example C), or parents' perceptions of the level of inclusion in given classrooms (which may not reflect the day-to day reality for students with and without disabilities). Thus, each of these distinct operational definitions for the construct "inclusion" leaves out dimensions related to common sense notions of what it means to be included in an educational environment.

2. Operational definitions may include features that are irrelevant or not central to the original concept. For example, an investigation of family adjustment issues associated with the onset of disability in children may be operationalized by including in the study families who have children with disabilities and who have sought support services. However, this operational definition of "family adjustment problems" includes elements that may be irrelevant and could influence the results of the study. Families may seek services for reasons unrelated to disability issues, such as poverty or illness. Also, seeking services is determined by many factors other than experiencing adjustment problems, including availability and expense of services, cultural attitudes toward seeking professional help, and encouragement from others. Thus, there is always a concern that the methods used to define the concept of interest include components that are not related to the original concept but that influence the study findings in ways that the researcher may not anticipate.

3. Often, individual researchers will operationalize the same construct in different ways. Consider the construct of anxiety. Anxiety may be operationalized as a self-report (paper and pencil measure), as skin galvanic response (physiological measure), or as a behavioral rating by an observer. Use of discrepant operational definitions of the same constructs in different studies often leads to different empirical findings, thereby making it difficult to compare studies to each other or to evaluate the credibility of findings in an area of research. Also, using different operational definitions for the same construct implies that the results of a study must be qualified or restricted to the specific operational definitions used. In other words, findings that are based on a particular operational definition of a key construct may not be generalizable to other, different approaches to measuring the same phenomenon. Fortunately, researchers and practitioners are not restricted to single studies in evaluating the status of knowledge in a given area. As research within a topic advances and becomes more complex, subsequent researchers incorporate the lessons of previous studies, and operational definitions acquire greater specification as knowledge accumulates (Heppner et al., 1992).

The concept of a *latent variable* is used in research to reflect the idea that the same variables can be measured in different ways (Bellini & Rumrill, 1999). The specific measures that are used are referred to as observed variables, or *indicators* of the construct of interest, whereas the latent variable is unobserved. It is not possible to measure a variable in "pure" form, divorced from the method of measurement. Rather, scores on a measured variable are a mixture or combination of variation caused by the trait or construct and variation associated with the specific method used to measure the variable (see Chapter 3). In that regard, scores are trait-method units (Campbell & Fiske, 1959). The notion of the operational definition implies that the findings of a study may be restricted (to some degree) to the specific methods used to measure variables, and that measurement, although essential for quantitative studies, also presents the possibility of a confounding influence. When a latent variable is measured in at least two different ways in a study, it is possible to separate the effects caused by the construct from the effects caused by the measurement method (Campbell & Fiske, 1959; Kazdin, 1998).

Sometimes the weak connections between concepts and quantitative operational definitions (or, between latent variables and their measured indicators) may underlie the characterization of social sciences as "soft," that is, less amenable to clear and convincing confirmation and disconfirmation by empirical tests than the "harder" physical sciences (Bellini & Rumrill, 1999). However, Kazdin (1992) noted that "clinical research is not in any way soft science; indeed, the processes involved in clinical research reflect science at its best precisely because of the thinking and ingenuity required to force nature to reveal its secrets" (p. 8).

Research Hypotheses and Statistical Hypotheses

Whereas research questions are stated in abstract, conceptual terms, research hypotheses are typically stated in terms of the expected relationships among the constructs in a study. They may also be stated in an if/then format that expresses the presumed causal relationship: If these specific conditions are met, then the following result is expected. For example, the research hypothesis tested in the Mills et al. (1998) study could be stated as "Children with disabilities who scored higher on pretest measures of cognitive and language development will perform better in mainstream classrooms than children with disabilities whose pretest scores on these measures were lower. Among the children who scored lower, on the pretest measures, the ones who were enrolled in non-integrated classrooms will perform better." The research hypothesis tested in the Tankersley et al. (1996) study could be stated as "Children who participate in the preschool-based prevention program will have fewer incidents of antisocial behavior when compared to children who did not participate in the program."

Statistical hypotheses refer to the specific operational definitions used to measure the variables of interest and the specific statistical approach used in the study. Typically, the statistical hypothesis is stated in its "null" form; in other words, it posits no significant differences on the variables of interest. This is because the logic of statistical tests, based on probability theory, is oriented toward *disconfirming* the hypothesis of no differences between experimental (the group that receives a treatment or intervention) and control (the group that receives no intervention or an intervention that is not relevant to the study purpose) groups (see Chapter 6). For example, Tankersley et al. (1996) could have addressed the following statistical hypotheses:

1. The experimental (children who received the Head Start preschool prevention program) and control (students who received traditional Head Start programming) groups do not differ significantly on the mean frequency or duration of social interactions.

2. The experimental and control groups do not differ significantly on the mean frequency of compliance with teacher directions.

3. The experimental and control groups do not differ significantly on the mean frequency of aggression.

4. The experimental and control groups do not differ significantly on the mean frequency of destruction.

Research Questions, Research Operations, and Knowledge Claims

Research questions are developed from a variety of sources, including casual observations and particular interests of the researcher, existing theory that specifies how variables may be related, and previous research in a given area (Bellini & Rumrill, 1999). To test particular hypothesized relationships developed from observation, existing theory, and/or previous research, it is first necessary to operationalize these abstract concepts, that is, make them concrete through specific procedures and measurement operations. In this way, the hypothesis is tested using empirical data. The findings of the study are then delimited by the particular definitions and measures used to operationalize the constructs of interest and the specific conditions in which the constructs were investigated. However, after the investigation is concluded and the results are analyzed, the researcher typically wishes to make statements about the more abstract level of concepts that inform the particulars of the research situation. In other words, science seeks generalized knowledge rather than knowledge that is limited to a particular experimental situation (Bellini & Rumrill, 1999). The strength of a knowledge claim depends on the quality of the operational definitions, measurement instruments, research design and implementation, the clarity or nonambiguity of the findings, and how the results of a particular study contribute to the weight of empirical evidence in a given research area.

IDENTIFYING RESEARCH VARIABLES

Most simply stated, variables are "characteristics of persons or things that can take on two or more values" (Bolton & Parker, 1998, p. 444). Types of variables are distinguished by their measurement characteristics. *Categorical* variables are those whose values may include a limited number of discrete categories. Examples of categorical variables include gender, which can take on two values, female and male, and marital status, which can have a number of values such as married, single, separated, divorced, or widowed. In given individuals, categorical variables may take on only one of a limited range of possible values. *Continuous* variables are variables that may take any value along a continuum of scores. For example, age (for human beings) may take any value ranging from 0 to approximately 100 years. Intelligence, as expressed in terms of intelligence quotient scores, can take on any value between approximately 20 (below which intelligence is generally regarded as unmeasurable) and approximately 180.

Variables may be directly observable (e.g., eye color) or nonobservable (e.g., self esteem). Many observable variables, such aggression or grabbing as identified in the previously cited Tankersley et al. (1996) study, may need to be defined so that all members of the research team are sure to notice the same occurrences of the behaviors. However, in the social sciences in general, and special education research in particular, many key variables of interest are nonobservable (e.g., attitudes toward inclusion of students with disabilities, psychosocial adjustment). These nonobservable variables must be inferred from indirect sources of measurement, such as self-report questionnaires, psychometric tests, and the reports of significant others.

Independent and Dependent Variables and the Logic of Experimentation

Variables are also distinguished by their role in the research process. *Independent variables* are the variables that the researcher manipulates in an experiment, or the variables that are theorized to predict or explain the variation of other study variables in correlational and causal comparative studies (Bellini & Rumrill, 1999; see Chapter 6). Synonyms for independent variables include input, cause, antecedent, predictor, process, and treatment variables (Bolton & Parker, 1998). In the logic of experimentation, the independent variable causes or produces changes in the *dependent variable.* Synonyms for the dependent variable include measured, consequent, criterion, outcome, and response variable (Bolton & Parker, 1998). In the Mills et al. (1998) study, the dependent variables were the measured outcomes that the researchers presumed to be influenced by level of inclusion in the classroom: cognitive and language development measures using the standardized assessment instruments (the McCarthy Scales of Children's Abilities General Cognitive Index and the Preschool Language Assessment Instrument).

The purpose of experimentation is to examine causal relationships among variables (Kazdin, 1998). In the logic of experimentation, a researcher attempts to examine causality by "systematically varying or altering one variable or set of variables and examining the resultant changes in or consequences for another variable or set of variables" (Heppner et al., 1992, p.40). The variable that is varied, altered, or manipulated in the study is the independent variable. Often, the independent variable is an intervention that is provided to one group but not to other groups. When the independent variable is an intervention, it is called a treatment or situational variable (Kazdin, 1992).

In experimentation, the term *manipulation* refers to the deliberate process of examining the effects of varying the value or level of an independent variable (Bellini & Rumrill, 1999). To examine these effects, resultant changes in the dependent variable (or set of variables) are observed. In the simplest experiment, this manipulation of the independent variable is accomplished by using two groups, a group that receives an intervention and a group that does not receive the intervention. If all preexisting differences between the two groups are minimized except for the difference in the value or level of the independent variable (an extremely difficult proposition to actualize), then the logic of experimental design permits the researcher to conclude that the measured differences between the two groups on the dependent variable (measured after the intervention is concluded) are the result of the independent variable.

In many, if not most, examples of special education research, it is not possible, because of ethical constraints or logical impossibility, to manipulate the independent variable. For example, it is not possible in the real world to randomly assign study participants to a disability status. Also, in "field" research (e.g., the classroom) it is often impossible to ensure that all preexisting differences between experimental and control groups are identified and controlled in the investigation. In these cases, it is more difficult to infer causal relationships between independent and dependent variables on the basis of the study findings (Cook & Campbell, 1979). It is the research design of a study, rather than the specific statistical analyses used in the investigation, that determines the inferential status, or strength of the causal inferences that can be made on the basis of a study's findings (Heppner et al., 1992). In its traditional meaning, independent variable refers to a variable that is amenable to experimental manipulation for the purpose of inferring causal connections.

Status or Individual Difference Variables

Variables that characterize or describe subjects but cannot be assigned or manipulated by the researcher are *status* or *individual difference variables* (Kazdin, 1998). These variables may be aspects of personality (e.g., self-esteem, locus of control, intelligence) aspects of a person's socioeconomic situation (e.g., education level, marital status, family income), or aspects of group membership (e.g., gender, race/ethnicity, sexual orientation). Characteristics of teachers, such as level and type of education, years of experience, and disability status, are also examples of status or individual difference variables that have been studied in special education research.

Often, status variables are labeled as independent variables in the research literature and perform the same role as predictors in a statistical analysis. In these cases, making causal inferences on the basis of observed results is problematic, because the status variable has not been (and, in fact, cannot be) manipulated. The purpose of using status or individual difference variables in a statistical analysis is to detect *association* between the status and dependent variables rather than to establish causal explanations. Also, we do not mean to suggest that causal explanation is impossible when the study does not include an experimental manipulation of independent variables. Causality can be inferred from the association between variables on the basis of logic, such as when the status variable logically occurs before to the "effect," when the status variable covaries with the effect (i.e., changes in the status variable are associated with changes in the dependent variable), and when there is a mechanism of explanation that rationally links the variation of the status variable to its consequences (Cook & Campbell, 1979; Kazdin, 1998). Causality can also be inferred on the basis of the total evidence gathered from a series of investigations. For example, the well-established causal link between smoking and lung cancer is supported by a wealth of research evidence rather than the result of any single experimental study or small group of studies.

Moderator Variables

Moderator variables are status variables that influence (i.e., moderate) the effect of an independent or other status variable on a dependent variable. For example, a researcher wishing to compare attitudes toward the inclusion of students with disabilities between general and special education teachers finds that gender is also related to respondents' attitudes. In fact, women in this hypothetical study report more positive attitudes than men, regardless of whether they are special education or general education teachers. In this example, gender serves to *moderate* the relationship between type of teaching setting and attitudes toward inclusion.

Moderator variables are often included in the design of a study when the researcher suspects that the relationship between an independent or status variable and a dependent variable is influenced by another status variable. Inclusion of moderator variables in the design of investigations permits researchers to identify more precisely the nature of complex relationships among independent and dependent variables.

SAMPLING ISSUES

In conducting a research study, scientists would ideally investigate all people to whom they wish to generalize their findings. These people constitute a *population*, meaning that they make up the entire group of individuals having the characteristic or characteristics that interest the researcher. For example, researchers who are interested in how adolescents adjust to acquired severe spinal cord injury (SCI) in the United States would ideally include all Americans between the ages of 12 and 18 who have acquired SCI. However, the time and expense needed to include all members of this population would make the research infeasible. Therefore, researchers must content themselves with studying a *sample* of people who presumably represent the population of interest. A sample is a given number of subjects who are selected from a defined population and who are presumed to be representative of the population (Bellini & Rumrill, 1999).

Using a sample subset of the population solves the problem of feasibility. However, a new problem is created for the researcher--whether he or she can generalize the results from the sample to the population of interest. In other words, it is possible that the results of the study may only be valid for the specific sample that is studied. The representativeness of a sample in relation to its population is a key issue in the conduct and evaluation of research investigations. The term *population validity* is defined as "the degree to which the sample of individuals in the study is representative of the population from which it was selected" (Borg & Gall, 1983, p. 99). The method of selecting a sample is vital to the entire research process. If research findings are not generalizable to some extent beyond the particular sample used in the study, the research does not provide us with new, practical knowledge. A study whose findings cannot be generalized to a population of interest may be considered a waste of time and effort.

Random and Systematic Sampling Error

Samples rarely have the exact same characteristics as the populations from which they are drawn. The differences between the characteristics of the sample and the characteristics of the population on the variables of interest are known as *sampling errors.* These may be of two types, random and systematic sampling error (Kalton, 1983).

Random sampling error refers to the "accidental" differences between sample and population characteristics that are likely to occur whenever a sample is drawn from a population of interest. The size of these errors, i.e. the magnitude of the differences between sample and population, tends to become smaller as one selects a larger random sample. Individuals who have characteristics that are unusual for the population will, if included in a small sample, have a larger effect on the average values for those characteristics. With a larger sample, more individuals will reflect the "average" value for the population on the given characteristic, whereas individuals with unusual characteristics will have a smaller effect on the average values of the characteristic. For this reason, researchers can be more confident in generalizing results from studies that use large random samples than they can in generalizing results from studies with small random samples.

A sampling procedure is random if each member of the specified population has an *equal and independent chance* of being included in the sample. An important advantage of random sampling is that the degree to which the sample differs from the population can be reliably estimated using mathematical procedures. For example, when results of surveys are reported, a margin of error is often included. This is the mathematical estimation of the range of difference between sample and population.

Often, researchers in special education use nonrandom samples in conducting studies. When nonrandom samples are used, there is always the chance that *systematic sampling error* is present. Systematic sampling errors result from variables not taken into account by the researcher, which nevertheless influence the results of sampling procedures. Systematic errors tend to be in a given direction and, unlike random sampling error, cannot be estimated by mathematical procedures. Systematic errors are more serious because they may distort research findings in ways that have not been anticipated and therefore may lead to false conclusions.

Types of Sampling

Random sampling is the best way of ensuring that the results of a study will generalize to the population of interest. Several distinct methods of random sampling may be used, depending on the purpose of the research and the resources available to the investigator. Four common types of random sampling are simple random, systematic, stratified, and cluster sampling. Researchers may also use nonrandom sampling procedures in gathering data; however, when nonrandom sampling is used, the results of a study are less likely to generalize to the population of interest. Convenience, or volunteer, sampling is a nonrandom approach to sampling that is common in quantitative research investigations, and purposive sampling is a nonrandom method that has widespread application in qualitative research (see Chapter 7).

SIMPLE RANDOM SAMPLING. One of the most effective sampling procedures in conducting research is simple random sampling. In simple random sampling, each member of a population has an equal and independent chance of being included in the sample. In this context, "independent" means that the selection of one individual does not affect in any way the chances that other individuals may or may not be selected. It is an effective sampling technique because it yields research data that can be generalized to the population of interest within margins of error that can be specified statistically.

SYSTEMATIC SAMPLING. Systematic sampling is similar to simple random sampling except that, in the former, there is an identifiable pattern to the process of participant selection. In systematic sampling, the first name is chosen from a list in random fashion, and then every third, eighth, or fifteenth name (for example) is selected, until the researcher has attained the sample size required for the study. Thus, after the first name is randomly chosen, all other members of the sample are automatically determined by their placement on the list. Systematic sampling is easier to accomplish than simple random sampling in cases in which all members of the population are known, such as when the researcher has access to a directory of members of a professional organization. However, it is possible for systematic error to be introduced into a systematic sampling procedure if there exists some bias (unknown to the researcher) in how names are arranged on the list.

STRATIFIED SAMPLING. Stratified sampling is a procedure for ensuring that members of the population who have certain characteristics are represented in the sample. The government often uses stratified sampling to ensure that a sample is as close to the national population as possible on a number of identified characteristics, such as gender, race, education, and socioeconomic status. One approach to stratified sampling is to draw random samples of different sizes from identified subgroups of a specified population so that the proportion of individuals in each group is the same as their proportion in the population. Consider research into the teaching strategies and job duties of special education teachers (Gartin, Rumrill, & Serebreni, 1996; Tankersley, et al., 1996). Researchers may know that the roles and functions of special education teachers differ on the basis of work setting, area of specialization, and level of education. Estimates (drawn from a registry) of the proportions of teachers at various levels of education and work settings may be available. It is therefore possible for researchers to use a sampling technique that stratifies the sample on the basis of education and work setting: A specified proportion of teachers is drawn from private schools, public schools, residential programs, specific speciality areas (e.g., learning disabilities, multiple disabilities, deafness), and different educational levels (e.g., bachelor's, master's, and doctoral degrees). This approach would ensure that teachers of certain types are not overrepresented or underrepresented in the sample so that systematic error related to the stratification characteristics is not introduced into the study. By ensuring that the sample reflects the population on these key characteristics, the generalization of study results is enhanced (Borg & Gall, 1983).

CLUSTER SAMPLING. Cluster sampling is a procedure that is often used in educational research. Whereas in simple random, systematic, and stratified sampling the sampling unit is the individual, in cluster sampling the cluster (or preexisting group of individuals) is the sampling unit. A classic example of a cluster sampling unit is the school district. A researcher who is interested in comparing the performance of students in various school districts may well choose a cluster sampling procedure to accomplish the study. The researcher would randomly select the districts for inclusion in the study rather than randomly selecting students from all possible school districts. A key advantage of cluster sampling is that the resources needed to accomplish the study may be conserved by applying them more selectively; thus, fewer resources are needed to carry out the investigation. A key disadvantage of cluster sampling is the possibility that, unknown to the researcher, clusters may differ on variables that influence the study findings. Therefore, the educational researcher who compares the performance of students in various school districts would likely use a combination of stratified and cluster sampling procedures to take into account such well-known influences as socioeconomic status of districts, student/teacher ratios, and dropout rates on school performance (Borg, Gall, & Gall, 1993).

CONVENIENCE SAMPLING. Research in any field is often limited by the availability of funds. Drawing large random samples can be very expensive and therefore infeasible in most special education research investigations. The use of large samples in research is generally possible only when research makes few or minimal demands on individuals such as in public opinion or market research. Random sampling is also difficult in most social science research because researchers have the legal and ethical obligation to obtain informed consent from human subjects (and, when children are being studied, from their parents) before involving them in a research project (see Chapter 4). Individuals can refuse to participate for any reason, and without consequence, which often limits the recruitment of large samples.

For these reasons, most research in special education is conducted with volunteer or convenience samples. The main problem with convenience samples is the possibility of introducing systematic sampling error into the selection process. When systematic error is introduced, the sample will have characteristics different from the population from which it is drawn, potentially limiting the ability of the researcher to generalize the results of the study to the population of interest. In fact, research on volunteer subjects reviewed by Rosenthal and Rosnow (1969) indicates that people who volunteer for research tend to be different in a number of ways--including being better educated, of higher social class, more intelligent, more sociable, and higher in need for social approval–from nonvolunteers.

The likelihood that systematic sampling error affects the results of a study that uses volunteer subjects can be evaluated by checking the ratio of individuals who agree to participate to individuals who are invited to participate, known as the response rate. It is common practice for researchers using questionnaires to report the percentage of participants who actually complete the questionnaire (Kalton, 1983). It is less likely that systematic sampling error is introduced when the response rate is high. If the researcher has access to additional data on the subjects invited to participate, he or she can provide a check on systematic sampling error by comparing participants with nonparticipants on selected characteristics that are presumed to be related to subjects' responses.

In evaluating the representativeness of a volunteer sample, the researcher and readers should consider the following questions: How likely is it that participants who volunteer for the study differ from the target population on selected characteristics? How relevant is this characteristic to the independent and dependent variables examined in the study? How would differences between the participants and the population on this characteristic be likely to influence the study results?

Because of the problems associated with volunteer samples and low response rates, skillful researchers work closely with personnel in the research setting, explain in full detail the nature of the research, solicit their ideas, and provide benefits to those who participate, all in an effort to increase the percentage of participants and reduce sampling bias.

PURPOSIVE SAMPLING. Qualitative researchers typically study only a few cases of individuals from a specified population (Bellini & Rumrill, 1999). Because the sample size in qualitative studies is often so small, the procedures used to select a sample in quantitative research are not applicable. For example, a qualitative researcher may select a respondent or setting to study because the individual or setting is an exemplary case of the phenomenon of interest, or a case from which the researcher feels he or she will learn the most (McReynolds & Koch, 1999). Purposive sampling refers to sampling decisions that are made in qualitative research on the basis of theoretical and practical considerations relative to the research question. For example, a researcher wishing to conduct a qualitative study of language acquisition patterns among preschool children with hearing impairments might begin by soliciting interest from members of a parent advocacy group. She could identify children to participate in her study from the group, and she could ask group members to recommend other parents whose children meet the sampling criteria for the investigation. The purpose of this approach would be to draw a sample of children with similar characteristics, but the concepts of randmomization and representativeness that are essential concerns in quantitative research do not apply in qualitative investigations.

SUMMARY

This chapter has addressed several key issues that are preparatory to the design and evaluation of special education research. Ideas for research come from a number of sources—including curiosity about a phenomenon, personal interests, teaching practice, existing theory or models, and previous research efforts. The idea that motivates a research project is typically expressed in broad, abstract terms, often in the form of a research question. To translate a research question into an empirical research project, the constructs inherent in the research question must be formulated into operational definitions. Operational definitions specify constructs on the basis of the particular activities and operations used to measure the construct in the investigation. Statistical hypotheses are grounded in the specific operational definitions used to measure the constructs of interest and the specific statistical approach used in the study. Typically, the statistical hypothesis is stated in the "null" form that posits no significant differences on the (dependent) variables of interest.

Variables are characteristics of persons or things that can take on two or more values. Variables can be categorized by their measurement characteristics (i.e., categorical and continuous) or by their role in the research process (i.e., independent, dependent, status, and moderator). In special education research, it is often not possible to manipulate independent variables to evaluate their causal relationships to dependent variables. Therefore, much of special education research is concerned with the relationships between status variables and dependent variables.

Sampling is essential to the research process because researchers rarely have the resources to access all individuals who constitute a population of interest. A sample is a given number of subjects who are selected from a defined population and who are representative of the population. The representativeness of a sample in relation to its population is a key issue in the reporting and evaluation of research findings. In simple random sampling, each member of a population has an equal and independent chance of being included in the sample. Simple random sampling is usually the preferred sampling strategy because sampling errors can be reliably estimated using statistical methods. Systematic sampling occurs when one member of a population is selected at random, then other subjects are selected on the basis of uniform spacing on a list or registry. Stratified sampling may be used to enhance the representativeness of a sample in relation to population characteristics that are known. Cluster sampling uses the random selection of groups of subjects (e.g., school districts) with each member of the selected group taking part for study. Convenience samples are used extensively in social science investigations, including special education research. The key problem with using convenience samples is the possibility of introducing systematic sampling error into the selection process, which limits the ability of the researcher to generalize the results of the study to the population of interest. Purposive sampling, typically used in qualitative research, is based on theoretical and practical issues involved in implementing the investigation.

Chapter 3

MEASUREMENT AND STATISTICS IN SPECIAL EDUCATION RESEARCH

James L. Bellini
Phillip D. Rumrill, Jr.
Bryan G. Cook
Shawn M. Fitzgerald

INTRODUCTION

THE PURPOSE OF THIS CHAPTER is to discuss key measurement and statistical issues involved in designing and evaluating special education research. Quantitative researchers in special education use standardized and nonstandardized instruments to measure observable phenomena and translate them into numerical data for the purpose of analysis. Therefore, in the quantitative research tradition, measurement issues are central to the operationalization of research hypotheses and the interpretation of research findings. Measurement issues also have important implications for statistical analyses of research findings, because research conclusions are only as good or credible as the quantitative data on which they are based (Bellini & Rumrill, 1999).

Once a sample is identified, appropriate measurement instruments are chosen, and data are collected; analysis of the data is the next step in the research process. The term "statistics" comprises a branch of mathematical operations pertaining to analyzing numerical data. Statistical methods of data analysis are pivotal to all quantitative research. Having an adequate conceptual understanding of statistical methods and the role of statistics in interpreting research results is necessary for evaluating the contributions of particular research studies to the special education literature. After an overview of measurement issues in the first part of this chapter, the second half will address selected statistical concepts that are important for designing and evaluating special education research. We will not address the mathematical formulas that are used to calculate statistics as would be included in a basic statistics course; rather, we will focus on conceptual explanations of key statistical principles and on various approaches to statistical analysis of quantitative data.

MEASUREMENT ISSUES

Measurement involves the ascription of numbers to the responses of individuals, objects, or events according to specific rules (Bolton, 1979). For example, a self-report questionnaire typically requires a scoring key (or computer software program) that provides the rules for how to sum the separate items into a total score, which item responses need to be reverse scored (as is the procedure for scoring negatively phrased items), which items go together to form an interpretable scale, and so forth. Other rules associated with measurement include standards for (a) administering tests and inventories and (b) for interpreting test results.

Levels of Measurement

In the social sciences, there exists a four-level hierarchy of measurement scales that is largely differentiated by the type of mathematical manipulations (i.e., statistics) that can be performed on the numbers assigned to variable characteristics and the amount of information that can be gleaned from the numbers (Stevens, 1946; 1951). The four types of scales are nominal, ordinal, interval, and ration.

Nominal Scale

The most basic type of measurement is known as the nominal scale. The nominal scale simply classifies characteristics of certain variables by assigning numbers to categories without consideration of a logical numerical ordering of the categories (Stevens, 1951); as the term "nominal" implies, variables are broken into categories on the basis of the names that are used for classification purposes. Gender is an example of a nominally scaled variable, whereby those designated as males would be grouped into one category, and those named as females would comprise the other. Anytime that categories need to be differentiated without one category representing more, higher frequencies, or greater value with respect to the variable of interest, the nominal scale is the appropriate choice. Variables such as eye color (e.g., brown, blue, green, hazel), type of educational placement (e.g., segregated special education classroom, inclusive classroom), and college major (e.g., psychology, English, nursing, education) are other examples of nominally categorized phenomena.

Returning to the gender example, a researcher might codify all males in a study using a "1" and all females using a "2." Again, this would not imply that females have twice as much "gender" as males, or that females are necessarily more important or accomplished than males on some other criterion. Rather, the numbers are simply used to differentiate the nominally derived categories of male and female. When variables are measured on the nominal scale, the researcher is restricted to simply determining how many (i.e., determining the frequency of) individuals, objects, or events have certain characteristics in common.

Ordinal Scale

When characteristics of a variable are categorized and follow a logical order (e.g., ranking of categories), the variable is considered to be measured on an ordinal scale. With ordinal measurement, the numerical values assigned to categories imply differences in the amount of the characteristic, and those values are assigned according to those amounts (Stevens, 1951). For example, the variable "life satisfaction" could be measured on an ordinal scale if research participants' levels of life satisfaction not only indicated different classifications of satisfaction toward life (i.e., satisfied/not satisfied), but were also ordered in some manner such that the degree or amount of life satisfaction (i.e., more or less satisfied) could be determined. Specifically, a measure of life satisfaction could be assessed using a five-point scale, whereby a 5 is assigned to the category "highly satisfied," a 4 to "somewhat satisfied," a 3 to "neither satisfied nor dissatisfied," a 2 to "somewhat dissatisfied," and a 1 to "highly dissatisfied." In this case, if an individual responding to this scale indicated that he or she was highly satisfied and another indicated that he or she was somewhat satisfied, not only could it be determined that these individuals differed in their life satisfaction, their amount or degree of life satisfaction could also be determined.

Unlike the nominal scale, the numbers assigned to ordinal measures imply that categories are lower, weaker, or worse than others. However, even though statements of "more" or "less" can be made regarding the characteristics of variables measured on an ordinal scale, it is not possible to determine "how much more" or "how much less" any characteristic of a variable is compared with another.

A good example of this distinction is the measurement of running performance using the order of finish as the (ordinal) scale. The measurement of performance in this case would clearly indicate which runner was better or worse than any other, but it would not be possible to determine how much better or worse any runner was compared with any other. That is, the first place runner could have preceded the second place runner to the finish line by several minutes or only by several seconds. The nature of the ordinal scale does not provide information regarding the magnitude of the difference between characteristics of a variable.

Interval Scale

The third level of measurement in the hierarchy is referred to as the interval scale. Variables measured on the interval scale are considered to have all the characteristics of the nominal and ordinal scales, plus one additionaal characteristic: the difference between any two points on an interval scale reflects an equal difference regardless of where on the scale the two points are located. Furthermore, because the difference between any two points on an interval scale is uniform throughout the scale, it is possible to determine the magnitude of differences between or among points (Stevens, 1951).

Ratio Scale

The highest scale of measurement is referred to as the ratio scale. In addition to the properties of the nominal, ordinal, and interval scales (i.e., classification, order or distances of equal intervals between points), the ratio scale has one additional property—a true zero point (Stevens, 1951). Age, time, and most physical measures such as height, weight, and length are examples of variables that are measured using this scale. The advantage of having a true zero point is that ratio comparisons can be made. For example, because time has a true zero point, it is possible to suggest that 10 minutes is twice as long as five minutes. For variables that are measured on an interval scale, these types of comparisons are not possible, because interval scales lack a true zero point. Take, for example, standardized intelligence tests, which are frequently used in educational and disability studies research. A score of zero on an intelligence test is theoretically not possible, because all people are assumed to have some degree of intelligence. In the social sciences, ratio levels of measurement are seldom used. In terms of statistical analysis, interval and ratio levels of measurement are often treated similarly (Wiersma, 2000).

THE PURPOSE OF MEASUREMENT IN
SPECIAL EDUCATION RESEARCH

Literally thousands of measurement instruments are used for the purposes of student assessment in special education, as well as for the design and implementation of special education research. These include measures of academic aptitude and achievement, peer acceptance, personality, emotional adjustment, medical and neurological functioning, speech and language capacities, hearing, vision, and vocational interests and values. Many of these instruments are available from commercial test developers, and other instruments are developed to measure selected constructs in the context of particular research projects. The first part of this chapter addresses several measurement concepts that are important for the design and evaluation of research, including standardization, reliability, and validity of measurement instruments.

Standardization

A measurement instrument is considered to be standardized if it has been carefully developed, its psychometric characteristics (e.g., reliability, validity) have been assessed and reported, and guidelines for administration have been provided–including minimum competency standards for those who administer, score, and interpret tests (Cronbach, 1990). Standardized test manuals specify in detail the procedures used in instrument development, as well as the steps to be used in administering, scoring, and interpreting test data. Standardization is vital for ensuring consistency in the administration and interpretation of test data. Standardized tests typically provide tables of *norms*, such as the means and standard deviations for people to whom the test developers initially administered the instrument (i.e., the standardization sample or norm group) along with descriptions of the characteristics of the norm group. These data facilitate the application of the measurement instrument to other, similar samples of people. They also provide valuable benchmarks for interpretation of the scores of people who complete the test or inventory at a later time. Standardized tests and inventories provide evidence that the scores are consistent, that everyone takes the same test under similar conditions, and that scores are meaningfully related to other important educational and social outcomes. This enhances the applicability of test scores to the educational and helping professions.

It should be noted that many special education researchers and teachers use nonstandardized tests and inventories to measure variables of interest. These measures may provide important ecological information about individual students in particular settings, but they are less credible in a scientific sense because they do not offer evidence of psychometric characteristics such as reliability and validity.

Reliability

Reliability refers to the consistency or precision of measurement and the extent to which measurement eliminates chance and other extraneous factors in resulting scores (Bellini & Rumrill, 1999; Hood & Johnson, 1997). Common synonyms for reliability include dependability, reproducibility, and stability. In classical test theory, the score that a person obtains on a test or inventory on a given occasion can be partitioned into two categories, a "true score" and an error component. A true score is a hypothetical concept that refers to the score the person would obtain under normal testing conditions. To grasp what is meant by true score, imagine that a student is administered a standardized intelligence test each day for 100 days. The individual would likely obtain a number of different scores (i.e., observed scores) over these occasions from which an average score (i.e., mean) could be computed. This mean score would approximate the person's true score around which the scores for all the testing occasions would vary (depending on the magnitude of the error component on each occasion). Thus, the person's true score remains the same on each testing occasion, but the observed score varies from occasion to occasion as a function of the magnitude of the error component for that occasion. Roughly stated, the error component is the difference between the person's true score and observed score on any given occasion (Bellini & Rumrill, 1999). The reliability of a measurement instrument is reflected in the approximate proportion of true score that is present in a person's observed score. In other words, the more reliable the test or instrument is, the smaller the error component will be. Fortunately, the conventional procedures used for estimating reliability usually make it unnecessary to subject a person to numerous administrations of the same test.

Where does error come from? Major sources of error in psychological and educational measurement include nonrepresentativeness of the instrument items; fluctuation in individual traits over time; lack of standardization in testing conditions; and subjective factors related to test performance such as stress, anxiety, depression, or annoyance (Bellini & Rumrill, 1999). These are designated as errors because they influence observed scores yet are irrelevant to the purpose for which the test was designed (Bellini & Rumrill, 1999; Bolton, 1979; Hood & Johnson, 1997). Thus, it is important to standardize testing conditions to reduce the incidence of extraneous errors and, thereby, to enhance the reliability or dependability of test scores.

Reliability, as applied to psychological and educational measures, is also a function of the relative stability of the personality trait being measured. All psychological traits are developed and expressed within specific contextual frameworks (e.g., family, friends, neighborhoods, schools, religious communities); we all act in different ways depending on the demands of the context. Yet, even for children, many psychological traits are relatively stable (e.g., extroversion, independence, tough-mindedness). Some traits, however, are more stable than others. For example, for most people there is considerable stability in the scores they obtain on intelligence tests at different times in their lives, whereas much less stability exists in scores obtained on a measure of depression, anxiety, or stress. Thus, the relative stability or instability of the source trait, which the test or inventory purports to assess, sets an upper limit for the stability of scores on a particular measure; a test can never be more stable (i.e., reliable) than the stability of the construct it measures.

Reliability of a test or inventory is reported in the form of a correlation coefficient. Reliability coefficients range from 0 to +1.0. Reliability coefficients at or greather than .80 are generally regarded as acceptable, because this means that at least 80 percent of the observed score represents true score according to classical test theory. However, what is considered to be acceptable reliability also depends on the purpose of measurement and the type of reliability. Reliability for instruments used in national testing programs (e.g., Graduate Record Examination, Stanford Achievement Tests) are typically greater than .90, whereas reliability coefficients for personality, interest, and attitudinal measures (which are usually less stable constructs than academic achievement) are often in the .70 to .90 range (Hood & Johnson, 1997).

Types of Reliability

Reliability can be estimated in a number of ways, including test/retest, alternate forms of a test, internal consistency, and inter-rater reliability. Each of these approaches to reliability represents an estimation of the *stability* of scores.

TEST/RETEST RELIABILITY. Test/retest reliability is a measure of the stability of individuals' scores on a test or inventory over time. The basic procedure is as follows: A sample of people complete a measure at a given time and then return at a subsequent time to retake the same measure. The test/retest coefficient is an estimate of the magnitude of the relationship between the scores for test occasion 1 and test occasion 2, averaged across all people who comprise the test/retest sample. The magnitude of relationship between individuals' scores on the two occasions is related to at least two factors that are independent of the test itself: (a) the stability of the trait being assessed and

(b) the time interval between the two testing occasions. One would not expect a particularly high test/retest reliability coefficient for a measure of depression, mood, stress, or other traits that typically fluctuate over time. If the time interval between testing occasions is short and the test is performance oriented, the reliability estimate may be inflated by memory and practice effects. If the time interval between testing occasions is long (e.g., one year or more) a lower reliability estimate is expected because participants may have matured, learned, or otherwise changed their status with regard to the construct being measured. Test/retest is generally regarded as a conservative estimate of the true reliability of a test (Bellini & Rumrill, 1999; Cronbach, 1990).

ALTERNATE FORM RELIABILITY. Alternate or parallel form reliability is a measure of the consistency of the same individuals' scores across comparable forms of a test. This approach is common in educational testing (e.g., Scholastic Aptitude Test, Graduate Record Examination, Stanford Achievement Tests) as a method of eliminating the influence of memory and practice effects on performance, especially when students are likely to take a test more than once. Alternate form reliability coefficients can be influenced by both (a) the stability of the construct being measured and (b) the quality and equivalence of the items that comprise the test's alternate form.

INTERNAL CONSISTENCY RELIABILITY. Internal consistency reliability is a measure of the stability of scores across the items that compose a test or scale within a test. This type of reliability can be estimated in a variety of ways–of which two, split-half and inter-item, are most common. These are popular forms of reliability estimation because they can be obtained from a single administration of a test (Hood & Johnson, 1997). Split-half reliability is computed by dividing a test or inventory into two comparable halves (typically odd and even numbered items) and then assessing the magnitude of relationship (i.e., correlation) among scores on the two halves for all individuals who took the test. Dividing the test into odd and even items is the most common approach to ensuring comparability of the two halves, because this eliminates possible effects of fatigue and practice that are likely to vary from the beginning to the end of the test. The general weakness of split-half reliability estimation is related to a principle of sampling, which holds that, all other things being equal (e.g., adequate item coverage, elimination of errors related to the conditions of test administration), the more items that comprise a test, the more stable or reliable are the scores. Thus, splitting a test into halves has the consequence of decreasing the reliability estimate. The Spearman-Brown prophecy formula may be used to correct for the shortened length of split halves and provide an estimate of reliability for the full test (Bolton, 1979).

Like split-half, inter-item reliability is obtained from a single administration of a test. Inter-item reliability differs from split-half in that it is computed by averaging all the intercorrelations among the items that compose the test or scale. Thus, inter-item reliability gauges the extent to which all items are related to each other, and it indicates the stability of scores across all items rather than across two halves. The Kuder-Richardson Formula 20 is used to estimate inter-item reliability when the test items require two-response answers (e.g., yes/no, true/false) and Cronbach's alpha coefficient is used when test items call for more than two response categories (Hood & Johnson, 1997). Inter-item reliability for most tests is often higher than reliability estimates using other methods (e.g., test/retest); hence, it should be considered a liberal (i.e., ceiling figure) estimate of reliability.

INTER-RATER RELIABILITY. Inter-rater reliability is used when the items that comprise a test or scale consist of ratings of individuals' behaviors that are made by an observer (e.g., special education teacher, school psychologist, parent, counselor). In these instances, it is important to have an estimate of the consistency of scores across a variety of observers or raters. Inter-rater reliability is computed by assessing the relationship (i.e., correlation) between ratings of two or more observers of the same individuals' behaviors. The consistency of observers' ratings can be improved by training the raters in the use of the test and by providing clear guidelines for assessment of the target behaviors before the estimation of reliability.

Standard Error of Measurement

As noted earlier in this chapter, reliability coefficients are estimates of the proportion of true score that is present in observed scores. Because we know that an individual's score on a test is composed of both true and error score components, it is useful to translate this knowledge to the interpretation of the observed score so as to compute a range of scores within which the person's true score likely falls (Hood & Johnson, 1997). The standard error of measurement (SEM) is an index of the estimated reliability of a test that is applied to an individual's test score. The SEM for an individual's score equals the standard deviation (for the standardization sample) multiplied by the square root of one minus the reliability of the test. Computing the SEM allows one to calculate from the observed score the approximate range of scores in which the person's true score probably falls. Thus, the SEM is useful in facilitating the interpretation of individuals' scores on measurement instruments as a probable range rather than as an absolute number. Consider the example of a student with mild mental retardation who receives a score of 70 on a standardized intelligence test. If the test's SEM is 3, the student's true score is most likely to fall between 67 and 73. Expressed in terms of probability, there is a 68 percent likelihood that an individual's true score is within one SEM unit above or below his or her observed score, a 95 percent likelihood that the true score falls within two SEM units, and a 99.9 percent likelihood that the true score exists within three SEM units of the observed score.

Validity

Validity pertains to whether a test measures what it purports to measure, or "the soundness and relevance of a proposed interpretation" (Cronbach, 1990, p. 150). The term "validity" shares a common root with "value," and validity is a judgment of the value of the test. Whereas reliability is an estimate of the consistency or stability of scores, the issue of validity in measurement addresses questions such as: "What does the test measure?," "What do the test scores mean?," and "What types of decisions are appropriate to make on the basis of the test scores?" (Bellini & Rumrill, 1999).

The Joint Technical Standards for Educational and Psychological Testing (American Educational Research Association, American Psychological Association, & National Council on Measurement in Education, 1985) states: "Validity is the most important consideration in test evaluation. The concept refers to the appropriateness, meaningfulness, and usefulness of the specific inferences made from test scores" (p.9). In other words, validity concerns the appropriate uses of tests, the interpretability of test scores, and the social consequences associated with their uses.

Validity is always a matter of degree. Tests may be useful and defensible for some purposes and populations but less useful or defensible for other purposes or populations. No test is 100% valid for every purpose and every population of potential users. Moreover, use of a test for a population on which it has not been normed, or for a purpose whose consequences have not been investigated, may constitute misuse of the test data (Hood & Johnson, 1997). Validation of a measurement instrument is a process of inquiry into the meaning of test scores as well as the test's uses and consequences for specific purposes.

Types of Validity

Establishing the validity of a test involves three separate but interrelated lines of investigation: content, criterion, and construct validity (Bellini &

Rumrill, 1999). All three aspects of validity are important for identifying the meaning and usefulness of a test. However, in evaluating the strengths and limitations of particular measurement instruments, the type of validity that is emphasized depends on the purposes and consequences of measurement.

CONTENT VALIDITY. As the term implies, content validity inquires into the content of the items of a test. The fundamental question in content validity is: Do the items adequately sample the content domain of the construct or constructs that the test purports to measure? (Bellini & Rumrill, 1999). Content validity is usually established by a careful examination of items by a panel of experts in a given field. For example, establishing the content validity of a measure of child intelligence would likely involve soliciting the judgment of experts (e.g., school psychologists, cognitive psychologists, learning and development specialists, teachers) regarding whether the items on the proposed test adequately sample the content domain of intellectual functioning within the developmental context of childhood.

CRITERION VALIDITY. Criterion validity inquires into the relationship (i.e., correlation) between scores on a test or inventory and other, external criteria to which the test or inventory is theoretically related. Criterion validity considerations involve the empirical basis for particular interpretations of test data. For example, because the Graduate Record Examination (GRE) was developed for use in selecting applicants for graduate schools, an important question related to this purpose is: Do GRE scores actually predict (and to what extent) academic performance in graduate school?

The two types of criterion validity are concurrent and predictive validity.

Concurrent validity refers to the relationship between test scores and an external criterion that is measured at approximately the same time. For example, concurrent validation of a rating scale measuring emotional disturbance in adolescents might involve comparing those ratings with psychologists' assessments (using different measures) of the same adolescents. The psychologists' assessments would be the external criterion against which the validity of the emotional disturbance scale is assessed. The size of the correlation coefficient between the two measures of emotional disturbance would indicate their degree of relationship, and it would therefore provide substantiation of the meaning and interpretability of scores on the emotional disturbance rating scale.

Predictive validity refers to the relationship between test scores and an external criterion that is measured sometime later. For example, one approach to investigating the predictive validity of the Strong Interest Inventory (SII) has involved assessing whether and to what degree individuals' scores on the SII predict subsequent career decisions. A number of long-term studies that assessed the relationships between individuals' scores on the SII and their subsequent career placements five to twenty years later have indicated that 55 percent to 70 percent of individuals who take the SII become employed in occupations congruent with their high scores on the SII Occupational Scales (Hood & Johnson, 1997). Those findings indicate that the SII may be a useful career planning tool for transition-age students with disabilities, especially as a means of identifying specific occupations that could be compatible with students' expressed interests.

Overall, validity coefficients are almost always lower than reliability coefficients (Bellini & Rumrill, 1999; Hood & Johnson, 1997). However, this does not mean that test scores that have low correlations with external criteria are invalid. Whenever the relationship between a test score and an external criterion is assessed, the degree of relationship obtained is a function of the measurement characteristics (e.g., reliability, validity) of both instruments, the sources of error that enter into the measurement of each variable, the similarities or differences in the methods used to measure the variables, and many other factors. Thus, measuring a criterion variable for the purpose of evaluating the validity of a measurement instrument introduces numerous additional sources of error that usually serve to reduce the magnitude of the observed relationship between the test score and the criterion.

CONSTRUCT VALIDITY. Construct validation studies are concerned with understanding the underlying constructs, dimensions, or attributes being measured by means of a test or other instrument (Cronbach & Meehl, 1955; Messick, 1980). Construct validity pertains to the linkages between the theoretical construct and its measurement. For example, consider a measure of self-esteem. The construct self-esteem is generally viewed in terms of individuals' appraisals of their physical, cognitive, social, academic, and emotional status. To evaluate whether the instrument accurately measures what it purports to measure, it is first necessary to understand the meaning of the construct. Construct validity questions might include the following: In comparison to people with low self-esteem, how do people with high self-esteem act in this or that situation? What characteristics typify people with high and low self-esteem? How do they handle stress? For what activities do they exhibit preferences? The meanings of the construct need to be spelled out. Articulating the construct domain takes place during the process of instrument development, and evaluating the degree to which the appropriate content is covered by the items that comprise the instrument is an issue of content validity. However, in inquiring about the overall validity of the measure, it is also necessary to evaluate whether the intended construct meanings are reflected in the patterns observed in empirical data.

For example, do people who are indicated as having high self-esteem on the basis of the underlying theory of the construct actually report high scores on the self-esteem measure? In the absence of explanatory theory and empirical evidence, there is no way to judge the appropriateness, meaningfulness, and usefulness of test scores (Messick, 1988).

Constructs are the building blocks of theories, and theories specify how particular constructs are related (Bellini & Rumrill, 1999; Cronbach, 1990). Thus, construct validity involves a back-and-forth movement between scores observed on a test and the (implicit or explicit) theory within which the construct is embedded. Construct validity seeks the mutual verification of the measuring instrument and the theory of the construct that the instrument is intended to measure. The theoretical conception of the construct dictates the nature of the data used to verify the specific inferences that are warranted from scores on an instrument (Bellini & Rumrill, 1999). In turn, the scores on a test are used to validate, refute, or revise the theory itself. In this way, all the data (both conceptual and empirical) that flow from a theory and its application are useful in the process of construct validation (Angoff, 1988; Cronbach & Meehl, 1955). The emphasis placed on construct validity in contemporary approaches to test validation reflects a renewed focus on and appreciation for the role of explanatory theories, particularly testable theories, in the development of scientific knowledge.

Messick (1980; 1988) made the point that construct validity is the unifying force that integrates content and criterion validity considerations into a common framework for testing specific hypothetical relationships among the construct in question, other indicators of the construct, and distinct constructs. The construct meaning provides a rational basis for hypothesizing the concurrent and predictive relationships with other variables and for judging content relevance and representativeness. For an instrument to be construct valid, appropriate content is essential. Concurrent and predictive studies are also needed to demonstrate the empirical bases for construct meaning, which, in turn, provide the foundation for the interpretation of test scores. In the end, all validity becomes construct validity (Cronbach, 1990).

Relationship Between Reliability and Validity

It should now be clear that measurement instruments that are used for assessing children with disabilities and conducting special education research ideally have high reliability and validity. However, it is possible for a measurement instrument to have high reliability (i.e., scores are dependable, consistent, and stable) yet not be valid for specific purposes. For example, a broken watch that yields the same time reading no matter what the correct time happens to be would have perfect reliability, because the measure is 100 percent dependable. However, the watch would have no validity, because the reading is inaccurate on all but two brief occasions per day (i.e., the reading does not correspond to the actual time).

This simple analogy reflects the correspondence between the reliability and validity of measurement instruments. Measurements must be reliable to be valid, but they can be reliable without being valid. Therefore, at the risk of inducing flashbacks to readers' high school physics courses, reliability is a *necessary but not sufficient* condition for validity. Reliability forms the upper limit for the validity of a test, because measurement must be dependable for it to be useful. However, validity is the single most important consideration in test use.

Looking at these concepts in another way, reliability is a general characteristic of test or inventory scores, whereas validity is specific to a particular purpose or use. For what purpose can the test be used and what are the consequences that flow from its use are the fundamental questions of validity. Thus, one does not validate a test per se or even the scores yielded by a test. Rather, one validates the inferences that the user draws from the test scores and the decisions and actions that flow from those inferences. The emphasis on inferences and uses of test data firmly places the responsibility for validity on the test user (Angoff, 1988). Conversely, responsibility for the reliability of test scores belongs to the test developer (Bellini & Rumrill, 1999).

Sources of Information About Instruments

Most tests and inventories that are available in the United States are published by a few large publishers such as Consulting Psychologists Press, the Psychological Corporation, and Pro-Ed. Publishers of tests distribute catalogs each year from which manuals, scoring keys, and the tests themselves can be ordered. Often, these companies offer specimen kits that include a copy of the item booklet, the test manual, and a scoring key. The test manual should include information regarding the construction of the test; scores (norms) and characteristics of the standardization sample; directions for administering, scoring, and interpreting the test; reliability and standard error of measurement estimates; and validity studies.

The single best source of information about tests is the *Mental Measurements Yearbooks* series, published by the Buros Institute of Mental Measurements at the University of Nebraska - Lincoln (Hood & Johnson, 1997). This series contains descriptive information about tests–including publishers, prices, and appropriate uses–as well as critical reviews of tests by one or more experts. Also, a complete list of published references pertaining to each test is included and updated with each new edition. *The Twelfth Mental Measurements Yearbook* (Impara & Plake, 1998) contains information on more than 350 newly released or revised tests and inventories.

Tests in Print (Murphy, Conoley, & Impara, 1994), also published by the Buros Institute, contains a listing of all tests that are available for purchase in English-speaking countries. The Test Corporation of America publishes *Tests* and *Test Critiques. Tests* provides updated information on more than 3,200 assessment instruments. The 10 volumes of *Test Critiques* offer in-depth reviews of psychological assessment instruments, and it includes information on both technical aspects and practical applications of tests (Bellini & Rumrill, 1999; Hood & Johnson, 1997).

Special educators may also find information on assessment instruments, particularly reports about the development and use of particular instruments in research, in professional journals, including the *Journal of Special Education, Exceptional Children, Remedial and Special Education,* and *Teaching Exceptional Children.* For additional information about assessment in special education, consult *Assessment of Exceptional Children* (Taylor, 1999).

STATISTICS: THE BASICS

Statistical methods consist of two types, descriptive and inferential. Descriptive statistics include methods of organizing, summarizing, and presenting data. Inferential statistics include procedures for reaching tentative conclusions, on the basis of probability theory, about population values from data that are derived from samples.

Descriptive Statistics

Descriptive statistics are concepts and tools that are useful in studying distributions of variables. As defined in Chapter 2, variables are "characteristics of persons or things that can take on two or more values" (Bolton & Parker, 1998, p. 444). A distribution is the "total set of values or scores for any variable" (Bolton, 1979, p. 15). Whenever quantitative data are collected in the course of a research investigation, these numerical scores are understood and described in terms of the characteristics of their distributions. Distributions are a natural starting point for understanding quantitative measurement and statistics because all statistical procedures are based on the distributions of variables.

DISTRIBUTIONS. Whenever a continuous variable is measured, the total set of values obtained takes the form of a distribution of scores. For example, if a sample of male and female adults is weighed, the distribution of scores is likely to range between the values of 100 and 300 pounds, although more extreme scores may also be observed. A number of concepts are useful in describing the characteristics of distributions, including shape, central tendency, variability, and relationship.

As the term implies, a frequency distribution is a *distribution* of the *frequency* of scores' occurrence within a particular sample. The familiar bar graph, or histogram, is a graphic display of a distribution of scores for a sample along horizontal (score or variable value) and vertical (frequency of scores' occurrence) axes. In a bar graph, the length of each bar reflects the frequency of the associated score in the sample. In a frequency polygon, the frequency of each score is plotted as a single point rather than a bar, and these points are then connected to achieve a simple representation of the shape of the distribution.

SHAPE. When a large sample of individuals is measured on a continuous variable (e.g., weight, height, intelligence, age), it is likely that the distribution of the sample's scores will approximate a *normal distribution.* A normal distribution looks like the familiar bell-shaped curve, with one high point in the center, where most scores are clustered, and tapering "tails" at either end, where fewer scores are distributed (Bellini & Rumrill, 1999). Although many physical and mental characteristics tend to be normally distributed, it is important to understand that no measurable characteristic is precisely normally distributed. The bell-shaped curve is a mathematical concept that appears to closely approximate the distribution of many variables in nature, but it is not a fact of nature and, therefore, is unlikely to represent the distribution of a given sample of scores. Non-normal distributions may have two or more "humps," (i.e., bimodal or multimodal distributions) rather than the familiar one, or the single hump may be off-center rather than in the middle of the distribution of scores (i.e., asymmetrical distribution). A distribution is said to be *skewed* when most scores occur at the low or high end of the score value range rather than in the center of the range as in a symmetrical, normal distribution.

The normal distribution is the foundation for descriptive and inferential statistics (Bolton, 1979). Most inferential statistical tests require an assumption that the variables to be analyzed are distributed normally, known as the normality assumption. Fortunately, many statistical tests are not severely influenced by violations of the assumption of normality and then can be applied with reasonable confidence to distributions that are non-normal (see subsection on nonparametric statistics later in this chapter). Hays (1988) and Stevens (1992) provided thorough discussions of the theoretical assumptions that underlie particular statistical procedures and the various ways that violations of the normality assumption affect the interpretation of statistical significance tests.

MEASURES OF CENTRAL TENDENCY. Measures of central tendency are used to describe the typical or average performance of a group on a measured characteristic. The *mode* is the numerical value or score that occurs most frequently in a distribution. If a distribution has two or more scores that occur most frequently, the distribution is said to be bimodal or multimodal. The mode is an appropriate measure of central tendency for both categorical (e.g., type of disability) and continuous variables (e.g., intelligence). The *median* is the middle-most score, or the score that divides the distribution in half, with 50 percent of scores falling below the median and 50 percent above the median. The median is an appropriate measure of central tendency when scores are rank-ordered or given percentile equivalents (e.g., scores on standardized achievement tests). The *mean* is the arithmetic average score. It is the most common measure of central tendency used to describe the distributions of continuous variables, and it is the basis for most inferential statistics. However, the mean score of a distribution is affected by extreme scores; a few extremely low scores will move the mean score downward, whereas a few extremely high scores will move the mean higher. For example, because the distribution of income in the United States indicates a small percentage of individuals with extremely high incomes, government agencies and the media report national income in terms of the median income rather than the mean. In distributions with extreme values, the median is a more accurate measure of central tendency because it is not as strongly influenced by the presence of extreme scores as the mean is. In the event that a distribution were precisely normal (which is a hypothetical, rather than actual, phenomenon), the mean, median, and mode would be identical.

MEASURES OF VARIABILITY. Measures of variability provide information about the dispersion or spread of scores in a distribution. Whereas central tendency measures tell the researcher where the typical or average scores fall in a distribution, variability measures provide insight into the distribution as a whole. The *range* is a rough measure of how compact or extended a distribution of scores is. It is computed by subtracting the lowest score from the highest score and adding 1 to the difference. For example, a distribution of scores on a 100-point geography test wherein the low score is 32 and the high score is 84 would have a range of 53 (84 − 32 + 1). Although the range is easy to compute, it is not particularly useful in describing the variability of scores in a distribution, because a single extreme score at the lower or higher end inflates the range yet may not accurately reflect the pattern of variability in the distribution.

Variance is a statistic that provides more accurate information than the range regarding how widely spread scores are from the mean score. The variance is a single index that reflects the average deviation (or distance) of scores from the mean score in a distribution. The *standard deviation* is the most useful and most commonly reported measure of the variability of a distribution. The standard deviation is the square root of the variance and, like variance, reflects the average deviation of scores from the mean score. The usefulness of the standard deviation as a measure of variability is that it is expressed in the same units as the mean score. When a mean and standard deviation for a variable are reported, it permits the reader to understand both the average value of scores and the average variability of scores around the mean value.

By definition, when a variable is normally distributed, 68 percent of scores will fall within one standard deviation of (above and below) the mean value, 95 percent of scores will fall within two standard deviations of the mean, and 99.9 percent of scores will fall within three standard deviations of the mean. For example, for each of the three components of the Graduate Record Examination (GRE)–verbal, quantitative, analytic–the mean score is approximately 500 and the standard deviation is around 100. This means that 68 percent of scores in any one event are likely to fall between 400 and 600, 95 percent are likely to fall between 300 and 700, and all scores fall between 200 (the lowest possible score for one event) and 800 (a perfect score). The characteristic variability of scores in a normal distribution (which is approximated in GRE scores) is the foundation for most inferential statistics.

MEASURES OF RELATIONSHIP. The correlation statistic is a measure of the linear relationship of two distributions of variables, or whether they covary. Bolton (1979) stated, "correlation indicates the extent to which persons are ordered in the same way on two different measures" (p. 20). The correlation statistic contains information about both the *magnitude* (or strength) and *direction* of the relationship between two variables. A correlation coefficient can range from +1.0 to − 1.0. A correlation of +1.0 means that there is a perfect, positive relationship between two variables. As the values of one variable increase, the values of the second value also increase in perfect proportion. However, there is rarely such perfect correspondence between two variables. In fact, a perfect correlation may be said to represent a tautology–two ways of expressing the same phenomenon. An example of a perfect correlation is the correspondence between weight in pounds and weight in kilograms.

Indeed, correlation coefficients are most informative when they are not perfect, that is, when they provide meaningful information about the relationship between two distinct variables. Consider measurements of height and shoe size. Most of the time, individuals who are taller also have larger feet. However, some tall individuals have small feet, and some short individuals wear larger shoes. The observed correlation between height and shoe size is approximately .85, a less-than-perfect but very strong linear relationship. A zero correlation between two variables means that they are not related in linear fashion; as one variable increases, the other may increase, decrease, or remain constant with no identifiable order to the relationship. Two variables whose correlation would approximate zero are the height of children and the number of pets they have at home; these variables likely coexist in random fashion, with no discernible relationship being evident. A negative correlation means that as the value of one variable increases, the value of the second variable decreases. For example, there is a relatively stable negative correlation between days absent from school and academic achievement. As absenteeism increases, academic achievement tends to decrease.

The Pearson product moment correlation coefficient is the most commonly reported correlation statistic and is appropriate as a measure of linear relationship when the two variables are continuous. Other measures of relationship are appropriate when different combinations of continuous, categorical, and dichotomous (i.e., having only two values) variables are the focus of analysis. Regardless of the type of correlational statistic used, a coefficient of zero always means that there is no discernible relationship between variables, and the closer the coefficient is to −1 or +1, the stronger the relationship. Readers should consult statistics texts by Harris (1985); Hinkle, Wiersma, and Jurs (1998); and Stevens (1992) for more detailed descriptions of correlational statistics.

Inferential Statistics

One of the primary purposes of quantitative research in the social sciences is to draw valid *inferences* about the status of a population of people on the basis of the relationships observed within a sample of that population's members (Drummond, 1996). Inferential statistical methods consist of a family of techniques for translating empirical data into probability statements that are used as the basis for reaching decisions about research hypotheses (Bellini & Rumrill, 1999; Bolton, 1979). In that regard, statistical significance tests are used to determine the likelihood that the findings obtained in the sample are also reflected (i.e., can be inferred) in the population from which the sample was drawn.

It is important to understand that significance tests focus on the confirmation or disconfirmation of the null hypothesis, not the confirmation or disconfirmation of the research question. In other words, the strategy of statistical significance testing is to reject the null hypothesis and thereby support (provisionally) the research hypothesis (Cohen, 1990). If the null hypothesis is rejected, on the basis of the significance test, it means that it is unlikely, at a specified level of probability, that the results obtained could be due to chance alone. Tentative confirmation of a research hypothesis by disconfirming, at a specified level of probability, its null inverse is the most that statistical significance tests can accomplish. The test does not confirm that the converse of the null hypothesis, the research hypothesis, is true, nor does it ensure that a similar result will be obtained if the study is replicated with a different sample (Cohen, 1990). These limitations underscore the tentative nature of all research conclusions based on statistical significance tests, the tentative connection between results obtained in a particular sample (and a particular research investigation), and the actual state of affairs that exists in the population.

STATISTICAL SIGNIFICANCE AND PROBABILITY VALUES. What is the basis for determining that a statistically significant result exists in the population on the basis of the sample data? The social sciences (including education) have adopted *by convention* a benchmark for determining when a result is statistically significant. The conventional benchmark is the probability value, or *p*- value, $p < .05$. When a *p* value less than or equal to .05 is obtained in hypothesis testing, it is interpreted to mean that there is likely to be a statistically significant relationship between the variables in the population of interest. When a *p*- value greater than .05 is obtained, it is interpreted to mean that there is likely no statistically significant relationship between the variables in the population.

In the logic of quantitative research, a statistically significant result in a sample at the $p < .05$ level means that there is a 95 percent probability that the decision of statistical significance obtained in the sample data accurately reflects a true, significant relationship between the variables in the population. It also means that 5 percent of the time it is likely that a decision of statistical significance may be obtained in the sample when no actual significant relationship between the variables exists in the population. In other words, when $p < .05$ is adopted as the benchmark of statistical significance, the researcher is willing to have the significance test be incorrect approximately 5 percent of the time. As noted previously, the $p < .05$ benchmark is only a convention that has been adopted among social scientists. Other benchmarks are sometimes adopted by individual researchers, which provide a more or less stringent decision rule for statistical tests, such as $p < .01$ for a more stringent test or $p < .10$ for a less stringent test. A more stringent benchmark enables the researcher to be more confident that the results obtained in a sample are true for the population, but the more stringent decision rule requires a stronger relationship among variables to infer statistical significance. Conversely, a less stringent benchmark provides less confidence that the results for the sample are true for the population, but the relationship among variables need not be as strong to infer statistical significance.

The value of any statistical significance test is that it provides the researcher with a decision rule for identifying relationships or differences between variables that are not due to chance (i.e., are significant) at a specified level of confidence. However, as Bellini and Rumrill (1999) and Bolton (1979) noted, statistical significance does not guarantee that results are meaningful; it only identifies results that are *likely* due to factors under investigation rather than chance.

TYPE I AND TYPE II ERRORS. Two types of "errors" or false conclusions—when the statistical hypothesis test yields findings that do not correspond to the actual state of affairs in the population—are possible in hypothesis testing. The first type of error, type I error, happens when the researcher finds a significant relationship between variables in the sample, but no true significant relationship between those variables exists in the population of interest. It means that the null hypothesis (i.e., no significant differences between the variables in the population) is rejected on the basis of the statistical significance test when the null hypothesis is actually true for the population. The type I error rate that the researcher is willing to accept is expressed as the alpha level that is selected *before* conducting the statistical analysis. As noted previously, by convention most researchers in the social sciences set the alpha level at .05. The observed level of significance (i.e., the *p*- value) is then compared with the preset alpha level to determine whether results are statistically significant. A *p*- value that is less than the preset alpha level indicates that results are unlikely due to chance and are, therefore, statistically significant.

The second type of error, type II error, occurs when the researcher finds that there is no significant relationship between the variables in the sample, but a significant relationship between the variables actually exists in the population. A type II error means that the null hypothesis (i.e., no statistically significant differences between the variables in the population) is accepted on the basis of the statistical significance test, when the null hypothesis is actually false in the population. In other words, type I errors occur when the statistical test is overly sensitive, and it results in a "false-positive" interpretation. Type II errors result when the statistical test is not sensitive enough to accurately detect true differences or relationships between the variables, thereby yielding a "false-negative" finding.

We want to remind the reader here that the basis for statistical significance tests is probability theory. Statistical significance tests yield only probability estimates about the nature of a relationship between variables in a population on the basis of the observed relationship in a sample. The only way to know for certain the actual nature of the relationship between those variables in the population of interest is to sample every member of the population, an impossible task in virtually every instance of research. For this reason, it is effectively impossible to know for certain when a type I or type II error has occurred in a statistical analysis. However, some conditions of the research situation and statistical analysis have been identified that make it more or less likely that a type I or type II error is responsible for the obtained results. See Cohen (1988) for a more thorough discussion of statistical power and the confidence that researchers can apply to statistical inferences.

CONDITIONS THAT MAKE TYPE I AND TYPE II ERRORS MORE LIKELY. Using a higher (i.e., less stringent alpha level) such as .10 or .20, makes it more likely that a researcher will make a type I error, that is, find a statistically significant result in the sample when no true, significant relationship between the variables exists in the population (Bellini & Rumrill, 1999). Also, type I errors are more likely when the researcher performs a large number of separate and independent statistical significance tests within a research study.

The principal condition that makes type II errors more likely is when statistical significance tests are based on a small sample of subjects. The actual size of the sample needed to reduce the likelihood of type II errors depends on the type of statistical analysis performed and the effect size that the researcher can reasonably expect between study variables (Cohen, 1998). The reason that quantitative analyses of small samples are more likely to result in type II errors is that statistical significance tests are highly sensitive to sample size; the larger the sample, the more sensitive the statistical test is for identifying significant relationships between variables. As an example, consider two investigations, one using a sample $N = 10$ and the other using a sample $N = 100$, that obtain the same magnitude of correlation between two variables, $r = .25$. In the case of the smaller sample, the correlation is found to be statistically non-significant $(p > .05)$, whereas in the second case the correlation is found to be statistically significant $(p < .05)$. However, the magnitude of the correlation $(r = .25)$ between the two variables is the same! Because the first study is based on a very small sample, and statistical tests are highly sensitive to sample size, it is likely that in this hypothetical study the test was not sufficiently sensitive, or powerful, to detect a true, significant relationship that exists between the variables in the population. The concept of *power* (Cohen, 1988) indicates the sensitivity of a statistical test to detect true relationships or differences. Given the different results of statistical significance testing in the two studies, it is likely that a type II error occurred in the former study. In the second study $(N = 100)$, the test was sufficiently powerful and a statistically significant result was obtained. Low statistical power has been found to be a pervasive problem in social science research, including special education and related fields such as rehabilitation counseling (Cohen, 1990; Kosciulek & Szymanski, 1993; Rosnow & Rosenthal, 1989).

EFFECT SIZE. Statistical significance tests are highly sensitive to sample size, such that very small correlations between variables or very small differences in the mean values for two groups are likely to be statistically significant given a large enough sample size. This characteristic of statistical significance tests has contributed to considerable confusion and some inaccurate conclusions about the stability of numerous findings in social science research (Cohen, 1990; Hunter & Schmidt, 1990). For example, a traditional review of studies on the effectiveness of a particular classroom management technique would likely use the method of tallying the number of studies that found a significant effect for the strategy against those studies that did not find a significant effect. This review would probably conclude that sometimes the classroom management technique appears to "work," and sometimes it does not (Hunter & Schmidt, 1990). However, an astute observer would note that the various studies under review used samples of different sizes with unequal power to identify significant treatment effects. Thus, the interpretation of research findings for classroom management efficacy, on the basis of the traditional benchmark of statistical significance, would be confounded by two separate issues, (a) the size of the effect of the identified technique in each study and across the various studies and (b) the influence of sample size on the likelihood of finding statistically significant relationships. More often than not, a simple evaluation of studies in a given area of social science based on statistical significance will result in inconclusive findings and a general impression that the social sciences are not capable of providing definitive solutions for pressing social problems (Hunter & Schmidt, 1990). This conclusion is both unfortunate and inaccurate because of the confounding issues previously identified.

The limitations of using statistical significance tests as the only benchmark for determining when research results are important has led to a focus on alternate measures of experimental effects, known as effect size measures, to complement statistical tests. Effect size is the proportion of variance in one variable or a set of variables that is accounted for by another variable or set of variables (Cohen, 1988). The square of the correlation coefficient (r^2), also known as the coefficient of determination, is the most common effect size measure (Bellini & Rumrill, 1999). In the case of a perfect correlation ($r = 1.0$), r^2 is also 1.0 and indicates that 100 percent of the variation of two variables is shared variation. If $r = .6$, then $r^2 = .36$; thus, 36 percent of the variation of the two variables is shared.

The d statistic is a numerical index of the size of the mean differences between two groups (e.g., treatment and comparison groups) on a variable of interest. Thus, d is a measure of effect size that is used for evaluating the size of treatment effects. It is computed by subtracting the comparison group mean from the treatment group mean and then dividing the difference by the standard deviation of the comparison group. In other words, d is the mean difference between the two groups expressed in standard deviation units of the comparison group. The advantage of the d statistic (and other measures of effect size) is that it allows a direct evaluation of research findings across various studies that use different-sized samples and outcome measures. This enables the reader to gauge, with a frame of reference that can be used across a number of studies, the practical significance of research findings. Many research articles now include effect size measures to facilitate cross-study comparisons, also known as meta-analyses (see Chapter 6).

Methods of Statistical Analysis

This section introduces a number of statistical techniques by which data are analyzed. The examples presented here are relatively common in special education research. These methods are tools, and statistical analyses are meaningful only when they are applied within an appropriately designed study and interpreted within the theoretical context of the research question. As Pedhazur (1982) stated, "Data do not speak for themselves but through the medium of the analytic techniques applied to them. Analytical techniques not only set limits to the scope and nature of the answers one may obtain from data, but also affect the type of questions a researcher asks and the manner in which the questions are formulated" (p. 4).

THE *T*- TEST. A number of different inferential statistical tests are used to analyze quantitative data in the social sciences. The simplest statistical test is known as the *t*- test, or test of mean differences between two samples (typically a treatment group and a comparison group). Consider the following example:

A researcher has developed a psychosocial intervention designed to enhance the self-esteem of children with visual impairments. She wishes to know whether the intervention is effective. She identifies a sample of children with visual impairments from several local school districts and negotiates the support of the districts (and consent of the participants and their parents) in implementing the investigation. She randomly assigns the participants to two groups, a group that receives the intervention and a group that does not receive the intervention. Then, she implements the intervention. After the intervention is concluded, she administers a self-report measure of self-esteem to both groups. She expects that the mean scores on self-esteem for the intervention group will be greater than the mean scores on self-esteem for the comparison group; this will signify that the intervention was effective in enhancing self-esteem.

But, how can the researcher determine whether a mean difference is large enough to be noteworthy or indicative of a treatment effect, rather than the spurious result of chance sampling fluctuations? The *t*- test is used in this case to make warranted inferences about treatment effects (e.g., receipt or nonreceipt of an intervention) for a population (e.g., children with visual impairments) on the basis of between-group differences in the distribution of a dependent variable (e.g., performance on a measure of self-esteem). The researcher anticipates that, as a function of the psychosocial intervention, the mean score on the measure of self-esteem for the treatment group will be higher than the mean score for the comparison group. Thus, in a *t*- test, the effect of the intervention is reflected in *between group differences* on the dependent variable. The researcher also knows, however, that individuals within each group will obtain different scores from each other on the self esteem measure. The differences between the individuals within each group are known as *within-group differences*, and they reflect the natural variability of individuals within a sample or subsample on any characteristic. The *t*- test is computed as a ratio of between-group differences to within-group differences on the dependent variable (Hinkle et al., 1998). If the ratio of between-group differences to within-group differences is large enough, the difference between the two group means is statistically significant; on the other hand, if the ratio of between-group differences to within-group differences is not large enough, the difference between the two group means will not be statistically significant. Simply stated, statistical significance is a function of three factors: the potency of the treatment (the between-group difference on the outcome variable), the amount of variability within each group (within-group difference), and the size of the sample. Thus, the researcher is likely to be rewarded with a statistically significant result when the treatment effect is relatively large (e.g., the intervention results in substantial differences between groups on self-esteem scores), when the variability of individuals' scores within each group is relatively small, and when a large sample is used.

In the language of inferential statistics, the treatment effect is known as systematic variance or variance in scores that results from a known condition or intervention (Bellini & Rumrill, 1999; Bolton, 1979). Variation that is due to other, unmeasured factors on which the two groups may differ *and* that affects scores on the dependent variable is known as error variance. Error variance may also reflect sampling fluctuations (i.e., sampling error) that occur whenever a sample is drawn from a population. The *t*- test is a statistical method for partitioning the variation of scores into systematic and error variance. It is then converted into a probability value that indicates the likelihood that differences between two groups of a specific magnitude are due to chance or due to the efficacy of the intervention being tested. The *t*- test is the appropriate inferential statistical test when comparing the mean scores of two groups on an outcome variable.

ANALYSIS OF VARIANCE. Analysis of variance (ANOVA) is the appropriate statistical strategy when more than two groups (a categorical variable with more than two "levels") are compared on an outcome variable. For example, the researcher may wish to compare the effectiveness of two distinct instructional interventions to increase mathematics achievement and compare both to a group that received no intervention. Like the *t*- test, ANOVA partitions the variation of the dependent variable in the three groups into systematic and error variance. A ratio of systematic to error variance is computed, known as the *F*-ratio, and it is converted into a probability value. The F-ratio for ANOVA provides the information needed to determine whether the means on the outcome variable (e.g., mathematics achievement for the three groups) are significantly different. Because, in this example, the goal of the researcher was to compare the efficacy of two different interventions with a nonintervention group, it is necessary to evaluate the mean differences of the three groups using "post hoc" (i.e., after the fact) tests. The post hoc test is used to determine whether the mean differences of each of three pairs of groups are statistically significant: group A is compared with group B; group A with group C; and group B with group C. Post-hoc tests can only be used when an ANOVA reveals that statistically significant differences exist between some combination of groups; they specify the groups between which differences occur.

Factorial ANOVA permits researchers to examine the separate and interactive effects of two or more categorical variables (typically an independent variable and a status variable) on an outcome variable. The separate effects of the independent and status variables on the outcome variable are known as main effects, and the moderating effects of combinations of independent and status variables are known as interactive effects. Factorial ANOVA provides a technique for partitioning the variation in the outcome variable into variance caused by the separate main effects, variance caused by interactive effects, and variance caused by error.

For example, a researcher wishing to compare reading achievement scores for a sample of special education students according to differences in disability category and type of placement. In this example, disability category (e.g., learning disability or behavioral disorders) would be considered a status variable, type of placement (e.g., inclusive classroom or segregated classroom) would be the independent variable, and reading achievement (e.g., scores on a standardized measure of reading performance) would be the dependent variable. The first two issues in the factorial ANOVA concern main effects: Does reading achievement differ as a function of disability category, and does it differ as a function of placement type? The researcher finds no significant main effects for disability category or type of placement; children with learning disabilities recorded reading scores that were not significantly different from those recorded by children with behavioral disorders, and scores were also similar for children in inclusive and segregated classrooms. Next, the researcher turns her attention to possible interaction effects between the status and independent variables on the dependent variable. Results indicated that children with learning disabilities who were placed in inclusive classrooms fared significantly better on the reading test than did their segregated counterparts with learning disabilities. Conversely, students with behavioral disorders placed in segregated classrooms achieved at a higher level on the reading measure than did their counterparts who were included. Therefore, a significant disability category by placement type interaction was observed.

MULTIPLE REGRESSION. Multiple regression analysis is a method of analyzing "the collective and separate effects of two or more independent (and/or status) variables on a dependent (or outcome) variable" (Pedhazur, 1982, p. 6). Akin to the factorial ANOVA technique, multiple regression provides a way to (a) assess the collective contribution of two or more variables to the variation in the dependent variable and (b) partition the variation in the dependent variable into variance explained by each separate independent variable and error variance. Multiple regression is an extension of the simple correlation. Whereas correlation assesses the relationship between two variables, multiple regression assesses the relationship, or multiple correlation, between a set of independent or status variables and one dependent variable. Multiple regression analysis has two primary purposes, prediction and causal explanation. These different purposes are distinguished not by different statistical procedures but, rather, by the role of theory in guiding the decisions of the researcher and the interpretation of the data.

Multiple regression has been widely used in special education research to predict a variety of educational and social outcomes. For example, Heiman and Margalit (1998) examined the multiple relationships among loneliness, depression, peer acceptance, social skills, and demographic variables such as age and gender for a sample of 320 students with mental retardation who were placed in self-contained special education classrooms (in public schools) and in special schools. Two separate multiple regression equations were computed to predict the dependent variable of loneliness, which was measured by scores on the Loneliness and Social Dissatisfaction Questionnaire (Asher, Parkhurst, Hymel, & Williams, 1990); one for students in self-contained special education classrooms and one for students in special schools. Independent, or predictor, variables were depression, social skills, peer acceptance, age, and gender. The combination of independent variables explained a significant proportion of variance in participants' loneliness scores for both groups of students.

Multiple regression is a highly flexible analytic technique (Pedhazur, 1982). It can be used with multiple continuous independent or status variables or a mixed set of dichotomous, categorical, and continuous independent or status variables. Typically, the dependent variable in a regression analysis is a continuous variable, but variations of regression (e.g., logistic regression) are used to predict dichotomous dependent variables. Output statistics from regression analysis include measures of effect size (i.e., multiple R for the multiple correlation and R^2 for the variance explained in the dependent variable by the set of independent variables), as well as statistical significance tests for the contribution of each independent variable to the prediction of the dependent variable.

MULTIVARIATE ANALYSIS. Multivariate analysis comprises a family of statistical techniques that examines the effects of one or a set of independent (including status) variables on a set of continuous dependent variables. Multivariate analysis is less common in special education research than other parametric analyses, although some researchers have advocated for the expanded use of these techniques. In a recent study that used multivariate techniques, Espin, Deno, and Albayrak-Kaymak (1998) examined the content of Individualized Education Programs (IEPs) of students with disabilities who were placed in resource rooms and inclusive settings. One aspect of the study investigated the effect of disability label and program type (i.e., placement) on four components of the IEP. The two independent variables were disability label and program type, each with two levels. Students were classified as having a learning disability or mild mental retardation and as being placed in a resource room or in an inclusive classroom. The dependent variables were number of minutes per week specified on the IEP that the student received special education services, number of long-range goals on the IEP, number of short-term objectives on the IEP, and number of sources used to formulate the IEP. A multivariate analysis of variance (MANOVA) indicated a significant main effect of program type and disability label and a significant interaction effect. The significant main effects of program type and disability label are explained by findings that higher levels of the dependent variables were generally observed for students in resource rooms and for students with mild mental retardation. The significant interaction effect reflects the finding that the number of short-term objectives was higher for students with learning disabilities in inclusive settings than it was for students with mild mental retardation placed in resource rooms.

Multivariate techniques, which are defined by the examination of multiple dependent variables, include factor analysis, MANOVA, multivariate multiple regression, canonical correlation analysis, discriminant function analysis, and cluster analysis. For additional information on multivariate statistics, see Stevens (1992).

NONPARAMETRIC STATISTICS. All of the statistical methods described to this point in the chapter are known as parametric statistics. Parametric statistics enable the researcher to draw conclusions about a population of people on the basis of information gathered from a sample within that population. For these conclusions, or inferences, to be defensible (i.e., valid) there is an underlying assumption that the dependent variables under study are approximately normally distributed in the population. Parametric statistics also require that samples or subsamples (i.e., groups) within a population have approximately equal or proportional variance with respect to the dependent variables of interest. When a dependent variable is not normally distributed, and/or when groups do not exhibit equal or proportional variance, *nonparametric* statistics are required to make warranted inferences on the basis of the sample under study. Commonly applied nonparametric statistics in special education research include the median test, chi square, Mann-Whitney *U* test, Kruskal-Wallis one-way analysis of variance, and the Wilcoxon matched-pairs signed-rank test.

Appendix A lists the variety of parametric and nonparamteric (i.e., inferential) statistical techniques discussed in this and earlier sections, the measurement characteristics of variables that are most appropriate for each procedure, and relevant research purposes for each technique. Readers who are interested in learning more about statistical analysis in the social sciences should consult *Applied Statistics for the Behavioral Sciences* (Hinkle et al., 1998) or other statistics texts (e.g., Harris, 1985; Stevens, 1992).

Practical Versus Statistical Significance

Statistical significance is a useful benchmark for determining when a research finding is likely to be the result of nonchance factors (e.g., treatment effects). However, statistical significance is not a useful criterion for determining when a research finding is likely to be relevant to practitioners. Given the known relationship between sample size and the probability of identifying statistically significant relationships among variables, the research consumer (i.e., reader) should always attend to the actual differences among means (when group comparisons are made) or other indicators of the magnitude of relationship that are independent of sample size (e.g., d, R^2) when assessing the practical significance of a research finding.

Evaluating the practical significance of research findings also involves reassessing the status of the theoretical proposition after the empirical test, as well as the heuristic and practical value of the theoretical proposition relative to the goals, activities, and procedures of the particular agency or school. As Bellini and Rumrill (1999), Serlin (1987), and Tracey (1991) all noted, research conclusions rarely apply directly to practice. Instead, research findings confirm or disconfirm particular theoretical propositions or models that, in turn, potentially enhance their credibility and usefulness for professional practice.

Notes on Samples, Populations, and Hypothesis Testing

As we have established, the ultimate purpose of inferential statistics is to make warranted inferences, on the basis of probability theory, about the nature of the relationships between or among variables in a population of interest on the basis of the relationships between or among these variables that are observed in a given sample. Once an inference about the relationships between or among variables in a population is made (on the basis of statistical analysis), a second inferential step–from the population of interest to the general hypothesis that was tested–is necessary to ensure the meaningfulness and generality of research propositions (Serlin, 1987). Whereas the inferential leap from sample to population is based on mathematical principles (i.e., statistics) the inferential leap from the population to the research hypothesis is based on the plausibility of the theory that provides an explanation for the results. It is the plausibility of theory that is supported by particular research findings and which, in turn, substantiates the contribution of research findings (Bellini & Rumrill, 1999). As applied to statistical procedures, the linkages among samples, populations, and hypotheses imply that theoretical considerations should guide the design, analysis, and interpretation of empirical results.

SUMMARY

In quantitative research, measurement issues are central to the operationalization of research hypotheses and the interpretation of findings. Three important characteristics by which researchers evaluate measurement instruments are standardization, reliability, and validity. Standardized tests provide evidence that scores are both consistent and meaningfully related to other important social outcomes. Reliability refers to the stability of scores, the extent to which measurement eliminates chance and other extraneous factors, and the approximate proportion of true score that is present in an obtained score. Several different strategies may be used to estimate reliability, including test/retest, alternate forms, internal consistency, and inter-rater. In aggregate, these methods assess to the stability of scores over time, across comparable forms of a test, across items of a test, and across different raters, respectively.

Validity is a judgment of the value of a test, or the appropriateness, interpretability, and social consequences of particular uses of a test. Three types of validity investigations are content, criterion, and construct validity. Content validity refers to whether the items of a test adequately sample the appropriate content domain. Criterion validity pertains to the relationships between test scores and other, external criteria. Construct validity deals with understanding the underlying constructs, dimensions, or attributes being measured by a test. Validity is the single most important consideration in test evaluation. Reliability is a necessary, but insufficient, condition for test validity; a test must be reliable to be valid, but not all reliable tests are valid.

Statistical methods of data analysis are used in quantitative research. Descriptive statistics are methods of organizing, summarizing, and presenting data. A number of concepts are useful in describing distributions of variables, including shape, measures of central tendency (i.e., mean, median, and mode), measures of variability (i.e., range, variance, and standard deviation), and measures of relationship (i.e., correlation). The normal distribution is the basis for both descriptive and inferential statistical methods. Measures of central tendency describe the typical performance of a group on a measured variable. Measures of variability provide information about the spread of scores in a given distribution. Measures of relationship furnish information about the magnitude and direction of the linear association of two variables.

Inferential statistics provide a basis for making inferences about the relationships among variables in a population based on the relationships that are observed in a sample. The probability value, $p < .05$, is the conventional benchmark for determining whether a research finding is statistically significant. However, two types of errors, type I and type II, are possible in hypothesis testing. A type I error occurs when the null hypothesis (i.e., no significant differences on the outcome variable) is rejected but is actually true in the population. A type II error occurs when the null hypothesis is accepted but is actually false in the population. Several conditions that make these errors more likely were identified. Given that statistical significance tests are highly sensitive to sample size, it is also important to evaluate research findings on the basis of effect size, which is the proportion of variance in one variable that is explained by a second variable, or the mean differences between two groups. Measures of effect size permit a direct evaluation of research findings across different studies.

A number of different inferential statistical techniques are used in special education research, including the *t*-test, analysis of variance, multiple regression, and multivariate analysis. When researchers are not able to meet the assumptions inherent in the parametric statistical paradigm (e.g., normal distribution, equivalent between-groups variance), they may use nonparametric statistics as data analytic tools. Appendix A presents the types of variables and research purposes associated with different inferential statistical approaches, both parametric and nonparametric. Practical significance of findings is a central issue in the evaluation of a research study. In assessing the practical significance of a study, the research consumer should attend to the actual differences among means when group comparisons are made or to other measures of the magnitude of relationships that are independent of sample size, (e.g. d, R^2). Evaluating the practical significance of research findings also involves assessing the pragmatic value of the theoretical proposition that was tested relative to the goals, activities, and methods of the school or agency to which the research consumer seeks to generalize. It is the practical value of the theoretical proposition, confirmed by the empirical test, that substantiates the contribution of research to special education practice.

Appendix A

TYPES OF STATISTICAL ANALYSES

Type of Analysis	Variables	Purpose of Analysis
Correlation	Two (may be any combination of continuous, dichotomous, or categorical)	Assesses the linear relationship of two variables
t- Test	One categorical independent, one continuous dependent	Tests mean differences between two groups
ANOVA	One or more categorical independent and/or status, one continuous dependent	Tests mean differences for more than two groups
ANCOVA	One or more categorical independent and/or status, one or more continuous moderator, one continuous dependent	Tests mean differences for two or more groups while holding moderator variable constant across groups
Multiple regression	Two or more categorical and/or continuous independent and/or status, one continuous dependent	Assesses collective and separate correlation of multiple predictor variables to single outcome
Multiple discriminant Analysis	One categorical independent or status, set of continuous dependent	Assesses the differences among two or more groups on a set of dependent variables

Logistic regression	Two or more categorical and/or continuous independent and/or status, one dichotomous dependent	Assesses collective and separate correlation of multiple predictor variables to single dichotomous outcome
Multivariate multiple Regression	Two or more categorical and/or continuous independent and/or status, two or more continuous dependent	Assesses collective and separate correlation of multiple predictor variables to two or more outcome variables
MANOVA	Two or more categorical independent and/or status variables, two or more continuous dependent	Tests mean differences on two or more outcomes for two or more groups
Canonical correlation	Two or more sets of continuous variables	Assesses the relationships among two or more variable sets
Factor analysis	Set of continuous variables	Assesses the dimensionality of a set of continuous variables
Cluster Analysis	Set of continuous variables	Assesses the dimensionality of a set of continuous variables

Chapter 4

ETHICAL ISSUES AND GUIDELINES FOR SPECIAL EDUCATION RESEARCH

PHILLIP D. RUMRILL, JR.

INTRODUCTION

ETHICS ARE A SET OF RULES or guidelines regarding what is "right" or appropriate conduct (Bellini & Rumrill, 1999; Corey, Corey, & Callanan, 1998). Although we all maintain our own core ethics that guide us in our everyday lives, most professions set forth ethical guidelines, or codes, that specify how people should conduct themselves as representatives of those professions. For example, the Code of Ethics and Standards of Practice for Special Education (Council for Exceptional Children, 1999) provides a structure for professional conduct with respect to such issues as instructional responsibilities, management of behavior, parent relationships, advocacy, professional employment, and interactions with other professionals.

Given the applied emphasis of research in special education, as described in Chapter 1 of this text, as well as the close contact that special education researchers have with children and youth with disabilities, ethical issues are of paramount importance in the design, implementation, and dissemination of research in our field. Indeed, the special education researcher has obligations to several constituency groups that have vested interests in ensuring that empirical studies are carried out under the highest ethical standards and circumstances. Specifically, researchers in special education have ethical obligations to participants in their research, to the parents of research participants, to other researchers collaborating on investigations, to their employers, to the agencies that support research projects, to professional consumers (i.e., readers) of research results, and to professional organizations with which they are affiliated.

The purpose of this chapter is to describe the considerations and standards that shape "right" or appropriate conduct in scientific inquiry as they apply

to special education. The chapter begins with an overview of ethical principles that underlie all aspects of special education, then follows with standards
concerning the treatment of human subjects in educational and social scientific research. The chapter concludes with a discussion of ethics as they apply
to the process of reporting and publishing special education research.

UNDERLYING ETHICAL PRINCIPLES OF
SPECIAL EDUCATION

Before the special education researcher begins to conceptualize and
design a study, he or she must become familiar with the abiding ethical provisions that guide all educational interactions with children with disabilities
and their parents. Reprinted with the kind permission of the Council for
Exceptional Children, Appendix B presents the Code of Ethics and
Standards of Professional Practice for Special Education.

In addition to the ethical guidelines set forth by the Council for
Exceptional Children to shape professional conduct in special education,
medical and social science professions share an overarching set of precepts
that serves to define the right and appropriate conduct in numerous settings
and circumstances (including research). Specifically, nonmaleficence, beneficence, autonomy, justice, and fidelity have been identified, by various ethicists, as hallmarks of professional behavior in human services (Beauchamp &
Childress, 1979; Howie, Gatens Robinson, & Rubin, 1992; Rubin & Roessler,
1995). The following paragraphs define and explain these concepts as they
apply to all aspects of special education practice and research.

Non-Maleficence

"First, do no harm." Known as nonmaleficence, the "do no harm" maxim
in applied education and psychology means that researchers must take every
precaution to ensure that participants are not subject to danger or negative
consequences (Bellini & Rumrill, 1999; Heppner et al., 1992). Most social science ethicists agree that non-maleficence is the most basic and important
guideline for the conduct of researchers and practitioners (Diener &
Crandall, 1978).

"Doing no harm" requires the special education researcher to do more
than simply avoid inflicting intentional harm. Researchers must also minimize unintended risks to every extent possible, inform participants of any
risks that cannot be controlled, and maintain vigilance in assessing any
potential harmful situations that may arise during the conduct of a study.

Furthermore, non-maleficence is seen as even more important than the ideal of providing benefit to (i.e., helping) the student, consumer, or participant. When a special education researcher is considering an intervention or procedure that could benefit one participant while potentially harming another, ethical standards dictate that he or she should not apply that intervention until the potential risks have been minimized and explained to the participant who may be subject to harm.

Beneficence

If nonmaleficence–the act or process of "doing no harm"–constitutes the most basic ethical obligation of the special education researcher, then beneficence–"acting in a manner that promotes the well-being of others" (Rubin & Roessler, 1995, p. 165)–must be viewed as the core principle that defines the purpose of any educational relationship. It should be noted that beneficence applies to the well-being of both research participants and other professionals.

For example, the applied special education researcher who demonstrates an intervention to enhance the self-esteem of children with disabilities upholds the principle of beneficence in two ways. Not only is a direct benefit provided to participants in the investigation (especially to those who report increases in self-esteem after completing the intervention), readers of the research report or published article who incorporate the researcher's strategies into their own practices stand to enhance their students' prospects for successful psychological adjustment and often positive outcomes. In other words, beneficence in special education research can be observed in terms of both direct benefits to participants in particular studies and the contributions that published research makes to the professional knowledge base.

Implicit in the principle of beneficence is the notion of competence. Teachers have an ethical obligation to ensure that they have had appropriate training and possess sufficient skills to help their students develop academic, social, vocational, and daily living skills. This also means that teachers must realistically appraise the limitations of their training and experience and not attempt to exceed their qualifications by providing services that would be the more appropriate purview of another professional. This self-assessment process is equally important for the beneficent special education researcher. When applying the designs and techniques described in subsequent chapters of this book, researchers must ensure that their methods and analyses are compatible with their current levels of proficiency. In that vein, beneficence includes not only the desire or intention to contribute to the well-being of people with disabilities by means of special education research but also the ability to carry out a responsible and scientifically sound investigation.

Autonomy

The concept of autonomy, defined by Kitchener (1984, p. 46) as "respect for the freedoms of choice and action of the individual to the extent that those freedoms do not conflict with similar freedoms of others," is a cornerstone of American laws, politics, and culture. The freedom to choose and act in accordance with one's own values, interests, and ambitions is among the most important liberties, and ethical standards in medical and social science research are imbued with the rights of subjects to participate (or not participate) of their own volition and without negative consequences.

Since the Nuremberg trials after World War II, the principle of autonomy has received steadily increasing attention from research ethicists (Heppner et al., 1992). Anyone who has conducted a research investigation at a college, university, or hospital during the past 25 years is familiar with the notion of informed consent, a mainstay requirement of ethical research practice, which holds that potential research participants must be informed about the nature and purpose of the investigation before to their voluntary enrollment.

As it applies to special education research, autonomy encompasses more than soliciting and securing informed consent from potential participants and their parents. The researcher must ensure that delivering an intervention or collecting data does not intrude any more than is absolutely necessary on participants' other pursuits (Howie et al., 1992). In the event that an investigation requires or is intended to result in a particular course of action, participants must be granted assurances that the ultimate locus of control for their choices rests with them and/or their guardians. Even if the study involves activities that appear to be inherently helpful as per the principle of beneficence (e.g., communication skills training, instruction to improve reading comprehension, community-based work experiences), participants must retain absolute perogative regarding whether, when, and to what extent they engage in the investigation.

Justice

In any field or sector of society wherein limited resources do not allow decisionmakers to provide for all of the needs of all people, difficult choices must be made regarding "who gets what and why" (Howie et al., 1992, p. 49). Such is certainly the case in special education. In making decisions concerning who gets what and why, the principle of justice often serves as the ethical benchmark (Corey et al., 1998; Heppner et al., 1999; Rubin & Roessler, 1995).

In education and other areas of human services, justice implies that resources and services are disbursed fairly and not on the basis of "advantaging" or "disadvantaging" characteristics (Howie et al., 1992, p. 50). In other words, just distribution of resources means that people who occupy a status of advantagement do not receive a disproportionate share of goods or services. It also means that people whose status is one of disadvantagement are not disproportionately excluded from accessing benefits or resources. Schriner, Rumrill, and Parlin (1995) noted that justice in disability policy is not simply a matter of dividing resources evenly among all people who have a need or claim; rather, they asserted the age-old maxim that the purpose of social services (including special education) is to "level the playing field" (Rubin & Roessler, 1995, p. 171) for people to access certain benefits or amenities of society. In that regard, however, Bellini, Bolton, and Neath (1998) noted that justice or equity for one person often results in injustice or inequity for another. For example, a medical researcher conducting a study with an experimental drug to treat attention deficit disorder limits her investigation to 18 children because of limited funding for the project. The nineteenth and subsequent children who enroll in the study are not provided with the treatment; rather, they form a "services as usual" comparison group. The treatment turns out to be highly successful, which is, of course, beneficial to the participants who received the intervention. One could make the point, however, that the comparison group incurred an injustice, albeit an unavoidable one, given the fiscal constraints of the study, by not having the opportunity to receive the experimental drug. As a means of more justly allocating the benefits of the intervention, the researcher might decide to administer the experimental drug to the comparison group sometime after the study has concluded.

Justice is a key principle in the delivery of special education services, and it poses key considerations for special education researchers as they design investigations, select participants, and apply consistent standards in determining "who gets what and why." By establishing a clear scheme and rationale for determining how research studies are justly and fairly carried out, special education researchers can add to the knowledge base in a manner that reflects the full spirit of ethical conduct in all social science disciplines.

Fidelity

The principle of fidelity is a core element of any effective helping or educational relationship. Fidelity means faithfulness, keeping promises and honoring agreements, and loyalty (Heppner et al., 1992). Being honest, not engaging in undue deception, and maintaining confidentiality are commonly accepted ways of manifesting fidelity in such relationships as supervisor/worker, teacher/student, counselor/client, and researcher/participant.

Being viewed as trustworthy, credible, and honest provides an essential foundation on which special education researchers design and implement investigations that are imbued with the ideals of nonmaleficence, beneficence, autonomy, and justice. In perhaps the most fundamental sense, the principle of fidelity serves as a building block of ethical practice and effective relationships in all aspects of scientific inquiry in our field.

TREATMENT OF HUMAN SUBJECTS IN SPECIAL EDUCATION AND SOCIAL SCIENCE RESEARCH

As should be clear from reading the preceding code of conduct and ethical guidelines, protecting the welfare of research participants is an absolute guiding mission for all social scientists. Implicit in any investigation wherein researchers collect data from human subjects (and especially children) is the assurance that participants have not been coerced and that they (and their parents) have made informed choices on the basis of the risks and benefits associated with participation. Key ethical issues related to the treatment of human subjects include protecting participants from harm, institutional review procedures, informed consent, privacy and confidentiality, deception and debriefing, and considerations related to applying and witholding treatment.

Protecting Participants from Harm

Although the principle of autonomy implies that research participants should have the freedom to choose whether and to what extent they will be involved in a study—even in one in which some degree of risk can be foreseen—the superseding nonmaleficence maxim dictates that researchers take precautions to ensure that potential risks have been minimized before inviting participants to join an investigation. Ary, Jacobs, and Razavieh (1985, p. 382) offered the following guidelines for educational researchers to use in developing studies that involve potential risk to participants:

A. Only when a problem is of scientific significance and it is not practical to investigate it in any other way is the psychologist (researcher) justified in exposing research subjects, whether children or adults, to physical or emotional stress as part of an investigation.

B. When a reasonable possibility of injurious aftereffects exists, research is conducted only when the subjects or their reasonable agents are fully informed of this possibility and agree to participate nevertheless.

C. The psychologist (researcher) seriously considers the possibility of harmful aftereffects and avoids them, or removes them as soon as permitted by the design of the experiment.

It is important for readers to understand that harm can take many forms in special education research and that it cannot always be easily foreseen. Harm includes such obviously negative consequences as physical injury and death, but it may also include embarrassment, irritation, anger, physical and emotional stress, loss of self-esteem, exacerbation of stress, delay of treatment, sleep deprivation, loss of respect from others, negative labeling, invasion of privacy, damage to personal dignity, loss of employment, and civil or criminal liabilities (Heppner et al., 1992). Harm can also emerge as either a direct consequence or an indirect result of participation in a research study. Direct harm is often seen in medical research in the form of unintended side effects of medication or treatments. Although more subtle, indirect harmful consequences of research can be just as serious. For example, a transition researcher who wishes to test the effectiveness of a job placement for young adults with disabilities includes in her intervention several prompts to direct participants to obtain employment. What she fails to account for is the fact that participants who are receiveing Supplemental Social Security Income benefits (which often include medical coverage) could incur the risk of having their income and insurance benefits cut if they mantain full-time employment for an extended period of time (which is the goal of the placement intervention). In this hypothetical study, the desired outcome of employment brings with it the risk of indirect harm, namely the loss of Social Security benefits. To address this possibility of indirect harm, the researcher may wish to provide a debriefing session for participants in which he or she informs them of work incentives in the Social Security Administration's programs that allow some beneficiaries to maintain employment without compromising their benefits.

Institutional Review Procedures

The National Research Act of 1974 requires institutions receiving Federal funds (e.g., colleges and universities, research centers, hospitals, public schools) to review the ethical and legal soundness of proposals for research to be conducted at those institutions. The primary target of this statute is research that involves human subjects. As a means of proactively protecting such rights of participants as privacy, dignity, freedom from harm, choice, consentual participation, and withdrawal without consequence, most institutions covered by the National Research Act convene Institutional Review Boards (IRBs) to evaluate research proposals and to monitor the execution of those studies (Bellini & Rumrill, 1999; Hepner et. al., 1999; McMillan & Schumacker, 1997). In most cases, these institutions do not allow the researcher to initiate a study without first receiving official clearance from the IRB. An example of the form that is used to consider research proposals involving human subjects is provided in Appendix C. Many institutions also require researchers to submit progress reports to the IRB at specified points throughout studies and to develop final reports after the conclusion of investigations.

Informed Consent

One of the most important issues that IRBs consider is informed consent. Informed consent is typically achieved by providing potential participants with a description of the purposes of the investigation, a statement of potential risks and benefits, an option not to participate without consequence, and the opportunity to withdraw from the study at any time and for any reason. Consent is officiated by asking participants (or parents of minors) to sign a form indicating that they understand their rights as human subjects and that they have agreed to participate voluntarily and without coercion. Appendix D presents an example of an informed consent document.

It is important to note that obtaining informed consent from participants is not necessary in all research investigations involving human subjects. Studies that examine extant data (i.e., data that have already been collected for another purpose) provide only summary data to the researcher(s) without linking individual participants' information with their names and/or require participants to provide anonymous information may not compel the researcher(s) to secure informed consent from each participant. An exception to the informed consent rule is also commonly invoked in legal research that interprets information that is a matter of public record.

Privacy and Confidentiality

As is specified in the informed consent document presented in Appendix D, research participants have the right to privacy with respect to information that they provide in a study. Researchers must keep personally identifying information about particular participants in strict confidence unless participants expressly waive their rights to confidentiality. McMillan and Schumacher (1997) identified several ways of safeguarding research participants' rights to privacy, including (a) collecting and coding data anonymously without ever knowing the participants' names; (b) using numerical or alphabetical coding systems to link data to participants' names, then destroying the system at the end of the investigation; (c) retaining a third party who links names and data and then provides the researcher with anonymous results; (d) using aliases or code numbers (e.g., a portion of one's Social Security number) in linking personally identifying information; and (e) reporting only summary or aggregate results for the entire sample or particular groups, rather than reporting information garnered from individual participants' responses.

Another level of safeguarding participants' rights to privacy is often used in investigations that involve case studies (Roessler & Gottcent, 1994; Roessler, Reed, & Brown, 1998). A common design in epidemiological medical research and in qualitative investigations in various fields, the case study approach involves gathering in-depth information about a relatively small number of individuals. Although aliases are almost always used in reporting these studies, the level of specificity in the information reported is such that participants may be recognizable to some readers. To minimize the prospects of unwanted recognition, researchers often send copies of the manuscript or research report for participants'(and their parents') review before the paper is submitted for publication. This gives the participant an opportunity to check the report for accuracy and to change any representations of his or her personal experiences that are objectionable.

Deception and Debriefing

The principle of fidelity implies honesty and trustworthiness, as noted in a previous section of this chapter. Fidelity does not, however, mean that a special education researcher must fully disclose all aspects of an investigation to participants at the inception of the study. In fact, to fully disclose all aspects of a particular study often biases the results or outcomes. The researcher should inform participants of the general purposes of the study, but degrees of deception are seen as necessary aspects of many, if not most, investigations. Deception can include witholding specific details of a study, not informing members of a control or comparison group what intervention or stimulus other participants will be exposed to, collecting data under some auspice other than a research study, and out-and-out lying to participants (Heppner et al., 1992; McMillan & Schumacher, 1997).

Of course, how much deception is too much from an ethical standpoint is always a matter of situational judgment. IRBs examine the level of deception that a researcher intends to use, with the primary consideration being how necessary deception is to the conduct of the study. McMillan and Schumacher (1997) asserted that deception should only be used in cases in which "(1) the significance of the potential results is greater than the determined effects of lying; (2) deception is the only valid way to carry out the study; and (3) appropriate debriefing, in which the researcher informs the participants of the nature of and reasons for the deception following the completion of the study, is used" (p. 194).

Most research ethicists agree that, regardless of whether or how much deception was used in executing a study, participants have the right to a full disclosure of the purpose, methods, and findings of an investigation after it is completed. Some researchers provide a summary report of the study to all participants as a matter of routine, whereas others prefer to hold in-person debriefing meetings with participants.

Applying and Witholding Treatment

In studies that involve the application of a treatment or intervention, the principle of beneficence often comes into conflict with limitations associated with resources, time, and scientific controls. Researchers are often faced with the difficult decision of choosing who will participate in an intervention and who will be excluded.

The ethics of applying and/or witholding treatment are almost always complicated, and they interact with some of the foundational principles of scientific inquiry. On one hand, it would seem that any researcher would want as many people as possible to benefit from a successful intervention. On the other hand, constraints of time and money often necessitate limiting an experiment to a specified number of participants. Moreover, "good science" in experimental design (Heppner et al., 1992; McMillan & Schumacher, 1997) dictates that a group receiving an intervention or treatment should be compared with a control group that did not participate in the intervention. In addition, the principle of statistical power (as was described in Chapter 3) implies that researchers should not exceed certain thresholds of sample size to effectively gauge the impact of their interventions or treatments.

So, because overall sample and intrasample group sizes are limited by time, money, and scientific protocol, the "who gets what and why?" question reemerges as per the principle of justice. Many researchers provide abbreviated versions (e.g., written informational packets, self-help brochures) of interventions to participants who are not assigned to an experimental condition (Bellini & Rumrill, 1999). Other researchers place such participants on a waiting list and provide the treatment or training to them at a later date. For example, Palmer (1998) demonstrated an effective model for training college students with disabilities to request classroom accommodations from their instructors. Social scientific protocol dictated that he withold the intervention from a number of interested participants who formed a comparison group. However, to the extent that the intervention presented useful information and resulted in valuable skill acquisition for those (randomly) selected to participate in the training, Palmer's study (as it was initially designed) effectively excluded half of the sample. Noting the inherent injustice in his original design, the researcher decided to provide the training to the comparison group after he had gathered baseline data from them concerning the hypothesized effects of the intervention.

ETHICAL CONSIDERATIONS INVOLVED IN REPORTING SPECIAL EDUCATION AND PUBLISHING RESEARCH

The role of ethics in special education research clearly and rightfully centers on the treatment of subjects or participants. Not only is the special education researcher responsible for upholding the fundamental ethical principles that underlie the profession and practice of special education (i.e., nonmaleficence, beneficence, autonomy, justice, and fidelity), he or she must ensure that defined ethical standards related to scientific inquiry and the treatment of human subjects (e.g., confidentiality, informed consent, institutional review) are followed. However, the ethical special education researcher's obligation is not completely fulfilled by virtue of ethical conduct in the execution of a study. There are also ethical considerations to be made in the process of reporting and publishing research results. Synthesizing ethical provisions promulgated by the American Counseling Association (1995), and the American Psychological Association (1992; 1994), Bellini and Rumrill (1999) set forth a number of recommended standards for ethical practice in publishing social science research. Summarized and paraphrased in the following paragraphs, those standards address such key issues as authorship credit, the roles of editors and peer reviewers, acknowledgment of contributions, plagiarism, and copyright laws.

Relationships with Research Participants

In many published research articles, the investigators document how they adhered to the ethical standards of their home institutions in conducting particular investigations. They must describe how informed consent was obtained, and the "Method" section of a published research article should include a description of the manner in which participants were recruited for the study. The article should also include only information that cannot be linked to a participant's name or other identifying characteristics. It is important to remember that research participants who are considered to be at greater risk for harm, because of disadvantaging characteristics (e.g., children, people with disabilities, prisoners), are afforded a higher degree of protection under the National Research Act than are participants who are considered to be at less risk.

Data Collection, Analysis, and Reporting

Special education researchers must report data as they were collected. Tampering with, fabricating, and exaggerating results are considered unethical conduct (Parker & Szymanski, 1996). Also, the norm of common ownership of information (Merton, 1968; as cited in Bellini & Rumrill 1999) requires that all data presented in a research article are essential to the full and accurate reporting of an investigation's results. Extraneous information may serve to distract the reader from the true meaning of the study and, therefore, should not be reported. Conversely, providing too little information in a research report or article renders it difficult for other researchers to replicate the investigation

The procedures that were used to analyze data must not mislead the reader, distort findings, or exaggerate the impact or meaning of research results. Many authors include a description of the scientific limitations of their studies in the "Discussion" sections of published articles. This serves as a means of accurately characterizing the overall contributions of their research, as well as a forum to honestly report the parameters in which research validity conclusions about a study can be drawn.

Procedures for Correcting Errors

If the author notices an error of fact or omission in a published article, he or she should make reasonable effort to notify readers by submitting a correction or retraction to be included in the next issue of the journal. To prevent foreseeable errors from appearing in print, many journals provide authors with "galley" page proofs just before the finalized publication of each issue. These proofs provide a likeness of how the article will appear in print, and they afford authors the opportunity to make any final changes to the article before the journal's printing.

Citation and Acknowledgement Procedures

When citing facts, findings, or ideas that are not their own, authors must afford credit to the originator(s) of previously published work. Short direct quotes should be attributed to the page number of their original published source. Longer direct quotes or reprinting of an entire article usually requires the permission of the author(s) and/or publisher of the original work. Failure to obtain an original author's consent or offer appropriate acknowledgment may be viewed as plagiarism and a violation of copyright law. Most journals in special education and disability studies adhere to the American Psychological Association's (1994) guidelines for citing and acknowledging the works of other authors.

The concept of plagiarism needs additional attention here. Plagiarism can range from unintentional omissions of necessary citations to willful "theft" of another author's words in an attempt to make them one's own. The issue of giving credit where credit is due becomes complicated in circumstances related to the origin of ideas. Given that a discipline's knowledge base is built in small increments with each advance serving as an extension of the one before it (Bellini et al., 1999; Heppner et al., 1992), it is sometimes confusing to authors (and readers) who originated a particular concept and who extended or amplified it. How much one must extend an existing theory or model before claiming a new one is not provided in current ethical guidelines, nor is any allowance for the possibility that two or more authors could independently develop similar ideas at approximately the same time. Given that plagiarism almost always amounts to a situational judgment call, the best advice for special education authors is that they take every step possible to credit others for the work that others have done and be sure that claims of original ideas are qualified by acknowledging authors whose works contributed to the development of new knowledge.

Authorship Credit

To be granted authorship credit for a published article, an individual must have made an appropriate, substantive contribution to the manuscript. According to Winston (1985), scholarly contributions to a research article that could merit publication credit include conceptualizing and refining research ideas, literature search, developing a research design, instrument selection, instrument construction/questionnaire design, selection of statistical analyses, collection and preparation of data, performing statistical analyses, interpreting statistical analyses, drafting manuscripts, and editing the manuscript (Heppner et al., 1992). Individuals who do not warrant authorship credit but who contributed to an article in a minor way are often credited in an "Acknowledgments" or "Author Note" section at the end of the article. Heppner et al. (1992) identified several activities as minor contributions that do not usually warrant authorship credit: providing editorial feedback, consulting on design or statistical questions, serving as raters or judges, administering an intervention, providing (even extensive) clerical services, and generating conceptual ideas relevant to the study without contributing to the writing of the manuscript.

Bellini and Rumrill (1999) opined that authorship also implies that the person has not had a role in the editorial process or peer review of that article. In the event that an editor of a journal submits a paper for review and possible publication in that journal, he or she should defer all editorial decisions to a co-editor or editorial board member.

In terms of the institutional affiliations of authors, these should be accredited to the institutions at which authors were employed or affiliated at the time work on the article was completed. If an author changes his or her institutional affiliation during the editorial or publication processes, he or she may elect to add the new affiliation to the former one. In that event, the author credits bear both institutional affiliations.

Ordering of Authors

If an article was written by two or more authors (which is the case in most articles published in special education journals), the first author listed should be the one who has made the most significant contributions to the development of the article. Secondary authors' names should be listed in descending order of their contributions, unless otherwise indicated in an Author Note. When two or more authors contribute equally to a co-authored article or book, it is common for authors to be listed in alphabetical or reverse alphabetical order, accompanied by a statement that the publication represents an evenly distributed collaborative effort. In those cases, senior or principal authorship is shared by all contributors.

Publications Resulting from Dissertations or Theses

When an article with more than one author is the product of a student's dissertation or thesis, the student should usually be listed as the first author (Bellini & Rumrill, 1999). Regardless of the student's institutional affiliation at the time of the article's publication, the institution that sponsored his or her study (where he or she earned the degree that was culminated by the dissertation or thesis) should also be included in the author credits.

Most experts agree that the student should be the first author of articles resulting from his or her dissertation, but whether and how the student's dissertation supervisor is accorded authorship credit can be complicated decisions. The American Psychological Association Ethics Committee (1983) specified how authorship credit should be ordered in the published forms of dissertations or theses. Cited by Heppner et al. (1992, p. 88), the guidelines are as follows:

  I. Only second authorship is acceptable for the dissertation supervisor.

  II. Second authorship may be considered obligatory if the supervisor designates the ` variables or makes major interpretive contributions or provides the data base.

  III. Second authorship is a courtesy if the supervisor designates the general area of concern or is substantially involved in the development of the design and measurement procedures or substantially contributes to the write-up of the published report.

  IV. Second authorship is not acceptable if the supervisor provides only encouragement, physical facilities, financial supports, critiques, or editorial contributions.

  V. In all instances, agreement should be reviewed before the writing for the publication is undertaken and at the time of submission. If disagreements arise, they should be resolved by a third party using these guidelines.

Ethics Regarding Dual Submission and Re-Publication

Submitting a paper for review by a journal implies that the paper is not under current consideration by any other journal. Authors may not publish the same article in two different journals without tacit agreement from both journals' editors that a reprint is warranted and permissible. Authors also must not publish multiple articles from the same data set or within the same content area unless they have (a) secured necessary releases from the publishers of previous work and/or (b) included (in the article) an explanation of how the new study differs in terms of purpose, research questions, or hypotheses.

Verification and Re-Analysis of Data

To every extent possible, authors should make their data available to other researchers who wish to reanalyze and/or verify the results of a published study. This does not mean that requests for verification need to be honored. Parker and Szymanski (1996) noted that issues such as participants rights to privacy, proprietorship, and the motives and/or competence of the researcher seeking to certify or reanalyze findings may preclude authors from sharing their data with others.

Accordance of Results with Research Questions and Hypotheses

Researchers must report all findings that are relevant to their research questions and hypotheses, not only those that are statistically significant or that support a particular perspective. Exaggerating some results while ignoring others as a means of supporting a particular point of view or prediction is ethically unacceptable and should be avoided at all times.

Editorial and Peer Review Processes

Special education professionals who serve as journal editors, editorial board members, or reviewers for grant competitions must protect the confidentiality of authors who submit their work for peer review. Moreover, editors and reviewers may not use information contained in prepublished work without expressed consent from the originating author(s). We also believe that an editor or reviewer should not be added to a list of authors during the review or publication process if he or she did not appear in the original manuscript's author credits—even if he or she makes substantial contributions in an editorial role.

SUMMARY

The special education researcher is subject to a number of ethical considerations in the design, implementation, evaluation, and reporting of empirical research. First, the researcher must conform to the rules of "right" conduct as they apply to the ethical principles that underlie the field of special education. Nonmaleficence, perhaps the most basic tenet of any helping or service profession, sets a priority on doing no harm to students or participants in research projects. Beneficence, a concept that serves to define the ultimate purpose of our field, implies that teachers and researchers should strive to help people in a way that improves their independence and quality of life. Autonomy provides a basis for absolute deference to individuals' (and their parents') rights to choose whether and to what extent they will participate in a service program or research investigation. Justice connotes fair and equal treatment of all participants without offering undue advantages to one participant or disadvantaging another. Fidelity in special education research means that the researcher is honest, trustworthy, and credible.

In addition to the overarching ethical considerations that special education researchers must make as representatives of the profession, it is important to abide by current ethical standards regarding the treatment of human subjects. Issues of informed consent, the use of deception, witholding treatment from a comparison or control group, and confidentiality are paramount concerns for responsible special education researchers, and most institutions have review boards that oversee how research participants are treated.

Finally, because the special education researcher seeks to disseminate his or her findings in professional journal articles, he or she is subject to rules of conduct associated with the publication process. In this chapter, we discussed such ethical concerns as authorship credit, plagiarism, copyright law, acknowledgment of contributions, and the roles of editors and peer reviewers.

Given the myriad of ethical issues that special education researchers face as they design, implement, evaluate, and disseminate their studies, it is essential to become familiar with the standards set forth by sponsoring institutions and professional associations. By maintaining vigilance in applying the highest standards of right and appropriate conduct in all interactions with research participants, one another, and those who review their work, special education researchers can continue a long tradition of responsible research practices whose ultimate purpose is to understand and improve the life experience of people with disabilities.

Appendix B

THE COUNCIL FOR EXCEPTIONAL CHILDREN (CEC) CODE OF ETHICS AND STANDARDS OF PRACTICE

CODE OF ETHICS FOR EDUCATORS OF PERSONS WITH EXCEPTIONALITIES

We declare the following principles to be the Code of Ethics for educators of persons with exceptionalities. Members of the special education profession are responsible for upholding and advancing these principles. Members of The Council for Exceptional Children agree to judge and be judged by them in accordance with the spirit and provisions of this Code.

A. Special education professionals are committed to developing the highest educational and quality of life potential of individuals with exceptionalities.

B. Special education professionals promote and maintain a high level of competence and integrity in practicing their profession.

C. Special education professionals engage in professional activities which benefit individuals with exceptionalities, their families, other colleagues, students, or research subjects.

D. Special education professionals exercise objective professional judgement in the practice of their profession.

E. Special education professionals strive to advance their knowledge and skills regarding the education of individuals with exceptionalities.

F. Special education professionals work within the standards and policies of their profession.

G. Special education professionals seek to uphold and improve where necessary the laws, regulations, and policies governing the delivery of

Reprinted by permission. Council for Exceptional Children, Reston, VA, 1997.

special education and related services and the practice of their profession.

H. Special education professionals do not condone or participate in unethical or illegal acts, nor violate professional standards adopted by the Delegate Assembly of CEC.

CEC STANDARDS FOR PROFESSIONAL PRACTICE IN RELATION TO PERSONS WITH EXCEPTIONALITIES AND THEIR FAMILIES

Instructional Responsibilities

Special education personnel are committed to the application of professional expertise to ensure the provision of quality education for all individuals with exceptionalities. Professionals strive to:

1. Identify and use instructional methods and curricula that are appropriate to their area of the professional practice and effective in meeting the individual needs of persons with exceptionalities.

2. Participate in the selection and use of appropriate instructional materials, equipment, supplies, and other resources needed in the effective practice of their profession.

3. Create safe and effective learning environments which contribute to fulfillment of needs, stimulation of learning, and self-concept.

4. Maintain class size and case loads which are conducive to meeting the individual instructional needs of individuals with exceptionalities.

5. Use assessment instruments and procedures that do not discriminate against persons with exceptionalities on the basis of race, color, creed, sex, national origin, age, political practice, family or social background, sexual orientation, or exceptionality.

6. Base grading, promotion, graduation, and/or movement out of the program on the individual goals and objectives for individuals with exceptionalities.

7. Provide accurate program data to administrators, colleagues, and parents, based on efficient and objective record keeping practices, for the purpose of decision making.

8. Maintain confidentiality of information except when information is released under specific conditions of written consent and statutory confidentiality requirements.

Management of Behavior

Special education professionals participate with other professionals and with parents in an interdisciplinary effort in the management of behavior. Professionals:

1. Apply only those disciplinary methods and behavioral procedures which they have been instructed to use and which do not undermine the dignity of the individual or the basic human rights of persons with exceptionalities, such as corporal punishment.

2. Clearly specify the goals and objectives for behavior management practices in the person's with exceptionalities Individualized Education Program.

3. Conform to policies, statutes, and rules established by state/provincial and local agencies relating to judicious application of disciplinary methods and behavioral procedures.

4. Take adequate measures to discourage, prevent, and intervene when a colleague's behavior is perceived as being detrimental to exceptional students.

5. Refrain from aversive techniques unless repeated trials of other methods have failed and only after consultation with parents and appropriate agency officials.

Support Procedures

1. Adequate instruction and supervision shall be provided to professionals before they are required to perform support services for which they have not been prepared previously.

2. Professionals may administer medication, where state/provincial policies do not preclude such action, if qualified to do so and if written instructions are on file which state the purpose of the medication, the conditions under which it may be administered, possible side effects, the physician's name and phone number, and the professional liability

if a mistake is made. The professional will not be required to administer medication.

3. Professionals note and report to those concerned whenever changes in behavior occur in conjunction with the administration of medication or at any other time.

Parent Relationships

Professionals seek to develop relationships with parents based on mutual respect for their roles in achieving benefits for the exceptional person. Special education professionals:

1. Develop effective communication with parents, avoiding technical terminology, using the primary language of the home, and other modes of communication when appropriate.

2. Seek and use parents' knowledge and expertise in planning, conducting, and evaluating special education and related services for persons with exceptionalities.

3. Maintain communications between parents and professionals with appropriate respect for privacy and confidentiality.

4. Extend opportunities for parent education utilizing accurate information and professional methods.

5. Inform parents of the educational rights of their children and of any proposed or actual practices which violate those rights.

6. Recognize and respect cultural diversities which exist in some families with persons with exceptionalities.

7. Recognize that the relationship of home and community environmental conditions affects the behavior and outlook of the exceptional person.

Advocacy

Special education professionals serve as advocates for exceptional students by speaking, writing, and acting in a variety of situations on their behalf. They:

1. Continually seek to improve government provisions for the education of persons with exceptionalities while ensuring that public statements by professionals as individuals are not construed to represent official policy statements of the agency that employs them.

2. Work cooperatively with and encourage other professionals to improve the provision of special education and related services to persons with exceptionalities.

3. Document and objectively report to one's supervisors or administrators inadequacies in resources and promote appropriate corrective action.

4. Monitor for inappropriate placements in special education and intervene at appropriate levels to correct the condition when such inappropriate placements exist.

5. Follow local, state/provincial, and federal laws and regulations which mandate a free appropriate public education to exceptional students and the protection of the rights of persons with exceptionalities to equal opportunities in our society.

PROFESSIONAL EMPLOYMENT CERTIFICATION AND QUALIFICATION

Professionals ensure that only persons deemed qualified by having met state/provincial minimum standards are employed as teachers, administrators, and related service providers for individuals with exceptionalities.

Employment

1. Professionals do not discriminate in hiring on the basis of race, color, creed, sex, national origin, age, political practices, family or social background, sexual orientation, or exceptionality.

2. Professionals represent themselves in an ethical and legal manner in regard to their training and experience when seeking new employment.

3. Professionals give notice consistent with local education agency policies when intending to leave employment.

4. Professionals adhere to the conditions of a contract or terms of an appointment in the setting where they practice.

5. Professionals released from employment are entitled to a written explanation of the reasons for termination and to fair and impartial due process procedures.

6. Special education professionals share equitably the opportunities and benefits (salary, working conditions, facilities, and other resources) of other professionals in the school system.

7. Professionals seek assistance, including the services of other professionals, in instances where personal problems threaten to interfere with their job performance.

8. Professionals respond objectively when requested to evaluate applicants seeking employment.

9. Professionals have the right and responsibility to resolve professional problems by utilizing established procedures, including grievance procedures, when appropriate.

Assignment and Role

1. Professionals should receive clear written communication of all duties and responsibilities, including those which are prescribed as conditions of their employment.

2. Professionals promote educational quality and intra- and interprofessional cooperation through active participation in the planning, policy development, management, and evaluation of the special education program and the education program at large so that programs remain responsive to the changing needs of persons with exceptionalities.

3. Professionals practice only in areas of exceptionality, at age levels, and in program models for which they are prepared by their training and/or experience.

4. Adequate supervision of and support for special education professionals is provided by other professionals qualified by their training and experience in the area of concern.

5. The administration and supervision of special education professionals provides for clear lines of accountability.

6. The unavailability of substitute teachers or support personnel, including aides, does not result in the denial of special education services to a greater degree than to that of other educational programs.

Professional Development

1. Special education professionals systematically advance their knowledge and skills in order to maintain a high level of competence and response to the changing needs of persons with exceptionalities by pursuing a program of continuing education including but not limited to participation in such activities as inservice training, professional conferences/workshops, professional meetings, continuing education courses, and the reading of professional literature.

2. Professionals participate in the objective and systematic evaluation of themselves, colleagues, services, and programs for the purpose of continuous improvement of professional performance.

3. Professionals in administrative positions support and facilitate professional development.

PROFESSIONALS IN RELATION TO THE PROFESSION AND TO OTHER PROFESSIONALS

To the Profession

1. Special education professionals assume responsibility for participating in professional organizations and adherence to the standards and codes of ethics of those organizations.

2. Special education professionals have a responsibility to provide varied and exemplary supervised field experiences for persons in undergraduate and graduate preparation programs.

3. Special education professionals refrain from using professional relationships with students and parents for personal advantage.

4. Special education professionals take an active position in the regulation of the profession through use of appropriate procedures for bringing about changes.

5. Special education professionals initiate, support, and/or participate in research related to the education of persons with exceptionalities

with the aim of improving the quality of education services, increasing the accountability of programs, and generally benefitting persons with exceptionalities. They:

a. Adopt procedures that protect the rights and welfare of subjects participating in the research.

b. Interpret and publish research results with accuracy and a high quality of scholarship.

c. Support a cessation of the use of any research procedure which may result in undesirable consequences for the participant.

d. Exercise all possible precautions to prevent misapplication or misutilization of a research effort, by self or others.

To Other Professionals

Special education professionals function as members of interdisciplinary teams, and the reputation of the profession resides with them. They:

1. Recognize and acknowledge the competencies and expertise of members representing other disciplines as well as those of members in their own discipline.

2. Strive to develop positive attitudes among other professionals toward persons with exceptionalities, representing them with an objective regard for their possibilities and their limitations as persons in a democratic society.

3. Cooperate with other agencies involved in serving persons with exceptionalities through such activities as the planning and coordination of information exchanges, service delivery, evaluation, and training, so that duplication or loss in quality of services may not occur.

4. Provide consultation and assistance, where appropriate, to both regular and special educators as well as other school personnel serving persons with exceptionalities.

5. Provide consultation and assistance, where appropriate, to professionals in nonschool settings serving persons with exceptionalities.

6. Maintain effective interpersonal relations with colleagues and other professionals, helping them to develop and maintain positive and accurate perceptions about the special education profession.

Appendix C

SAMPLE INSTITUTIONAL REVIEW BOARD DOCUMENT

APPLICATION TO THE INSTITUTIONAL REVIEW BOARD FOR THE PROTECTION OF HUMAN RESEARCH SUBJECTS

ANSWERS **MUST** BE TYPED

DATE SUBMITTED:_____ IRB#_____
(The above to be completed by IRB Secretary)

SUBMITTED BY: (**NOTE:** If this application is submitted by a student, it must also have the name of the faculty member who will assume responsibility for seeing that the research is carried out in accordance with regulations.)

_____   Dept._____Phone_____
(Faculty Member)

_____   Dept._____Phone_____
(Student)

Undergraduate_____Graduate_____Program of Study_____

TITLE OF
PROPOSAL:_____

CHECK APPROPRIATE REPLY:

A. Will the research be submitted as a grant or contract proposal?

Yes____No____

Note. From *Research in Rehabilitation Counseling*, by J. Bellini and P. Rumrill, 1999, Springfield, IL: Charles C Thomas • Publisher, LTD. Copyright 1999 by Charles C Thomas • Publisher, LTD. Reprinted by permission.

If the answer is Yes, who is the proposed sponsor?_____

Submission Deadline_____

B. Is the research currently being funded, in part or in whole?

Yes___No___

State_____Federal_____University_____Other (specify)_____

C. Has the research been reviewed before the IRB?

Yes_____No_____

If yes, please give the date of the review_____and the IRB# (if known)_____.

D. Is this research to be performed for a master's thesis?

Yes___No___

Is this research to be performed for a doctoral dissertation?

Yes___No___

Is this research to be performed as part of a course requirement?

Yes___No___

Is this research to be performed as an honor's thesis?

Yes___No___

Other (explain)_____

PLEASE READ INSTRUCTIONS BEFORE COMPLETING THIS FORM

To avoid delays, all questions must be answered. Incomplete forms will be returned to the investigator for additional information.

1. **Summary of proposal.** In concise, nontechnical language, describe the rationale and methods (experimental tests and procedures) to be

used. (**DO NOT USE JARGON**) State clearly what the subjects will be required to do or be subjected to in the experiment. Use the space below. Applications without a summary in the space allotted will not be considered by the Board.

A. Rationale

B. Methods
(The source of questionnaires and surveys should be indicated, whether published, adapted, or newly formulated.)

2. **Who will have direct contact with the subjects? Who will administer tests, conduct interviews, etc.?** State their qualifications specifically with regard to the procedures to be used in this study.

3. **Characteristics of subjects.**

A. Sex M____F___Both___

B. Age_____Any subjects under age 18?

   Yes___No___

C. Special ethnic group_____

D. Institutionalized Yes___No___(See item #4 below.)

E. General state of health_____("unknown" unless you will obtain health data on subjects *prior* to beginning the study.)

F. Source of subjects_____

G. How will subjects be identified and Recruited_____

_____

NOTE: *If the research is conducted at an off-campus institution (e.g., a school, hospital, etc.), attach a statement signed by an appropriate official authorizing access to subjects (e.g., school district superintendent), or current approval from that institution's review committee. Full approval cannot be given without this authorization.*

4. **Special groups** - If subjects are either (1) **children**, (2) **mentally incompetent**, or (3) **legally restricted** (i.e., institutionalized), please explain the necessity for using this particular group. *Proposals using subjects from any of these groups cannot be given expedited review, but must go to the full Board.*

Yes___No___ If yes, please attach memo explaining who and why.

5. **Type of consent to be obtained.** Informed consent requires that subjects be informed of and understand, by oral or written form, the procedures to be used in the research, and that they may refuse to participate or withdraw from the investigation at any time without prejudice. If oral consent is used, the investigator must explain to the subjects all of the points as required on a written consent form. A written version of what will be said when requesting oral consent must be attached to this application. **If written consent is used, the procedures must be clearly stated on the form signed by the subject. A copy of the written consent must be included as the last page of this application. All consent forms must be on university letterhead unless exempted by the IRB. APPROVAL WILL NOT BE GRANTED WITHOUT A COPY OF THE CONSENT FORM!**

A. Oral___Written___Obtained and explained by whom_____

B. From whom will consent be obtained and by what means for minors (minors or children aged 7 and older must be asked for ASSENT) or the mentally incompetent?

6. Confidentiality

A. What precautions will be taken to insure the privacy and anonymity of the subjects, and the confidentiality of the data, both in your possession and in reports and publications?

B. Will audio, video or film recording be used? Yes____ No____
Specify which _____ . If yes, what will be the description of the records when the research is complete? (All tapes, audio or video, MUST BE DESTROYED.)

7. Risk to Subjects
NOTE: *Investigators should complete this portion as succinctly as possible. If the Board has to request additional clarification or explanation, approval may be delayed a full month until the next meeting.*

A. Describe in detail *any possible* physical, social, political, legal, economic, or other risks to the subjects, either immediate or long range. Estimate the seriousness and extent of the risk. *Risk may be minimal but never totally absent. Do not say "No Risk."*

B. Describe what procedures will be used to minimize the risk you have stated above.

8. **Benefits**
Assess the benefits of research to:

A. The subjects

B. Society at large

C. Explain how the benefits outweigh the risks involved.

9. **Signatures**

A. Faculty

This is to certify that the procedures involved in this study are appropriate for minimizing risks to the subjects and acknowledges that I take full responsibility for the conduct of the research.

Signed_____ Date _____
                    (Faculty member)

Name typed _____

Campus phone _____ Campus address _____

B. Student**

Signed _____ Date _____

Graduate _____ Undergraduate _____

Name typed _____

Campus phone _____ Campus address _____

Please note: *If this study is being conducted by a student, a faculty member must sign in the space provided. A form without a faculty member's approval will be returned for signature.*

Appendix D

SAMPLE INFORMED CONSENT FORM

Purpose

The Center for Disability Studies conducts research on the lived experiences of people with disabilities. This research is conducted to learn more about how to improve educational and employment outcomes for people with disabilities. Information from participants is maintained by the Center and will be used for research purposes only.

Agreement

By signing this form, I agree to participate in research conducted by the Center as described below:

A Study of Accommodation Needs and Activities

I agree to participate in a study of my experiences in requesting and using reasonable accommodations in the high school classroom and in the workplace. The study will involve no more than two personal visits of less than one hour each with a trained interviewer. The interviewer will request information on my perceptions of barriers in education and employment as well as possible reasonable accommodations. I will also provide information regarding my background and personal views of my current life and situation in no more than two telephone contacts with the interviewer.

I understand that the Center may provide research data to qualified persons and/or research centers subject to ethical restrictions. If such information is shared with qualified persons or organizations, I understand that it will not be possible to connect my name with the information that I provide. Information from this investigation may be published anonymously in a case study format. I have the right to approve any information developed for publication.

I also understand that I have the option of withdrawing this consent and release of information and withdrawing my participation in this research process at any time. Should I withdraw, I understand that this will not affect my participation in any service program.

_____

Signature of Participant   Date

Participant's Age _____

Parent's or Guardian's Signature (if participant is under the age of 18)

_____

Participant's Mailing Address_____

_____Daytime Phone #_____

Chapter 5

RESEARCH VALIDITY

James L. Bellini,
Phillip D. Rumrill, Jr. and
Bryan G. Cook

INTRODUCTION

IN THIS CHAPTER, WE DISCUSS THE CRITERIA by which quantitative research investigations are evaluated and apply the concept of research validity to the methods that social scientists use to make warranted knowledge claims. Throughout this chapter, it is important to remember that the designs researchers use to ensure validity (e.g., experimental, single-subject, survey, correlational) are determined primarily by the research question or problem being addressed. No approach to empirical research is inherently better than any other, but each contributes in different ways to the development of scientific knowledge.

The purpose of all research is to generate warranted (i.e., valid) conclusions about the relationships among variables (Bellini & Rumrill, 1999; Kazdin, 1998). Whereas test validity (as discussed in Chapter 3) refers to knowledge claims related to measurements or observations, the terms validity and invalidity as applied to research design refer to "the best available approximation of the truth or falsity of propositions, including propositions about cause" (Cook & Campbell, 1979, p. 37). Thus, validity in research pertains to the warrant for a knowledge claim on the basis of the characteristics of the entire study, including the quality of sampling procedures, measurement, research design, statistical analysis, and conclusions drawn from the findings (Krathwohl, 1993).

A research investigation may result in a weak knowledge claim if the types of inferences the investigator wishes to draw are not substantiated adequately in the design and implementation of the study. From the standpoint of methodology, the better the design and implementation of an investigation, the more implausible it makes alternative explanations for the results, and the stronger, or more valid, the knowledge claim of the investigator therefore becomes (Cook & Campbell, 1979). With that in mind, an exemplary research design is one in which the researcher's explanation for the findings is buttressed by the elimination, or falsification, of rival, alternative explanations (Popper, 1959). The falsificationist approach to evaluating knowledge claims underlies quantitative hypothesis testing and emphasizes the difficulty inherent in definitively confirming causal hypotheses. Moreover, it encourages a modest, incremental approach to the development of scientific knowledge, which (over time) enhances the stability and credibility of a particular profession (Bellini & Rumrill, 1999).

TYPES OF RESEARCH VALIDITY

The four major types of research validity are internal, external, construct, and statistical conclusion validity (Bellini & Rumrill, 1999). Together, these issues form the set of considerations that researchers address when they design a research investigation (Kazdin, 1998). Awareness of the various threats to valid inference and the methods of minimizing these threats is central to designing and evaluating special education research.

Internal Validity

Internal validity refers to the approximate certainty with which researchers infer that a relationship between two variables is causal (Cook & Campbell, 1979) or the extent to which an investigation rules out alternative explanations for the results (Kazdin, 1998). Possible causal factors other than the independent variable(s) that are not accounted for in the research design but that may also explain the results are called threats to internal validity (Bellini & Rumrill, 1999). Overall, random assignment of research participants to experimental and control groups provides the best protection against threats to internal validity, because random assignment reduces the possibility of systematic group differences that may influence scores on the dependent measures. We will discuss the major threats to internal validity, including history, maturation, instrumentation, selection, attrition, and ambiguity about the direction of causal influence. Readers interested in a more comprehensive discussion of these issues should consult texts authored by Cook and Campbell (1979) or Kazdin (1998).

HISTORY. History as a threat to valid causal inference refers to (a) historical events that are common to all research participants in their everyday lives or (b) unplanned events occurring during the process of implementing an experimental procedure that plausibly represent rival explanations for the results (Kazdin, 1998). For history to be a threat, the event must impinge on the experimental situation in some way and influence scores on the dependent variable.

Consider the example of a researcher who uses a posttest-only experimental design (see Chapter 6) to test whether an intervention improves the attitudes of school principals toward the inclusion of children with disabilities. She recruits 50 principals and assigns them at random to two groups, a treatment group and a control group. The researcher implements a number of activities to enhance the sensitivity of treatment group members to disability issues. The control group receives a lecture on strategies to prevent school violence, a topic unrelated to the treatment condition. After these separate activities, the principals in both groups complete a standardized measure of attitudes toward inclusion. The researcher hopes to demonstrate that the intervention is effective in improving the attitudes of treatment group members, as indicated by higher scores on the attitude measure by the treatment group compared with the control group. However, in the interim between completion of the two interventions and administration of the posttest, a highly publicized Supreme Court decision mandates substantial changes in the way that public schools arrange educational placements for children with disabilities. Because this ruling requires members of the study sample (i.e., school principals) to make changes in the way children with disabilities are served, the researcher has no way of knowing whether changes in participants' attitudes toward inclusion are the result of her intervention or the Supreme Court's verdict. Thus, history represents a rival explanation for the results of the investigation, which undermines the study's internal validity.

MATURATION. Maturation is a threat to internal validity when an observed effect may be due to respondents' growing older, wiser, stronger, or better adjusted during the course of the study, when this maturational process is not the target of the investigation. Maturation is most likely to represent a rival explanation for results when there is a long time period between pretest and posttest. For example, consider a hypothetical intervention designed to increase the expressive language capacities of pre-school children (ages three to four) with mild hearing loss. The treatment, a language-rich preschool curriculum and training for parents of the children in speech-enhancement strategies, is implemented over a nine-month period. In this case, posttest expressive language scores, which are intended to measure the effect of the intervention, may instead reflect normal, childhood maturational processes (which, even without an intervention, could dramatically increase a young child's language facility over a nine-month period). Thus, the researcher's conclusion that the language-based intervention increased the treatment group's expressive language scores may be challenged on the basis of the rival explanation of maturation.

INSTRUMENTATION. Instrumentation is a threat to causal inference when an effect, as measured on the dependent variable, is due to systematic changes in the measuring instrument from pretest to posttest. This threat is most likely to occur when the dependent variable consists of observers' ratings of others' behaviors (e.g., sociability, aggression) and the raters either (a) become more experienced, more strict, or lenient over the course of the data collection efforts or (b) otherwise apply ratings criteria inconsistently from pretest to posttest. In either event, observed changes in ratings from pretest to posttest may be attributable to changes in raters' performance rather than the treatment or intervention that is the focus of the research. The rival explanation of instrumentation is particularly problematic in single-subject and applied behavior analysis research (see Chapter 6).

For example, a researcher conducts a classroom-based experiment to determine the effect of a token economy reinforcement system on the aggression of several children with behavioral disorders. In evaluating the dependent variable of aggression, he on several occasions makes a subjective interpretation of different children's physical contact with other children; a slap on the back is recorded as aggression in one instance but not in another, even though the researcher's operational definition of an aggressive act is any physical contact with another child. In this example, instrumentation becomes a threat to internal validity because the researcher cannot rule out the possibility that changes in aggression are attributable, at least in part, to his inconsistent (i.e., unreliable) measurement of the dependent variable.

SELECTION. The effect of an intervention can only be unambiguously attributed to the independent variable when the researcher is assured that treatment and control groups do not systematically differ on other variables that may influence the dependent measure. Random assignment to treatment and control groups provides the best safeguard against selection biases (Bellini & Rumrill, 1999). We want to emphasize, however, that random assignment of participants to groups does not ensure that treatment and control groups are equal or matched.

The threat of selection as an alternate explanation for results often occurs in educational research when intact groups (reflecting unknown and possibly systematic biases) are used rather than groups composed of randomly assigned individuals. A common mode of inquiry in education is to assess the effects of an intervention by applying it to one classroom of students while withholding it from another. The problem with this "intact group" approach is that the reasons why particular children were placed in each class, often unknown to the researcher, could influence students' performance on outcome measures irrespective of the intervention. Selection may also be an issue when participants are selected for treatment and control groups on the basis of severity of presenting issues (e.g., degree of mental retardation), because severity may systematically influence group means on the outcome variable (Kazdin, 1998).

ATTRITION. Attrition (also termed mortality) is a potential threat to causal inference when the effect of an intervention (i.e., differences between treatment and control groups on a posttest) may be attributable to systematic differences associated with the characteristics of individuals who withdrew during the course of the experiment. Attrition may result in a selection bias even when groups are initially chosen by random assignment, because, as a function of differential mortality, the treatment and control groups at posttest consist of different kinds of people.

Let us suppose that a school district wishes to test a rigorous standards reform program in which high school students must pass a difficult performance examination before advancing to the next grade. Half of the high schools in the district take part in the initiative (i.e., treatment group), whereas the remaining high schools proceed as usual (i.e., control group). After the first year of implementing this initiative, the superintendent pridefully announces to the school board that schools assigned to the treatment group reported a 17 percent increase in the rate of students who were promoted to the next grade. He adds that this increase is significantly higher than the 1 percent increase reported by schools assigned to the control group. What this administrator did not report was the fact that treatment schools observed a significantly higher dropout rate than did control schools, and that those students who dropped out did not, of course, take the year-end examination. Therefore, it is impossible to attribute higher promotion rates to the standards reform program because differential attrition (of students who, presumably, would not have done well on the examination) is a plausible, alternative explanation for the findings.

AMBIGUITY ABOUT THE DIRECTION OF CAUSAL INFERENCE. Sometimes, it is not possible to determine with certainty whether variable A causes variable B or variable B causes variable A. For example, a researcher may hypothesize that the increased stress often associated with acquiring diabetes mellitus in childhood causes increased depression. The data analysis reveals a significant relationship (i.e., correlation) between stress and depression within a sample of children with Type I (i.e., insulin-dependent) diabetes. He has also ruled out other threats to internal validity on the basis of research design features and logic, which strengthens the warrant for the claim that the relationship between the variables is causal. However, the possibility remains that the direction of causal influence is reversed, that having higher levels of depression results in greater susceptibility to stress. Lack of certainty with respect to the direction of causal influence is most likely to be a problem in correlational studies in which the conceptual foundation of the investigation is unclear or provides insufficient direction (Bellini & Rumrill, 1999).

External Validity

A fundamental purpose of research in all social sciences is to establish valid knowledge that transcends the particular context of a given investigation. External validity addresses this issue of generalization–the extent to which an observed relationship among variables can be generalized beyond the conditions of the investigation to other populations, settings, and conditions (Cook & Campbell, 1979; Kazdin, 1998). External validity is a particularly important issue for practitioners who wish to use research findings in teaching practice and, therefore, need to evaluate whether the findings associated with a particular sample, procedure, and research setting will generalize to their own schools and classrooms. Whereas random assignment to experimental groups provides the best protection against threats to the internal validity of findings, *random selection* of research participants from the population of interest affords the strongest likelihood that results will generalize to other individuals in that population (Bellini & Rumrill, 1999). However, random selection does not ensure that findings will generalize to different populations, settings, or conditions. The most persuasive demonstration of generalization (i.e., external validity) occurs when empirical findings of several studies are consistent across various types of subjects (e.g., children of different ages and different disability status), settings (e.g., classroom, laboratory, and diverse community settings), and other conditions (e.g., different researchers, diverse cultures).

Potential threats to the generalization of research findings include those associated with the specific sample, stimulus, context, and assessment procedures used (Kazdin, 1998). Many of these threats can be excluded or minimized on the basis of commonsense considerations. It is important for consumers of research to consider the context and findings of an investigation, as well as how a particular threat may restrict the applicability of observed results. If a particular threat does plausibly apply, caution in generalizing findings should be exercised.

SAMPLE CHARACTERISTICS. One vital question in assessing generalization is the extent to which findings may apply to people who vary in age, race, ethnic background, education, or other salient characteristics from those who constituted the research sample. For example, a services coordinator in a transition program for adolescents with severe behavioral disorders has read an article on a social skills training program that was found to be highly effective for a sample of young adults with a label of mild mental retardation. How generalizable are the findings for adolescents with severe behavioral disorders? External validity may be undermined as a direct function of the differences between the study sample (people with mild mental retardation) and the population to which findings are sought to be generalized (people with severe behavioral disorders). The two groups in this example are likely to be quite different, which means that findings reported for one group may not generalize to the other.

STIMULUS CHARACTERISTICS. Stimulus characteristics refer to the specific features of a given treatment or intervention that may restrict generalization of experimental findings. These features include the characteristics of the setting, experimenters, or interviewers–or how the stimuli are presented in an experiment. The external validity concern is that the specific stimulus conditions of an experiment may restrict the validity of findings to those conditions only. Experimental features that could limit external validity include using only one experimenter to implement an intervention, showing only one videotaped vignette to illustrate the experimental condition, and using a specific setting that may have different characteristics and conditions than are found in other settings. For example, a researcher wishing to demonstrate a self-advocacy training program for college students with disabilities uses a videotaped "model"–a person with a spinal cord injury who demonstrates appropriate self-advocacy in discussing her classroom accommodation needs with a "model" history professor. Even if the training appears to have a significant impact on the treatment group's self-advocacy skills, there is no way to separate the content of the training from the specific examples used to illustrate the content. In other words, the training may be interpreted by participants not as self-advocacy training in general, but as training on how people with spinal cord injuries request accommodations in history courses. One way to reduce this threat to external validity would be to present model self-advocates with several different disabling conditions and/or to vary the subject matter of the class settings depicted in the vignettes.

CONTEXTUAL CHARACTERISTICS. The specific conditions in which an intervention is embedded or the arrangements that are key to implementing an investigation may restrict findings to those conditions or arrangements only. The responses of participants who are aware of the fact that they are participating in a research study or correctly guess the purpose of the investigation may be influenced by this knowledge. In other words, study participants may react to the specific investigative arrangements in ways that influence their responses. Participants who correctly guess the purpose of the study may also seek to please investigators by (a) avoiding responses that they believe will result in negative evaluation or (b) providing "correct" responses. The external validity concern is: Would these same results be obtained if the subjects did not know they were being studied or did not correctly guess the purpose of the investigation? If it is plausible that subjects' responses were affected by their knowledge of the study purpose, then results should be restricted to the specific conditions of the study.

For example, a university professor wishes to survey preservice special education teachers regarding their attitudes toward inclusion. She uses a cluster sampling, whereby students in three classes are selected to participate. This professor is well known to students in the special education program as a zealous advocate of full inclusion, and one of the classes selected to participate in the survey is her own course, "Inclusion and Human Rights in Education." Given this professor's strong opinions regarding inclusion, it is impossible to determine whether respondents (especially those students in her class) are expressing their own perspectives on the issue or reflecting what they think the professor would like them to report.

Another potential threat to external validity related to contextual characteristics of a study concerns multiple treatment interference. In some research contexts (particularly in real world settings), subjects may be exposed to several different treatments in addition to the intervention, which is the target of the investigation. For example, children with attention deficit disorder (ADD) may be receiving drug therapy and psychological counseling at the same time that they are participating in a social skills training program. *Multiple treatment interference* refers to the difficulty of drawing warranted conclusions about the target intervention when it is being evaluated in the context of other treatments (Kazdin, 1998). In these cases, the generalization of findings may be restricted to those conditions in which multiple treatments are administered. Bringing back our ADD example, the impact of the social skills intervention could not be isolated because participants (almost invariably) would be receiving other treatments. Therefore, findings could only be generalized to settings in which children with ADD are receiving other treatments in addition to social skills training.

ASSESSMENT CHARACTERISTICS. The method of assessing the dependent variable in an investigation may also influence participants' responses and therefore restrict the generalization of findings to similar conditions of assessment. Many research investigations in special education and disability studies use self-report, paper and pencil measures to assess change in the dependent variable of interest. When self-report instruments are used, participants are typically aware that their performance is being evaluated, and what is being assessed is often made obvious by the nature of the specific items that comprise the instrument. These assessment characteristics can alter subjects' responses from what they would be under different conditions. When subjects are aware that they are being assessed, the evaluation is said to be *obtrusive*. When this awareness affects clients' responses, the measures are said to be *reactive* (Kazdin, 1998). Use of obtrusive and reactive measures may restrict the findings to those specific data collection conditions.

Assessment can also lead to subjects becoming sensitized to the constructs that are the target of the investigation, particularly when self-report assessments are administered before to the implementation of an experimental intervention to measure participants' baseline status. When a pretest causes subjects to become more sensitive to the construct that is the focus of the intervention, it can alter both the effect of the intervention and subjects' responses to the intervention at posttest from what would be obtained under different conditions (i.e., real world conditions in which sensitization does not take place). Posttest sensitization is a threat to the generalization of findings because it raises the question of whether results can be extended to those situations in which prior sensitization to the construct of interest does not take place.

Construct Validity

Internal validity is an evaluation of the status of the observed relationship between independent and dependent variables or whether change (as measured by the dependent variable) can be attributed to an intervention (the independent variable) rather than to other factors (e.g., history, maturation, selection). Construct validity of research operations focuses on the specific causal factors or mechanisms that are responsible for the observed change in the dependent variable.

As explained in Chapter 2, empirical research depends on translating key abstract concepts into specific research operations for the purpose of generating knowledge. Operational definitions form the essential linkage between the abstract, conceptual definition of a construct and the concrete procedures that comprise the study. For example, the construct intelligence, which can be defined in abstract terms as a person's ability to learn, might be operationalized in a research study by students' standard scores on an established intelligence test such as the Weschler Intelligence Scale for Children III. Once data are analyzed, researchers typically wish to induce general conclusions from the specific case that was the focus of the investigation. The process of scientific investigation, then, is a circular movement from abstract constructs (research planning and conceptualization phase) to concrete exemplars of these constructs (implementation of procedures, data gathering, and data analysis phases) and back to the conceptual level (interpretation of findings phase). Two linkages in this circular movement are vital in the generation of valid scientific knowledge: (a) the linkage between the abstract constructs and the concrete research procedures and (b) the return linkage between concrete procedures and the conceptual interpretations that are made on the basis of the findings (Bellini & Rumrill, 1999). Construct validity pertains to both of these linkages. On one hand (linkage between conceptual foundations and research operations), construct validity pertains to the "fit" between (a) the operational definitions and research procedures and (b) the hypothetical constructs that are assumed to underlie them (Kazdin, 1998). On the other hand (linkage between specific findings and conceptual conclusions), construct validity is the approximate validity of the generalizations about the higher order constructs that the researcher makes on the basis of the concrete research operations (Cook & Campbell, 1979). Taking both linkages into account, construct validity of research is an evaluation of the specific nature of the relationships that are demonstrated within a quantitative study. The threats to construct validity are confounds that call into question the researcher's interpretation regarding the specific factors that account for the study findings (Bellini & Rumrill, 1999; Kazdin, 1998).

A number of aspects of a study's design and procedures may make it difficult to accurately attribute the causal relationships indicated by the results to the constructs of interest. Threats to the construct validity of research conclusions include inadequate explication and operationalization of constructs, single operations and narrow stimulus sampling, experimenter expectancies, and cues associated with the experimental situation.

INADEQUATE EXPLICATION AND OPERATIONALIZATION OF CONSTRUCTS. One key consideration in construct validity pertains to the "fit" between (a) the conceptual and operational definitions used by the investigator and (b) how the construct is typically defined in the literature and operationalized in research. If there is a poor match between the commonly accepted definition and the researcher's definition, this is likely to raise questions about the warrant for specific interpretations that the researcher makes regarding the relationship between variables. For example, the construct of achievement, as it is defined in most literature, is the extent to which students learned what they have been taught. Yet, most standardized achievement tests (e.g., Peabody Individual Achievement Test-R, Woodcock-Johnson Test of Achievement-R, Wide Range Achievement Test-3) do not necessarily correspond to the instruction that students receive in school classrooms. In other words, the content of these tests may more closely reflect constructs such as general knowledge or test-taking ability than the actual content of grade-level curriculum.

SINGLE OPERATIONS AND NARROW STIMULUS SAMPLING. The definition of achievement cited in the previous paragraph raises questions about the advisability of using a single measure taken at one point in time as a sole indicator of the construct. The use of a single indicator to operationalize a construct is a problem, because indicators underrepresent constructs and contain irrelevant variation that is mixed with the variation that is due to the construct of interest (Bellini & Rumrill, 1999; Cook & Campbell, 1979). Method of measurement may represent one major source of irrelevant variation in a measured variable (see Chapter 3). Using two or more indicators that represent different methods of measurement allows the investigator to triangulate the construct, that is, separate the variation that is due to the construct from the variation associated with the method of measurement (Bellini & Rumrill, 1999). When a construct is confounded with a second, irrelevant construct (e.g., achievement and test-taking ability), the researcher can eliminate the effect of the confounding construct on the dependent variable by (a) including a standard measure of the confounding construct in the investigation and then (b) correlating this variable with the target construct to estimate the variation that can be attributed solely to the construct of interest.

Construct validity may also be limited by the use of a single exemplar or stimulus to operationalize a treatment of interest. For example, a researcher wishing to evaluate possible differences in case management practices between male and female special education supervisors presents participants with one case study of an 11 year-old female student who is profoundly deaf. Examining how special education supervisors would engage this student in case planning and service delivery activities provides limited insight into special education case management practice. Would respondents react differently to a 14 year-old boy with asthma and a specific learning disability, irrespective of gender differences in case management practices? With only one stimulus being presented to the supervisors, the researcher cannot answer that question, or others related to the representativeness of the case example vis á vis other students with disabilities. Therefore, respondents' reports of case management practices (the dependent variable) do not fully represent the construct of case management practice, because those reports pertain only to the single case study presented during the investigation.

Construct validity may also be limited by the use of a single individual to implement a treatment or intervention. Even if the treatment proves effective compared with a no-treatment control or comparison group, a reader who is conversant with construct validity issues may raise an alternative explanation to the findings; specifically, that the special character of the instructor may be responsible for the observed change in the dependent variable rather than the intervention itself (Bellini & Rumrill, 1999).

EXPERIMENTER EXPECTANCIES. In research situations where the principal investigator—or someone else knowledgable about the study's purpose—directly implements a treatment, the researcher's expectations regarding the intervention may confound the interpretation of findings (Kazdin, 1998). For example, a researcher who is enthusiastic about the effects of a token economy on decreasing the disruptive behavior of adolescents with severe behavioral disorders may wish to contrast it with an alternate approach (e.g., behavioral contracts). However, the experimenter's enthusiasm for the preferred strategy, coupled with her intention to demonstrate its efficacy, could lead to differences in how she implements the different interventions. The construct validity issue in this case highlights the possibility that the experimenter's expectations and enthusiastic implementation of the intervention provide a plausible, alternate explanation for the causal mechanism responsible for the observed change in the dependent variable of disruptive behavior.

CUES ASSOCIATED WITH THE EXPERIMENTAL SITUATION. Research participants may inadvertently receive cues, such as rumors about the experiment or information provided during the recruitment phase, that are incidental to the experimental treatment but that may contribute to the study results (Bellini & Rumrill, 1999). Hypothesis guessing by subjects–the basis of the Hawthorne Effect–may lead to enhanced motivation on the part of the experimental group (and alter their performance) to please the researcher. Incidental contact between members of the treatment and comparison groups may also lead to (a) compensatory rivalry, whereby comparison group members are especially motivated to perform as well as or better than the treatment group on the outcome variables; or (b) demoralization, when cues of the experimental situation result in lower than normal motivation on the part of the comparison group and adversely affect their standing on the outcome variables. Each of these situations may be a threat to construct validity, because they represent plausible, alternative explanations for the causal mechanisms that are presumed to account for the experimental findings. Depending on the specific context of the investigation, these threats to construct validity can be minimized by providing fewer cues that permit participants to guess the precise nature of the research hypotheses, reducing the incidental contact between treatment and comparison groups, and providing a "treatment" to the comparison group that is valued and, hence, less likely to result in demoralization.

Statistical Conclusion Validity

Covariation between an independent and dependent variable is a necessary first step in establishing that their relationship is causal. Statistical conclusion validity pertains to the approximate validity of conclusions about the covariation of variables on the basis of the specific research operations and statistical tests used in an investigation (Kazdin, 1999). When research conditions or statistical tests are not sufficiently rigorous, the conclusions that are based on those procedures may be erroneous. Common threats to statistical conclusion validity include low statistical power, violated statistical assumptions, "fishing" and error rate problems, low reliability of dependent measures, and low reliability of treatment implementation.

LOW STATISTICAL POWER. As defined in Chapter 3, the power of a statistical test is the probability of detecting a significant relationship between two variables in a sample when the variables are related in the population. Power is a function of the interaction of three characteristics of a study: sample size, the size of the "effect" (i.e., the size of mean differences between groups on the variables of interest or the magnitude of variable relationships), and the researcher's preset alpha level or benchmark of statistical significance (Cohen, 1990). Low statistical power is most likely to result when the sample size and effect size are small and the preset alpha level is conservative (Bellini & Rumrill, 1999). Low power may result in an invalid statistical decision (type II error), whereby the investigator concludes that two variables do not covary (e.g., a decision of no statistical significance) for the sample when, in fact, the two variables are significantly related in the population. Poor statistical conclusion validity resulting from low statistical power is a common problem in social science research in general (Cohen, 1990) and special education and disability studies research in particular (Kosciulek & Szymanski, 1993). However, low power is a problem that researchers can minimize by (a) using larger samples in their research, (b) enhancing the size of the "effect" between groups, and/or (c) choosing (before the statistical analysis) a less rigorous Alpha level as the benchmark of statistical significance (e.g., $p < .10$ rather than $p < .05$). Also, researchers are encouraged to perform a power analysis before to their main analyses to estimate the likelihood that their statistical conclusions will be valid (Cohen, 1990; Kosciulek & Szymanski, 1993).

VIOLATED STATISTICAL ASSUMPTIONS. The conclusion validity of most tests of statistical significance requires that certain statistical assumptions are met. When these assumptions cannot be made for the sample data, the statistical test is less accurate and the interpretations based on the analyses are less valid. For example, a key assumption for most mean comparisons between groups (e.g., *t*-tests, ANOVA, MANOVA) is that groups represent separate samples from the same population and, therefore, have roughly equal variance as indicated by the standard deviation of dependent variables. Specific assumptions for various statistical tests can be found in most introductory statistics textbooks (e.g., Hinkle, Wiersma, & Jurs, 1998).

We believe that the extent to which statistical assumptions have been met is one of the most underaddressed issues in special education research. Rarely do published research articles in our field specify the underlying assumptions of the statistical tests used by the author(s) or whether the distribution of study variables adheres to those assumptions. The danger inherent in this omission is that readers often find it difficult to discern whether the researcher(s) chose the correct statistical procedures to answer the research questions. Ambiguity concerning the appropriateness of selected statistical tests creates a threat to validity, because study findings can be only as meaningful as the precision of the researcher's data analytical techniques.

"FISHING" AND ERROR RATE PROBLEM. When multiple statistical tests are performed on a single data set, each comparison may be evaluated at a given, preset alpha level (e.g., $p < .05$), but the alpha level for the investigation as a whole (i.e., investigation-wise alpha) is the sum of all comparisons made. Therefore, performing multiple statistical tests without correcting for the number of comparisons increases the probability of concluding that covariation exists in the sample when, in fact, no covariation exists in the population from which the sample was drawn. In that event, the statistical test yields a false-positive result or type I error. The fishing and error rate problem refers to the situation in which the investigator goes "fishing" for statistically significant differences among variables in a data set and makes all possible comparisons among variables, which increases the likelihood that the statistical tests will yield false-positive results. When making multiple comparisons, the researcher can reduce the likelihood of false-positive results by applying a more rigorous alpha level for each separate test. For example, if five separate *t-* tests (comparing five separate dependent variables for two groups) are each evaluated at the $p < .01$ level of significance, then the $p < .05$ level of significance is maintained for the study as a whole, and the investigator can be reasonably assured (within a 5 percent margin of error) that a false-positive result has been avoided (Bellini & Rumrill, 1999). The researcher can also reduce the likelihood of type I errors by making a few, carefully planned statistical comparisons that are guided by theory rather than making all possible comparisons.

RELIABILITY OF MEASURES. Because measurement instruments with low reliability have a larger component of error as part of the observed score, they cannot be depended on to register true changes in the dependent variable. Using measures with low reliability as the basis for statistical tests can result in both type I and type II errors (Bellini & Rumrill, 1999). Thus, a large error component in the measurement of the dependent variable may increase the likelihood that (a) an insignificant mean difference between treatment and control groups does not reflect true differences in the population or (b) an observed significant relationship between two variables is not a true relationship. In the case of correlational studies, low reliability in the measurement of independent and/or dependent variables may attenuate or exaggerate the magnitude of variable relationships.

RELIABILITY OF TREATMENT IMPLEMENTATION. When different people or agencies are responsible for implementing an investigation, a lack of standardization in the execution of the study may result. For example, one critique of the "efficacy" studies, which attempted to determine the relative efficacy of segregated special education placements and inclusive placements, is that the treatments were not reliably implemented. In other words, the instruction and environment associated with one segregated special classroom does not necessarily occur in other segregated special classes. There may also be differences from occasion to occasion even when the same person implements the treatment or intervention. This lack of standardization—both within and across persons and agencies—can inflate the error variance in the dependent variable and decrease the accuracy of the statistical inference to the population of interest. As Cook and Campbell (1979) noted, this threat is pervasive in field research in which the researcher may be unable to control the quality of implementation of the intervention. The investigator should use all available means (e.g., extensive training of individuals and agencies) to ensure that the intervention is as standard as possible across individuals, agencies, and occasions.

RELATION AMONG THE FOUR TYPES OF RESEARCH VALIDITY

Although each type of research validity is important in its own right, and the warrant for a knowledge claim is based, in part, on how well the researcher addresses these issues in an investigation, there is a logical order of consideration (Bellini & Rumrill, 1999; Cook & Campbell, 1979). Before it can be shown that two variables have a causal relationship, it is first necessary to establish that they covary. Hence, statistical conclusion validity, or the demonstration that two variables are related statistically, is the initial criterion by which a knowledge claim is evaluated in quantitative research. Internal validity is the second issue in research, which is to determine whether a causal link between two related variables can be inferred. The third issue of research, construct validity, is to determine the particular constructs or mechanisms that are involved in the demonstrated causal relationship between variables. External validity, the final issue in research, involves the question: How generalizable is the relationship and causal mechanism to other populations, settings, and conditions? Each dimension of research validity contributes to causal explanation, which is the ultimate goal of scientific inquiry.

At the risk of being redundant, we want to remind readers here that no single research investigation can address each of these validity issues equally well. Limited resources often require an investigator to make compromises in designing research, which is why the growth of scientific knowledge in any profession or discipline is measured by tentative steps of incremental progress. The specific procedures that strengthen the internal validity of an investigation (i.e., experimental control) may unavoidably serve to reduce the generalizability of findings to real world settings (i.e., external validity) (Cook & Campbell, 1979). Ideally, the types of validity that the researcher chooses to emphasize in designing a particular investigation are a function of the global research context—that is, the totality of relevant studies in the given area, the degree to which relationships among variables have been established in previous research, and the extent to which generalizability of findings has been investigated. When the specific relationships among variables are not well understood, the research focus should be placed on statistical conclusion validity and internal validity: Do the targeted variables covary, and can a causal relationship be demonstrated? Once the warrant for these conclusions has been established, the research program moves on to address issues of construct and external validity: What is the specific causal mechanism at work, and do results generalize to other populations, settings, and conditions? The variety and complexity of research validity issues cannot be addressed in a single study or even a small group of related studies. Rather, valid scientific knowledge can only be established through multiple investigations carried out by many researchers spanning a long period of time (Bellini & Rumrill, 1999).

SUMMARY

In this chapter, we discussed the four types of research validity as criteria for establishing the warrant for scientific knowledge claims in the quantitative research paradigm. Each type of validity—internal, external, construct, and statistical conclusion—addresses a different aspect of the knowledge claim. Internal validity pertains to the strength of the inference that the relationship between two variables is causal. Threats to the internal validity of an investigation are rival explanations for the results that are not ruled out on the basis of the research design. External validity is the degree to which research findings can be generalized to other populations, settings, and conditions. Threats to external validity are those aspects of the study that could restrict findings to the specific circumstances of the investigation. Construct validity pertains to the specific causal mechanisms that are theorized to underlie the study findings. Threats to construct validity are those aspects of research design and procedures that make it difficult to accurately attribute the causal relationships indicated by the results to the constructs of interest. Statistical conclusion validity is the approximate certainty of conclusions about the covariation of variables on the basis of the specific research operations and statistical tests used in an investigation. Threats to statistical conclusion validity are aspects of research design and implementation that may result in erroneous interpretations of observed findings.

Taken in aggregate, the four types of research validity form the basis for building a scientifically oriented professional knowledge base. By understanding how internal, external, construct, and statistical conclusion validity interact, as well as how they sometimes interfere with one another, readers will be better informed consumers of the empirical research that is printed in special education journals.

Chapter 6

QUANTITATIVE RESEARCH DESIGNS

Bryan G. Cook,
Phillip D. Rumrill, Jr.
James Webb, and
Melody Tankersley

INTRODUCTION

In the quantitative research paradigm, researchers use the numerical expression of information for purposes of summarization, classification, interpretation, and generalization. Fundamental principles of scientific inquiry covered in previous chapters–such as sampling and population issues, validity and scientific control, probability and statistics, power, significance, and generalizability (see Chapters 1, 2, 3, and 5)–are all critical aspects of quantitative research designs. Although quantitative research approaches share in common the formulation of words and observations into numbers, great variance exists within the paradigm regarding the designs and methods that researchers use to address their questions and test their hypotheses. This chapter is organized around three broad categories of quantitative investigations: intervention/stimulus studies, relationship studies, and descriptive studies. It is our belief that the most important consideration in determining the suitability of a particular design or set of methods is the researcher's curiosity, that is, the question(s) or problem(s) that his or her research is devised to examine. Thus, designs or analytic techniques associated with one category of quantitative investigation are not inherently more sound than other types of investigation. Rather, appropriateness of a research design is determined by how well it addresses the researcher's question. As described in the following sections, each of the different types of quantitative research designs addresses different research questions and purposes.

INTERVENTION/STIMULUS STUDIES

One key purpose of research is to assess the effects that interventions and stimuli have on individuals' behaviors, knowledge, attitudes, and emotions. Whether examining the effects of self-advocacy training programs, assessing the impact of disability labels on teachers' attitudes toward and interactions with students, or determining the effectiveness of different teaching techniques with students with disabilities, special educators have a long history of intervention/stimulus studies that attempt to answer the question, "What happens when...?" Intervention/stimulus studies–including such approaches as true experiments, quasi-experiments, analogue studies, and single-subject research–have played a role in shaping policy initiatives, preservice teacher training, and instructional practice in the field of special education. This section describes each design subcategory, illustrated with examples from the special education literature.

Experimental Designs

True experiments are probably what most people imagine when they think of scientific inquiry in the social and physical sciences. Indeed, the quantitative research paradigm is deeply ingrained in experimental design– to the extent that experiments are often viewed as the highest or "best" form of investigation into new knowledge (Heppner et al., 1992). In fact, whereas we have divided quantitative designs into three major categories–intervention/stimulus studies, relationship studies, and descriptive studies, some experts categorize all research as either experimental or nonexperimental. Although dichotomizing research into experimental and nonexperimental categories provides a useful rubric for explaining what experimental design is and what it is not, this may inhibit a full appreciation of the breadth of approaches that are used within the overarching umbrella of quantitative methodology. As previously noted, we believe that researchers should not view designs in a hierarchical, "this one is better than that one" fashion. Having said that, it is important to recognize that true experiments do provide the strongest warrant for valid knowledge claims because of the systematic way that the effects of an intervention are isolated in "cause-and-effect" fashion.

The logic of experimental research is relatively simple. One hypothesizes: If X, then Y (e.g., if class size is reduced, then student achievement increases). The researcher uses some method to manipulate or measure X (i.e., the independent variable) which is usually posited (on the basis of existing theory) to result in changes in a dependent variable and then observes Y, (i.e. the dependent variable), to see whether concomitant variation occurs (Ary, Jacobs, & Razavieh, 1985; Heppner et al., 1992; Kazdin, 1992; McMillan & Schumacher, 1997). Concomitant variation is the amount of variation or change in Y that is attributable to (or, in the case of an experiment, caused by) variation or change in X. If sufficient concomitant variation occurs (as determined by the magnitude of relationship between X and Y and the size of the sample (i.e., a test of statistical significance) the experimental, "If X, then Y" proposition is assumed to be valid. Statistically significant results in an experimental investigation indicate, then, that the controlled or manipulated variation of X predicts or causes variation in Y.

In nonexperimental research, Y is observed, and an X or a number of Xs is also observed before, after, or concurrently with Y. The researcher does not control or manipulate X. This does not mean that the "If X, then Y" hypothesis is not tested in nonexperimental research. It does mean that the strength of the knowledge claim on the basis of nonexperimental confirmation of the hypothesis is not as strong as it is in an experimental research design. Researchers use a number of non-experimental techniques to ascribe *logical* validity to the proposition that Y concomitantly varies with X. For example, a researcher theorizes that placement in an inclusive classroom causes higher achievement for students with disabilities. To test her theory in an empirical study, the researcher hypothesizes that scores on standardized achievement tests (the dependent variable or Y) is a partial function of class placement (the independent variable or X). In a nonexperimental investigation of this hypothesis, both X and Y are observed as they occur without any manipulation or control of X. Let us assume that a significant relationship was found between academic achievement and class placement (i.e., students in inclusive classes scored higher than students in special classes). In terms of *empirical* validity, the warrant for new knowledge on the basis of the linear relationship of two variables as in this nonexperimental example is not as strong as it would be in the event that there is a cause-and-effect relationship between them. The primary reason for the limited empirical validity of non-experimental research is that nonexperimental research does not account for alternate explanations for variation in the dependent (i.e., Y) variable. In the example described previously, the linear relationship between class placement and student achievement might be explained (or caused) by other factors such as differences in intelligence and/or teaching methods used between the two groups.

To make the strongest warrant for a cause-and-effect relationship between the independent (i.e., X) and dependent (i.e., Y) variables, the researcher must systematically control or manipulate the independent variable **and** randomly assign participants to groups (Kazdin, 1992). In a typical "true" experiment, individuals are randomly selected to receive varying degrees of the independent variable. The simplest example is the two-group experiment, in which one group of individuals from the entire sample of participants is randomly selected to receive an intervention (i.e., the treatment group) and individuals not randomly selected for the treatment group do not receive the intervention (i.e., the control group). Random assignment ensures that the two groups are more-or-less equal along demographic, psychological, and functional dimensions, and that any differences between the two groups are due to chance. Then, sometime after the treatment group has completed the intervention, the researcher compares the two groups on whatever dependent variable(s) theory dictates should be influenced by the intervention. The "If X, then Y" proposition is supported if the treatment group performs, as predicted by theory, at a higher level than the control group on outcome or dependent measures. In a well-designed and executed experimental study, superior outcome performance of the treatment group is seen as the result of the intervention rather than other factors or alternate explanations.

For example, Sinclair, Christenson, Evelo, and Hurley (1998) investigated the effects of a "check-and-connect" intervention designed to keep adolescents with disabilities in school. It was hypothesized that receiving the intervention for a prolonged period of time would result in improved outcomes (e.g., staying in school, earning more school credits, completing assignments, perceiving school as important to their future). The "check" component of the intervention consisted of daily monitoring of students' tardiness, skipping classes, absenteeism, behavior referrals, detentions, suspensions, course failures, and accrual of credits. Basic "connect" services included sharing information about the monitoring system with the students, providing regular feedback about the students' educational progress, regularly discussing the importance of staying in school, and problem solving with students. Intensive "connect" interventions consisting of extended problem solving, academic support, and recreation and community service exploration were provided for students who were designated as high-risk on the basis of monitoring. These services had been administered to 94 students with learning and behavioral disabilities in grades 7 and 8. Forty-seven of the participants were randomly selected to then receive the intervention of continuing these services throughout grade 9. The other 47 students comprised a randomly assigned control group and did not continue receiving the intervention beyond grade 8.

Results indicated that students in the treatment group, as compared with the control group, were significantly more likely to be enrolled in school at the end of the year, were significantly more likely to complete assignments, earned significantly more credits, and were rated by teachers as significantly more academically competent and as exhibiting significantly fewer behavior problems. However, students in the treatment group did not differ from control students in their expectations for graduation, and neither group of students tended to perceive education as important to their future. The authors suggest that use of the extended "check-and-connect" intervention is likely to reduce the dropout rate and improve the educational experiences of students with learning and behavioral disabilities. However, other efforts, such as "increas[ing] the relevancy of high school curriculum" (Sinclair et al., 1998, p. 17), are likely needed in conjunction with this intervention to more completely ameliorate the school-related problems of this population of students.

After researchers have identified their independent and dependent variables on the basis of existing theory, several important issues emerge in designing experiments to establish causal relationships among variables. The first issue involves how to manipulate the independent variable. Researchers often use an "all-or-nothing" approach whereby one group receives the full intervention whereas the other group does not. On some occasions, however, researchers wish to examine the impact of several treatment conditions on an identified outcome (or set of outcomes). Multigroup experiments have the benefit of comparing a number of treatment modalities or intervention strategies within the same study. These experiments typically involve a pure control group and two or more treatment conditions. The treatment conditions may involve different levels of the same intervention (e.g., in an experiment examining the effect of instructional assistants on the behavior of included students with disabilities, students in the first treatment group may have one instructional aide present while they are included and the second treatment group has two aides present) or two or more different interventions (e.g., in another experiment examining the behavior of included students with disabilities, students in the first treatment group are in classrooms using a token economy reward system and students in the second treatment group are in classrooms using a response-cost discipline procedure in which recess is taken away for students exhibiting inappropriate behavior). These approaches allow the researcher to expand the research question from "Is Intervention A better than nothing (i.e., the control condition)?"–as in the two-group experiment–to "Is Intervention A better (or more effective) than Intervention B, and is either Intervention A or B better than nothing?"

Experimental researchers also face the issue of how outcomes will be assessed. Pretests are often given at some point before an intervention has begun to establish a baseline for each participant's performance on the same or a similar measure administered subsequent to the intervention (i.e., a posttest). These measures provide the researcher an opportunity to gauge the degree to that participants have benefited from the intervention, as indicated by the average differences between pretests and posttests for treatment and control groups or on posttest scores which have been statistically adjusted to control for differences in pretest scores.

For example, seventeen middle school students enrolled in a remedial mathematics class (five of whom were identified as having disabilities) were separated into control and experimental groups by Bottge (1999). The purpose of the study was to investigate the effects of contextualized mathematics instruction. Students were ranked according to their scores on a computation pretest. Pairs of students with adjacent rankings were formed. One student from each pair was randomly assigned to the contextualized problem group, and one was assigned to the control group. For the control group, mathematics instruction was based on word problems rather than on the contextualized method described later. Students first took a computation pretest, a word problem pretest, and a contextualized problem pretest (in which students solved a multiple-step problem involving buying a pet and building a home for it). Ten days of instruction followed, during which the contextualized problem group (a) received instruction from two video series using "an 'embedded data design' in which the problems are not explicitly stated or well formulated as they usually are in standard word problems" (Bottge, 1999, p. 85) and (b) were trained in a five-step process for solving problems. The word problem instruction (control) group received instruction regarding "typical word problems found in many basal mathematics textbooks" (p. 87).

After instruction, students took a posttest on the three measures. After statistically controlling (or covarying) for pretest scores, a significant effect of instruction was evidenced for the contextualized task, indicating higher adjusted posttest scores for the contextualized instruction group. Posttest scores on the computation and word problem tests did not significantly vary as a function of instructional grouping. Ten days after the cessation of the intervention, students completed another contextualized task, regarding purchasing and building a kite. A significant main effect of instruction across groups indicated that students in the treatment group performed better than their peers in the control group on this task as well. In aggregate, results were interpreted as supporting the efficacy of contextualized instruction in mathematics.

Pretest-posttest designs have the advantage of taking initial differences on the dependent variable between the groups into account. In some cases, however, administering a pretest, in and of itself, may have an effect on posttest measures that is unrelated to the intervention. Take the example of a researcher who wishes to assess the impact of having a parent of a child with a disability co-teach a workshop for practicing teachers on IDEA. Half of the teachers in a school are randomly assigned to take a workshop that is co-taught by a parent of a child with a disability who provides "real- life" examples of her child's educational experiences. The other teachers take a standard workshop that discusses the various components and requirements of IDEA. The researcher plans to measure the dependent variable, teachers' knowledge of IDEA, using a 20-item questionnaire. Although administration of the questionnaire to both groups before the in-service would allow the researcher to control for initial differences between the groups, taking the pretest might cause the teachers in the treatment group to pay more attention to or ask more questions about the legal aspects of the discussion (instead of getting caught up in the parent's stories regarding her child's education) than they would have had they not taken such a pretest. Moreover, practice effects might be evident in both groups, whereby familiarity with the test and its format could affect participants' posttest scores. The researcher in this example therefore concludes that a pretest would likely bias the results of the posttest.

To eliminate this possible pretest bias, researchers may opt for a "posttest only" design. Our researcher in the example described earlier might decide to administer the questionnaire regarding knowledge of IDEA only at the end of the workshop. Because participants were randomly assigned to the two groups, the researcher can assume that any characteristics that could influence performance on the posttest (e.g., knowledge of IDEA) are randomly distributed across the two groups. Of course, the posttest-only design does not allow the researcher to assess gain scores (i.e., change in scores from pretest to posttest), but it does enable the researcher to answer the question, "Did the group who took the workshop co-taught by a parent of a student with a disability have higher levels of knowledge regarding IDEA than the group who took the typical workshop?" If the answer to that question is "Yes," the researcher can conclude, given manipulation of the independent variable (i.e., type of workshop) and random assignment to groups, that higher performance on the examination is attributable to the co-teaching of the parent.

However, random assignment of participants to groups does not completely ensure that the groups do not differ on variables that might affect the dependent variable. For example, it is possible that, by chance, teachers with greater experience working with students with disabilities were assigned to the treatment group in the example presented previously. Results showing the treatment group had greater knowledge of IDEA than the control group might not, then, be attributable to the intervention of having a parent co-teach the workshop; instead those differences could be a function of teachers' prior experiences. Researchers may conduct statistical comparisons between groups to show that they do not significantly differ on variables that are theoretically associated with the dependent variable(s). For example, if the researcher had collected data from participating teachers regarding their amount of previous experience working with students with disabilities and had demonstrated that the two groups had relatively equal amounts of such experience, the alternate explanation that posttest differences were caused by differences in teaching experiences between the groups could be ruled out. Another technique to control for relevant differences between groups is for the researcher to match participants on one or more relevant variables when randomly assigning participants to groups. Bottge (1999), for example, paired each participant with the other student with the most similar pretest computation score and then randomly selected one individual from each pair to be in the treatment group and the other to be in the control group. In this way, the researcher ensured that posttest differences in the treatment and control groups were not due to initial differences in computation performance and were therefore more likely a function of receiving the intervention.

Quasi-Experimental Designs

Using a true experiment, characterized by random assignment of participants to groups, limits the effects of extraneous variables and enables the researcher to ascribe causation to the independent variable. However, it is often not possible to randomly assign participants to experimental conditions. Sometimes, it may not be practical to assemble all participants before the inception of the study to randomly assign them to groups. For example, when conducting research on the effects of field experiences on the knowledge of college students enrolled in an Introduction to Special Education course, a researcher may wish to randomly select students to participate in field experiences in local schools in conjunction with the course and then assess the effects of such participation on their learning. However, because field experiences must be arranged a semester in advance at the researcher's university and students may enroll in this course up to the day the course begins (which means that some students will not be able to participate in field experiments), it is impossible for the researcher to randomly assign students to treatment and control groups. Random assignment may also not be possible for ethical reasons. For example, one prominent question that special education researchers seek to answer is, "Do inclusive placements result in higher achievement for students with disabilities (compared with segregated special classes)?" However, randomly assigning some students with disabilities to inclusive placements and others to placements in special classes without regard to their characteristics or needs is contrary to the ethical standards of special educators. For these reasons, researchers often test the "If X, then Y" hypothesis by comparing two or more groups that are not randomly constituted using quasi-experimental methods.

Quasi-experiments involve one or more treatment groups and a comparison group (i.e., the nonrandom synonym for a control groups) who are subjected to varying levels of the independent variable, just as in experimental designs. The same issues related to how the independent variable will be manipulated and how to assess outcomes apply to both experimental designs and quasi-experiments. However, nonrandom assignment to groups affords less protection against the various threats to causal inference (i.e., internal validity). This means that alternate explanations for results such as history, maturation, and selection cannot be ruled out as readily in quasi-experimental designs.

For example, Schaller and Parker (1997) used a quasi-experimental design to examine the effects of instruction regarding research methods on graduate students' perceptions of their own anxiety regarding research, their perceptions regarding the usefulness or value of research, and their confidence in their own research skills. Twenty-three master's-level students in special education and rehabilitation counseling comprised the sample. Fifteen of these students had enrolled in an "Applied Research in Special Education and Rehabilitation Counseling" course, whereas eight students had signed up for an "Instructional Designs Using Assistive Technology" course. Schaller and Parker hypothesized that the independent variable (i.e., course taken) would have an impact on the dependent variables of research anxiety, perceptions of the usefulness of research, and confidence in research skills. Specifically, it was hypothesized that students who had completed the applied research course would have relatively greater decreases in research anxiety and relatively higher increases in perceived research usefulness and research confidence. In prestest/postest comparisons, students enrolled in the applied research course did, as predicted, experience significantly larger decreases in research anxiety than those who took the assistive technology course. However, no significant differences were shown between the two groups of students on changes in the other two dependent variables. It is possible that the small number of participants contributed to the lack of significant differences for perceived usefulness of research and research confidence. Another explanation could lie in the nonrandom nature of the group assignments. Students who took the research course could have been characteristically different from those who took the assistive technology course, and those differences could have influenced participants' gain scores.

In another quasi-experiment, Lederer (2000) investigated the efficacy of reciprocal teaching in social studies. The study involved six inclusive classrooms, two each at the fourth-, fifth-, and sixth-grade levels. One inclusive classroom at each grade level was taught by the researcher using reciprocal teaching techniques. The comparison classrooms were taught by their usual teachers, who tended to use teacher-directed instruction. Assignment to the groups was not random. Instead, the reciprocal teaching treatment was administered in the classrooms of teachers who were most interested in having the intervention take place in their classes. The reciprocal teaching intervention lasted for 15 to 17 days. During this intervention, students met in groups of four or five. They completed the assigned readings and proceeded through a step-by-step process of student-led questioning, summarizing, predicting, and clarifying the reading material. In these groups, students also practiced how to identify main points in the text and form basic summaries of their reading. Dependent variables were participants' scores on weekly comprehension assessments that evaluated their ability to answer questions, generate questions, and compose summaries.

One aspect of the investigation examined potential differences between the outcomes of students with learning disabilities (LD) who attended the treatment ($n = 15$) and comparison ($n = 10$) classrooms. Three separate analyses were conducted to determine whether the two groups performed significantly different on tests of answering questions, generating questions, and composing summaries. No significant differences were found between the two groups of students with LD regarding their scores for answering and generating questions. However, students with LD who had been in the classrooms where reciprocal teaching was used scored significantly higher than students with LD in comparison classrooms on composing summaries. Because the composition of summaries demonstrates in-depth comprehension of materials (i.e., students must pick out key concepts and then cohesively integrate them), the author suggested that reciprocal teaching can be an effective instructional approach for teachers of included students with LD.

Analogue Studies

Many researchers in special education and other social science fields have applied experimental and quasi-experimental techniques using a design that has come to be known as the analogue study (Heppner et al., 1992). The distinguishing feature of analogue studies is that they approximate, describe, or "mirror" phenomena that occur rather than having participants actually experience that phenomenon in a natural setting. This enables the researcher to exercise more consistency and control in the way the study is executed, thereby enhancing the internal validity of the research. Analogue studies may involve simulations of particular teaching techniques, fictitious written descriptions of students, and/or contrived videos of students or classroom situations. Typically, as is the case with experimental and quasi-experimental designs, analogue studies involve exposing one or more groups to a stimulus or intervention while withholding the treatment (or providing a different stimulus or intervention) to another group. Although analogue studies can use almost any kind of dependent variable, teacher or peer attitudes toward hypothetical students are commonly used outcome measures in special education analogue research.

In one example of an analogue study, Bak and Siperstein (1987) investigated the peer acceptance of students with mental retardation. Eighty fourth-through sixth-grade students were shown two videotapes. The first was a short vignette of a child reading. In one condition, a typical-appearing student read age-appropriate material competently. In another condition, a typical-appearing student read age-appropriate material with some difficulty (representing a student with mild mental retardation). In the final condition, a student with Down syndrome read below-age material with difficulty (representing moderate mental retardation). The students also viewed a video of the non-disabled child and the child with Down syndrome being interviewed by an adult. Both children being interviewed gave similar, age-appropriate answers. Dependent variables were students' ratings of the attributes of the child they viewed on the videotape and their ratings of the likelihood that they would befriend the child on the video. Rating scales were completed after viewing each of the two videos. Independent variables were level of mental retardation (i.e., non-disabled, mild retardation, moderate retardation), gender of students, and type of video seen (i.e., first or second).

A significant main effect of level of mental retardation was evidenced for participants' ratings of the attributes of the children on the videos. Specifically, participants rated the nondisabled child more positively than the child with mild and moderate mental retardation. In addition, a significant main effect was found for video type on the attribute ratings (i.e., children were rated more positively after participants viewed the second video). Finally, a main effect of gender for the attribute ratings indicated that girls rated the children in the videos significantly more positively. No significant differences were found regarding participants' intentions to befriend the children in the videos. On the basis of the finding that participants judged the children more positively after the second video, it was recommended that students in inclusive classrooms be given as much information about and exposure to students with mental retardation to facilitate peer acceptance.

Cook and Landrum (2000) also used an analogue study to investigate the attitudes of teachers toward the vocational competencies of students with a variety of disabilities who had undergone different school experiences. One hundred and seventy-three preservice and practicing special education teachers who were enrolled in college courses were asked to rate the job skills of a (fictional) soon-to-be-graduating high school student. The student was described as having a learning disability (LD), a behavior disorder (BD), or mild mental retardation (MMR). In addition, one of three school experiences was described. In the control condition, the student was described as having attended a career awareness class and as having been infrequently included in general education classes. In the inclusion condition, the student was described as having attended a career awareness class and as having been fully included in general education classes. In the transition condition, the student was described as having been infrequently included in general education classes, having attended a career awareness class, having completed "job shadowing" experiences at a number of job sites, and having earned course credit for holding a part-time job under the supervision of a job coach. The descriptions were randomly distributed to participants, who rated the vocational competence of the fictional student in the areas of reliability, productivity, social coping, organizational coping, and safety. Results indicated a significant effect of disability category (i.e., the student described as having a BD was rated significantly lower on social coping in compared with the student described as having a LD). Ratings of vocational competencies did not, however, differ as a function of school experience. The authors suggested that one interpretation of this lack of differences between school experiences may be that special educators do not view students with mild disabilities as needing or benefiting from community-based job experiences. If that is the case, these teachers may be less likely to advocate for such experiences for their students with mild disabilities.

The primary strength of analogue studies is that they provide important insights into the processes by which teachers and other stakeholders in special education form attitudes, develop relationships, and make instructional and policy-related decisions regarding students with disabilities. Analogue studies are especially useful when conducting research in which it is impossible for participants to naturally experience the intervention. However, analogue studies are typically limited by a lack of external validity. In other words, findings generated from a simulated situation do not necessarily generalize to students' or teachers' behaviors and attitudes in actual settings.

Single-Subject Research

In the preceding discussions of experimental, quasi-experimental, and analogue studies, there is an underlying assumption that the effects of interventions or stimuli are best assessed by comparing groups of people. In those research designs, participants in an investigation are grouped depending on the level or type of treatment or information that they receive. Conversely, single-subject research is designed to consider how an intervention might affect an individual or a group of individuals who are treated as one group. The term "single-subject" does not necessarily refer to the number of people who participate in this type of research but rather indicates the way comparisons are made. In single-subject research the analysis focuses on intra-subject, not inter-subject, comparisons (Kazdin, 1992). That is, the performance of one subject (whether constituted by one participant or one group of participants) is compared only with its own previous performance on the same measures. Measures of the subject's performance are not compared with measures of another person's or another group's performance. Because single-subject research is intended to focus on the change in behavior within the subject, the results are interpreted in terms of clinical rather than statistical significance. Changes in the dependent variable are evaluated in relation to the improved performance of the subject and whether the change in performance will benefit the subject rather than whether change in performance is statistically significant.

Single-subject designs evaluate changes in dependent variables across time in relation to the application, withdrawal, or modification of the independent variable. Typically, single-subject studies evaluate the progress of a subject before changing conditions in the environment—referred to as baseline—and then throughout the course of instituting the intervention. Single-subject designs differentially apply, withdraw, or modify the intervention to verify that changes in the dependent variable are due to manipulations of the independent variable and not the result of chance factors or confounding variables in the environment. When systematic changes in the dependent variable are associated with manipulations of the independent variable, the research demonstrates a functional relationship between the variables (Barlow & Hersen, 1984).

Single-subject research designs have several requirements. First, the dependent variable must be one that can be measured repeatedly over time (Kazdin, 1992). Often, dependent variables in single-subject research are measured daily or even more frequently so that the performance of the subject can be well documented during the baseline and intervention phases. Research in special education that uses single-subject techniques often looks at performance of subjects on dependent variables associated with academic skills (e.g., proficiency, accuracy on assignments, attention-to-task), social behavior (e.g., initiating interactions, aggression, self-stimulation), work-related skills (e.g., productivity, job performance, reliability), and independent living skills (e.g., making a bed, preparing a meal, riding a bus). The dependent variables are often behaviors that can be observed in the environment and defined in measurable terms so that more than one observer can agree on its occurrence. Such agreement on the occurrence of the dependent variable helps establish the trustworthiness of the research.

Single-subject research designs must first assess baseline performance of the subject. A baseline phase of the design provides information about the level of the dependent variable before the onset of treatment. Therefore, baseline data serve to describe the current extent of the behavior in question

and to predict performance of this behavior if no intervention is implemented (Kazdin, 1982). Single-subject designs then require an active intervention
phase, throughout which data are collected on the performance of the dependent variable. Comparisons of performance of behavior during baseline to
performance during the intervention phase determine the effectiveness of the
intervention.

Another requirement of most single-subject research designs is that at least
one replication of these results (i.e., changes between baseline and intervention phases) is instituted within the design (Alberto & Troutman, 1999). For
example, the reversal design (commonly referred to as the ABAB design) is
one in which the intervention is sequentially applied and withdrawn in four
phases: baseline performance of the dependent variable is collected first (the
first A phase), followed by assessment of the dependent variable while intervention is in place (the first B phase), followed by the withdrawal of the intervention to return to baseline conditions (the second A phase), and finally the
reinstatement of the intervention (the second B phase). This design is illustrated in Figure 6.1. A functional relationship between the dependent and
independent variables is established by not only the dependent variable
occurring more frequently in the first intervention phase compared with the
first baseline phase but also by returning to a level close to the original baseline data (or the trend of the data appears in the opposite direction of the data
in the first intervention phase) during the second baseline phase and again
increasing during the second intervention phase.

Figure 6.1

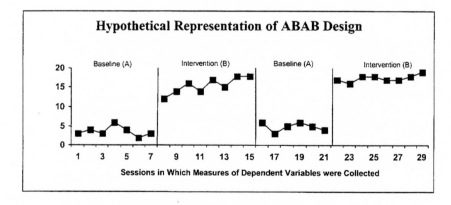

Carr, Newsom, and Binkoff (1980) used an ABAB design to evaluate
changes in aggressive behavior of children with developmental disabilities as
specific demands were placed on them. Bob, a 14-year-old boy, and Sam, a

nine-year-old boy, were both nonverbal and often engaged in self-stimulatory and aggressive behaviors. Each incident of aggressive behavior, defined to include scratching, hitting, kicking, biting, pinching, and/or hair pulling, was recorded during five- and 10-minute sessions. Because the purpose of this research was to assess whether the removal of demands would reduce the aggressive behavior of the children, baseline conditions required each student to be engaged in a particular behavior and the intervention conditions made no demands on the children. Therefore, during baseline conditions, Bob was required to sit in a chair and Sam was required to fasten buttons to a board. Throughout intervention conditions, the children were not engaged in any structured activity. For the three sessions that constituted the initial baseline condition, Bob demonstrated a mean of 121.7 aggressive acts for the five-minute observation sessions. When the demand of sitting was taken away during the first intervention condition, the number of aggressive acts reduced to zero. During the second baseline condition, aggressive acts rose to 128.3 and fell to 0.8 during the second intervention condition. The results were similar for Sam. During the initial baseline condition, which was composed of 12 separate 10-minute sessions, Sam demonstrated an average number of 43.3 aggressive acts. When the demand of fastening the buttons was withdrawn during the first intervention condition, the average number of aggressive acts reduced to 1.0. When baseline conditions were reinstated, aggressive acts increased to 53.7 and were then reduced to 0.3 during the second intervention. On the basis of these compelling clinical findings, Carr et al. (1980) concluded that aggressive behavior may be used as a way to escape certain demands of the environment.

Another single-subject research design is the multiple baseline design. The multiple baseline design incorporates a baseline and an intervention phase (AB) for more than one subject (i.e., multiple baseline across subjects design), for more than one dependent variable (i.e., multiple baseline across behaviors design), or in more than one environment (i.e., multiple baseline across settings design). Once baseline levels of the dependent variable have been established for each subject, behavior, or setting, the intervention is sequentially introduced to the next subject, behavior, or setting (Alberto & Troutman, 1999). In this way, if the dependent variable(s) increases across individuals, settings, or behaviors at the various times when the intervention is introduced, the researcher has confidence that it is the functional relationship between the independent and dependent variable—rather than some other explanation—that has caused the change in the dependent variable(s). (See Figure 6.2 for an illustration of a multiple baseline design.) The multiple baseline design enables the researcher to establish a functional relationship without withdrawing the intervention (as is required in the reversal design). Therefore, this design is especially useful when the dependent variable is one that cannot be reversed because it has been learned (e.g., the effects of an intervention that has taught the subject to read cannot be withdrawn) or should not be reversed because it is dangerous for the subject or others (e.g., self-injurious behaviors).

Figure 6.2

Hypothetical Representation of Multiple Baseline Design

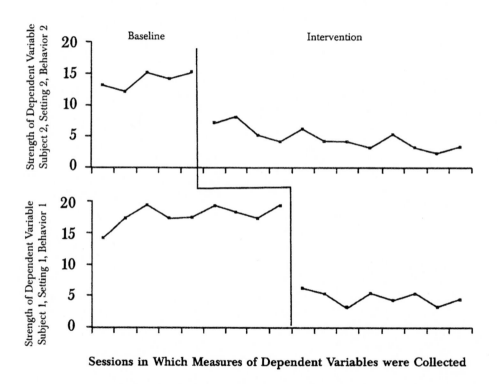

Sessions in Which Measures of Dependent Variables were Collected

Alber, Heward, and Hippler (1999) used a multiple baseline across subjects design to examine the effects of teaching four partially included middle school students with learning disabilities to recruit positive teacher attention in their inclusive settings. Training regarding how and when to appropriately recruit teacher attention (e.g., raise hand, ask questions such as "Are these answers right?") was provided for students over two to three days. Training occurred after 12 days of baseline measurement for two of the participants and after 19 and 31 days for the other two students. Following the training, students were prompted by their special education teacher two or three times per class period to use the procedures to gain their general education inclusion teacher's positive attention. Three of the students were also given prompting cards, kept in their notebooks, that enabled them to self-monitor their recruitment efforts. During the beginning of the recruitment intervention, the special education teacher reinforced the students' recruitment efforts each day. This reinforcement was eventually reduced to two days per week, and then was removed. Results indicated that the students recruited more teacher attention, received more teacher praise and instructional feedback, and produced more accurate and complete work during the intervention conditions than during the baseline conditions. The authors concluded that "[t]eaching students to recruit teacher attention is one strategy for promoting successful inclusion by enabling students with disabilities to actively influence the quality of instruction they receive" (Alber et al., 1999, p. 269).

The results of single-subject research are typically graphed and then evaluated through visual inspection of the data (Kazdin, 1982). Data are graphed within phases of the design (i.e., baseline or intervention) for each session in which the dependent variable is measured. Changes in strength of the dependent variable in relation to the presence or absence of the independent variable are assessed during each phase according to several criteria. For example, the mean level of the dependent variable is calculated (i.e., an average for all data within the phase is obtained) for each phase of the design, and performance on the dependent variable is compared. If performance during the intervention phase is better than performance during the baseline phase, the intervention may have clinical significance. Another aspect of determining the effectiveness of the intervention is assessment of the change in trend of the data. If the dependent variable is a behavior that the researcher wants to increase, for example, then an ascending trend during intervention phases would be important in determining the clinical significance of an intervention.

RELATIONSHIP STUDIES

The intervention/stimulus studies discussed so far in this chapter exemplify the purposeful and active spirit of scientific investigation aimed at drawing causal inferences concerning educational phenomena. By systematically manipulating the independent variable and randomly assigning participants to treatment and control groups, the use of experimental techniques permits the strongest warrants for new knowledge, that is, a causal link between the intervention or stimulus and outcomes. However, in many situations it is not possible or even desirable to manipulate the independent variable as a means of establishing a causal relationship. Many investigations test relationships among variables as they occur or have occurred. Because an independent variable is not manipulated in relationship studies, causality cannot be inferred from an individual study. Thus, the researcher is not able to conclude "X causes Y" or "if X, then Y" as with intervention/stimulus studies. Instead, the strength or magnitude of association between two or more variables is examined without regard to the potential causal link between the variables being explored.

In this section, we describe two categories of relationship studies, correlational and causal comparative designs. As in the preceding sections of this chapter, the designs are first described, and then examples from contemporary special education literature are provided.

Correlational Designs

A correlation is a statistic that expresses the direction and magnitude of the relationship between two quantitatively coded variables (this relationship is expressed by the correlation coefficient, see Chapter 3). In special education research, the correlation is one of the most frequently used methods for measuring the relationship between two variables. Investigations using correlations are often referred to as prediction studies, because the variability associated with one variable corresponds to or predicts variance in another, although causality is not empirically established. For example, performance and behavior in school are closely related, and a relatively high correlation exists between measures of these two variables. However, this association does not confer causality. Without manipulating one of these variables and observing related changes in the other variable, we do not know whether high performance causes appropriate behavior, whether appropriate behavior causes high performance, or whether other variables cause high performance and appropriate behavior.

It is important to keep in mind that although individual correlational studies do not attempt to infer causal relationships between variables, covariation is a necessary precondition of causality. Research consumers may, in fact, draw causal inferences on the basis of the total evidence generated in a number of correlational studies, particularly if a theory supports a causal relationship or if the one variable occurs before the other. For example, a researcher wishing to determine the relationship between scores on the Graduate Record Examination (GRE) and academic performance in graduate school conceptualizes GRE scores as the independent or predictor variable and graduate school performance as the dependent or criterion variable. Because the GRE is taken before enrollment in graduate school, scores are hypothesized to predict academic success rather than vice versa. Therefore, if a positive relationship between the two variables is observed (i.e., as GRE scores go up, performance in graduate school tends to increase), it is assumed that variable X (GRE scores) predicts variable Y (graduate school performance). Even though the relationship between predictor and criterion variables cannot be considered causal (because there was no manipulation of the independent variable), a positive association of the variables, which supports the researcher's theory-based hypothesis, could lead readers to conclude that (in general) high GRE scores indicate or predict a higher probability of success in graduate school than do lower scores. In fact, the positive relationship between GRE scores and performance in graduate school, which has been observed in numerous studies, has led many graduate-level special education programs to adopt minimum GRE scores as an admissions requirement.

The example presented previously describes a simple correlation, that involves one predictor and one criterion variable. Researchers may also use multiple correlations, or regression equations, which involve two or more predictors and one criterion (Pedhazur, 1982). In studies with larger samples and more complicated theoretical hypotheses, researchers may also opt for canonical correlations to interpret interrelationships among multiple predictors and multiple criterion variables. Correlational studies may examine the psychometric properties (e.g., reliability and validity) of standardized measurement instruments, be used to develop equations to explain or predict important outcomes in special education (e.g., graduation rates, scores on achievement tests), and evaluate the "relatedness" of measurable constructs when the researcher cannot or does not wish to manipulate an independent variable that is theorized to be causally related to a dependent variable.

For example, Cook, Gerber, and Semmel (1997) investigated the assumption that educational reforms aimed at increasing the achievement of nondisabled students also improve the achievement of students with disabilities, particularly students with mild disabilities who are frequently included in general education classes. The researchers theorized that because students with disabilities require instruction on different levels and at different rates than nondisabled students, teachers and schools cannot simultaneously improve the performance of both groups of students. Reading achievement of nondisabled students and students with mild disabilities was measured separately across two years' time in 33 elementary schools and 23 junior high schools. The predictor variable in the correlational design was change in school-level reading among nondisabled students. The criterion variable consisted of change in school-level reading performance among students with mild disabilities. Two separate correlation analyses were conducted, one for elementary schools and one for junior high schools. In elementary schools, results showed a significant inverse relationship between the change in performance of students with mild disabilities and nondisabled students in the same schools. In other words, as reading performance of nondisabled students increased in a school, the reading performance of students with mild disabilities tended to decrease in the same school. In junior high schools, the correlation was not significant. According to the authors, these findings indicate that, at least in elementary schools, it should not be assumed that students with mild disabilities will be successful when included in environments that are effective for nondisabled students.

In another study using a correlational design, Lin (2000) investigated predictors of family adaptation among 274 families of people with cerebral palsy. Family is a major influence in the growth and development of all children, perhaps especially those with disabilities. Successful family adaptation to having a child with a disability is, therefore, critically important, although frequently problematic. The criterion variable in the investigation, family adaptation, was measured by a 12-item scale measuring "the overall health or pathology of the family" (Lin, 2000, p. 205). On the scale, primary caregivers in the families rated their agreement with statements such as "we can express feelings to each other," and "we avoid discussing our fears and concerns." The predictor variables were derived from primary care givers' ratings indicating their families' status on 30 attitudes and behaviors regarding problem solving. The instrument yielded scores on five dimensions or factors: positive family appraisal (e.g., "accepting that difficulties occur unexpectedly") support from concerned others (e.g., "sharing problems with neighbors") spiritual support (e.g., "attending religious services/activities") personal growth and advocacy (e.g., "learning more about cerebral palsy through reading, attending a workshop, etc.") and positive social interactions (e.g., "doing recreational activities with our family member with cerebral palsy") Results of a multiple regression analysis indicated that two of the predictor variables, positive family appraisal and spiritual support, were significant predictors of family adaptation. On the other hand, support from concerned others, personal growth and advocacy, and positive social interactions were not significantly related to family adaptation. Fifty-six percent of the variance in family adaptation was explained by positive family appraisal, and an additional and unique one percent of the variance in the criterion variable was explained by spiritual support. The authors suggested that the results can be used in designing interventions promoting family adaptation.

Causal Comparative Studies

Causal comparative studies *compare* differences between derived or existing groups on measures of selected dependent variables. As with correlational studies, causality is not inferred in individual causal comparative studies because no intervention or treatment is delivered and group membership (i.e., the independent variable) is not systematically manipulated. Rather, phenomena are observed as they occur or sometime after they have occurred. Researchers typically use between-group comparative methods (e.g., *t*- tests, analyses of variance, multivariate analyses of variance) to gauge differences in the dependent variable between the groups under study.

Consider the example of a researcher who wants to examine differences in the self -esteem of boys and girls with behavior disorders in a large school district. She measures the self-esteem of 124 students with behavior disorders, 85 boys and 39 girls, using a popular standardized instrument. Statistical analysis indicates that boys with behavior disorders have, on average, higher self-esteem than girls with behavior disorders. On the basis of these results, can the researcher conclude that gender causes the level of self-esteem in students with behavior disorders? No, because there is obviously no systematic way to control and manipulate the independent variable in this example—the gender of students with behavior disorders. What she can conclude is that, in her sample, girls with behavior disorders have lower self-esteem than their male counterparts. The researcher may, then, rely on relevant theory to postulate explanations for the findings. For example, these results may be due to the tendency of schools to identify more boys than girls as having behavior disorders. Girls who are identified as such may, then, tend to have more severe problems and be likely to have lower self-esteem.

Conclusions reached through causal comparative research are limited by the passive nature of the between-group analyses (i.e., the independent variable is not manipulated, nor is there random assignment to groups). However, many characteristics that we use to group and label special education students (and teachers) are not subject to manipulation or random assignment. Investigations of differences between intact or predetermined groups using causal comparative designs are, therefore, frequently performed in special education research and provide valuable information about the impact of educational policies and instructional interventions on different groups of teachers and students.

For example, Lago-Delello (1998) sought to compare the classroom experiences of students at risk for serious emotional disturbance (SED; a term synonomous with behavior disorders) to similar students who did not exhibit behaviors associated with SED. Thirteen first- and second-grade students identified as being at risk for SED were compared on a number of variables to 13 not-at-risk classmates who were matched with the at-risk students on a number of demographic variables. Results indicated that teachers rated at-risk students significantly lower on ideal pupil attributes, that students who were at-risk for SED spent significantly less time academically engaged in their general education classroom, and that at-risk students received greater amounts of negative and neutral teacher feedback. However, no differences were found between the two groups regarding their perceptions of teachers' expectations, amount of positive teacher feedback, number of student public response opportunities, and number of social behaviors initiated and received. Thus, even before they are referred and identified for special education, it appears that the educational experiences of students who are at-risk for SED differ from their peers in some, but not all, aspects of schooling. The author stated that "these results suggest a 'window of opportunity' for effective classroom intervention that addresses the learning and behavior problems of these children before peer rejection and negative teacher bias have a direct effect on their school outcomes" (Lago-Delello, 1998, p. 490).

Baranek (1999) also used a causal comparative design to determine whether differences could be detected in the behaviors of infants who were later categorized as autistic, developmentally disabled, and normally developing. Thirty-two children (11 with autism, 10 with developmental disabilities [DD], and 11 typically developing) whose families had ample and high-quality videotapes of their children from nine to 12 months of age were the participants in the investigation. Randomly selected portions of the videos featuring each child were compiled into two five-minute segments. These segments were then observed, and quality and frequency of children's behaviors in a number of categories (e.g., gaze aversion, response to name, social touch responses) were recorded. One aspect of the analysis involved a series of ANOVAs that were conducted with the group (i.e., autistic, DD, and typically developing, as the independent variable) and the various quality and frequency ratings of children's behavior served as the dependent variables. Results indicated that students with DD engaged significantly more often in stereotyped, inappropriate play than the other two groups; that children with DD looked at the camera significantly less frequently than the other two groups; that children with autism and DD evinced unusual posture significantly more often than typically developing children; and that children with autism needed significantly more adult prompting to respond to their names than the other two groups of children. The author concluded that behaviors of children at a very young age may be highly indicative of disabilities not typically diagnosed until much later.

DESCRIPTIVE STUDIES

As noted in Chapter 1, one important purpose of scientific inquiry is to describe or explain observable phenomena in a manner that adds understanding or insight to a question or problem. The special education professional literature contains many examples of investigations whose primary goal is to describe events, experiences, attitudes, and observations regarding students with disabilities rather than to establish a causal or predictive relation between variables. Although the qualitative descriptive techniques presented in Chapter 7 have been used to describe various facets of special education with increasing frequency in recent years, researchers have also used a number of quantitative approaches in descriptive studies.

Descriptive research involves collecting data to test hypotheses or answer questions regarding the past or current status of selected variables. A descriptive study simply asks "what is" or "what was" and reports conditions or people the way they are at a point or several points in time. Researchers conducting descriptive studies examine such phenomena as achievement, attitudes, opinions, behaviors, and professional literature that are collected or observed from individuals or groups of participants. It is important to note that descriptive designs do not manipulate variables in an attempt to draw causal inferences, as is the case in intervention/stimulus studies–nor do they apply statistical tests to gauge relationships among variables or groups of participants, as is the case in correlational and causal comparative studies. By simply reporting what exists, descriptive studies help to amass evidence concerning a particular phenomenon and can make a valuable contribution to a discipline's knowledge base.

Researchers use a variety of sources to gather information for descriptive studies, including self-reports from research participants, reports from significant others, direct observations, and review of documents. As in other types of research, the techniques chosen are determined primarily by the research questions or hypotheses that are drawn from existing literature and theory. A number of descriptive methodologies exist in quantitative research, each of which has many possible iterations depending on the specific research question being asked and the resources available to the investigator(s). We have divided descriptive designs into seven categories: surveys, case studies, program evaluations, historical/archival research, longitudinal studies, empirical literature reviews, and meta-analyses. This section provides general overviews of these descriptive designs, illustrated with examples from professional journals in special education.

Surveys

Surveys have been a very common type of descriptive research in recent special education literature. By use of self-report data that are collected in interviews with respondents (in which the researcher records data on the instrument) or by means of questionnaires (in which the respondent records his or her own answers on the instrument), surveys have become a part of virtually every aspect of life in contemporary American society. The primary purpose of survey research is to gauge the status of particular variables within a sample of respondents (e.g., attitudes of general educators toward inclusion) or to draw inferences regarding the constitution of a population of people on the basis of the characteristics of a sample of individuals drawn from that population (e.g., ethnic composition of students with learning disabilities). Surveys elicit relatively brief measures from relatively large numbers of people (Babbie, 1995), in contrast to the more in-depth case study designs that involve collecting large amounts of information from smaller samples.

For example, Hollenbeck, Tindal, and Almond (1998) sent surveys regarding (a) teachers' knowledge of accommodations on "high-stakes" state proficiency tests, (b) teachers' use of accommodations for students with disabilities, and (c) testing conditions (i.e., standard, modified, or exempt) for students with disabilities to 633 randomly selected general and special education teachers in the state of Oregon. The sample included teachers at the elementary and middle school levels. The 1997 reauthorization of the IDEA mandated the involvement of students with disabilities in large-scale assessment programs (i.e., state proficiency tests). Hollenbeck et al. (1998) used the survey method to address questions raised by this mandate regarding what accommodations will be provided, how modified tests will be interpreted, and who will make the decision whether students with disabilities are exempt from the test. One hundred and sixty-six (166) teachers returned completed surveys (26% return rate).

In Oregon, specific types of accommodations on the state proficiency test may be used without the test being marked as having been modified (e.g., extended time, testing in a separate location, provision of a dictionary or calculator). Use of other accommodations (e.g., allowing arithmetic tables, dictated responses, alternate responses) require that the test be marked as modified. On average, respondents correctly indicated whether 16 different accommodations would require a test to be marked as modified slightly more than half of the time (54.8%). A wide range of use of accommodations for students with disabilities was reported. Only 13.1 percent of respondents indicated that they used extended time for students with disabilities on the proficiency tests, whereas 81.7 percent had provided an alternate form of the test for students with disabilities. It was also reported that students with learning disabilities were the most likely to take the state proficiency test, modified and unmodified. Students with mental retardation were the most likely to be exempted. The decision regarding whether students with disabilities would take the test and, if so, whether the test would be modified, was most frequently decided by a group of educators. The authors concluded that "teachers' knowledge of allowable accommodations was limited enough to jeopardize the validity of score interpretation ..." (Hollenbeck et al., 1998, p. 181). Extensive preservice and in-service training was recommended to address these problems.

In another recent example of survey research, Palmer, Borthwick-Duffy, and Widaman (1998) devised an instrument to investigate parents' perceptions of inclusion for their children with severe cognitive disabilities. The survey was completed by parents of 995 students. Students with severe disabilities have been increasingly placed in general education classrooms, or included, in recent years. Yet little information exists regarding parents' perceptions of inclusion for these students. The survey measured three factors of parents' perceptions: quality of educational services, mutual benefits of inclusion (benefits to both students with and without disabilities), and child acceptance and treatment. Responses to all questions were on a six-point Likert scale, with one being strongly disagree and six being strongly agree; thus, the theoretical neutral mean was 3.5. The mean response value to items comprising the factor regarding quality of education services was 2.80, indicating that parents tended to be slightly negative regarding the quality of education that their children did or would receive in an inclusive classroom. Parents were, on average, slightly positive regarding the mutual benefits associated with inclusion, as indicated by a mean response of 4.01 to items comprising the second factor. The mean response of 3.62 to items on the child acceptance and treatment factor suggested that parents were neutral or undecided on how well their children were or would be accepted by nondisabled classmates in inclusive classrooms. Results were interpreted to show that parents of students with severe disabilities held varying and multidimensional views toward inclusion. The authors further concluded that the instrument can be used by schools to identify and appreciate parents' feelings about the inclusion of their children with significant cognitive disabilities.

Case Studies

Whereas survey research typically involves taking measures at one point or over a short period of time from a large number of participants, case studies typically involve an in-depth or prolonged examination of one person or a small group of people (Heppner et al., 1999). Rooted in epidemiological research in the medical field (particularly as a means of understanding uncommon conditions or illnesses), the quantitative case study design has been frequently applied in special education research to provide insights into many aspects of the education of students with disabilities. By reporting a large volume of data about a limited number of individuals, case studies can lend an understanding to a particular phenomenon that may not be attainable using other quantitative designs. It is important to recognize, though, that attempts to generalize findings to the broader population from which participants were drawn are not warranted. Because case studies deal with only a small number of participants (who are typically not randomly selected from the population of interest), their external validity is severely limited. Nonetheless, preliminary information generated from a quantitative case study can be used to focus or guide more systematic inquiry in a particular area of research. The picture painted by a case study regarding an individual or group and their educational experience can be extremely useful in highlighting the potential effectiveness of an intervention method or the need for change in policy and practice in a given area.

For example, Deno, Foegen, Robinson, and Espin (1996) examined a middle school teacher's experiences in implementing inclusion in a school that was attempting to develop an inclusion program without the use of additional resources. Two years before the researchers' involvement with the teacher, it had been mandated that all schools in this district develop a collaborative model of inclusion. To assist the instructor in targeting students in need of assistance and focusing instruction, the researchers developed criterion-referenced tests for each of the nine weeks of a unit on fractions that Ms. Franklin (a psuedonym) was teaching in three of her inclusive classes. Students took a pretest at the beginning of the week and a posttest at the end of the week to determine whether they had mastered the skills on which they received instruction. Each of the classes was large (between 30 and 35 students) and contained a great deal of diversity. At the end of the nine weeks, the posttests indicated that 69 percent of the included special education students mastered zero or one of the weekly skills, whereas 84 percent of the nondisabled students mastered two or more of the weekly skills. Moreover, on average, the included students with disabilities mastered less than one quarter of the concepts covered in the class. Only three of the 94 students in all the classes had mastered all nine of the skill areas.

The authors expressed concern not only with the outcomes achieved by the students in these inclusive classrooms, but also with the teacher's planning. The researchers had hoped that providing weekly data on how each particular student was progressing through the unit on fractions would allow the teacher to individualize her instruction for students who had not achieved mastery of the skills. However, the teacher was observed to make "few attempts to adjust instruction to the needs of students who were having difficulty" (Deno et al., 1996, p. 348), and all students received similar instruction regardless of their mastery of prerequisite skills. On the basis of their findings in this case study, the authors questioned whether inclusion can result in benefits for students with disabilities without intensive supports that might enable teachers to individualize instruction.

Ryndak, Morrison, and Sommerstein (1999) investigated the changes in literacy of one student with a disability before and after inclusion, also using a case study design. Melinda was first described as a 15-year old girl with moderate to severe disabilities (at different times she had been labeled as having severe learning problems, mental retardation, neurological impairment, and multiple disabilities) who had been placed in a segregated special day class for the past 10 years. Emerging views on literacy suggest that "a learner acquires literacy skills more quickly when instructional content correlates with the written and spoken language that is required in the learner's real life" (Ryndak et al., 1999, p. 6). It is possible, then, that being placed in an inclusive environment in which students are expected to routinely produce appropriate written and spoken language may improve the literacy achievement of students with disabilities. The authors collected information about Melinda over a seven-year period through observations at school, at home, and in the community; reviews of Melinda's educational records; interviews with Melinda's service providers and administrators; conversations with Melinda and her parents; examination of Melinda's work; and audio- and videotapes of Melinda's public presentations.

Before being included, standardized tests indicated that Melinda had a receptive vocabulary of six years and 10 months (at the age of 15) and an oral vocabulary of three years five months. Few people could understand Melinda's verbalizations, and she often relied on gestures and/or the translations by friends to communicate. Melinda's reading comprehension was judged to be at the second-grade level, and she experienced frustration in all academic areas. Moreover, according to her mother, Melinda had almost no writing skills. Melinda also exhibited a number of undesirable behaviors (e.g., peeling back the skin on her fingers, being off-task in her special day class, yelling, and "falling apart").

During the seventh grade, Melinda began to be included in general education classes at the request of her parents. After being included, Melinda demonstrated "tremendous growth in articulation and vocabulary" (Ryndak et al., 1999, p. 13). For example, toward the end of high school, Melinda began to express complex thoughts and memories, such as the time she described her experiences in special education at a local conference on inclusion: "I was very angry and frustrated. ... I didn't like that place. It felt like a prison to me" (Ryndak et al., 1999, p. 15). In addition, her father claimed that Melinda's behavior was a thousand times better after being included. Melinda received a high school IEP diploma at the age of 20 and went on to attend college for two years. While at college, Melinda authored an article for her school paper using a strategy developed in high school in which she worked with a friend to facilitate the development of her thoughts into complete sentences. Melinda would then copy the sentences originally written by her friend. The authors conclude that "[t]his study suggests that literacy development can be affected positively by immersing the learner in genuine opportunities to speak, listen, read, and write in contexts that are real" (Ryndak et al., 1999, p. 20), that is, in an inclusive classroom.

Program Evaluation

The primary goal of program evaluation research is to describe programs so that others may emulate their successes and learn from their shortcomings. A primary distinguishing feature of program evaluation research is that it does not purport to yield generalizable findings. Rather, the focus is placed on using a variety of measures to generate clear, concise descriptions of the methods by which the program was developed and delivered, specific parameters for evaluating the program's impact, and a measure of the program's cost-benefits in terms of fiscal and/or personnel resources relative to realized outcomes (McMillan & Schumacher, 1997). Program evaluations typically feature analyses of both processes and outcomes, also known as formative and summative evaluations. Program evaluations in special education may involve a wide range of programs, including those that educate students with disabilities or that train preservice special education teachers and graduate-level special educators.

McMillan and Schumacher (1997) identified four criteria by which educational programs should be evaluated: utility, feasibility, propriety, and accuracy. In examining these criteria, program evaluators use a variety of methods and data sources. These include direct observations, documentary evidence, participant interviews, and end-user surveys (i.e., information solicited from participants after the program has concluded). Because the intent of program evaluation research is to describe rather than generalize, researchers typically report quantitative program evaluation data using descriptive (e.g., frequencies and means) rather than inferential (e.g., correlations and ANOVAs) statistics. The following paragraphs summarize the methods and findings of two program evaluation studies that have recently appeared in the special education literature.

Early intervention has shown great promise for improving the outcomes and futures for people with a variety of disabilities, including autism. In their program evaluation, McGee, Morrier, and Daly (1999) provided "a brief description of the Walden Toddler Program" by reviewing "the empirical and philosophical foundations that comprise the bottom lines of the incidental teaching toddler model" (p. 133). The Walden Toddler Program opened in 1993 and provides 30 hours per week of home- and center-based early intervention services to eight toddlers with autism (four in the morning session, four in the afternoon session) per year. The toddlers with autism attend the center with eight nondisabled toddlers and receive incidental teaching. Incidental teaching, as used in this program, is described by six attributes: (a) teachers and environment encourage student initiation; (b) rigorous speech shaping in which students are rewarded for successive approximations; (c) active social instruction; (d) wait-ask-say-do chaining sequence of prompts; (e) promotion of engagement; and (f) use of a checklist for staff to maintain consistency of curriculum and techniques. A family liaison also provides up to four hours per week of in-home intervention demonstration to each family. Parents must commit to providing at least 10 hours of additional home-based instruction on their own. On the basis of five minutes of videotaping during the first and last 10 days of each of the year-long programs, only 36 percent of the 28 students with autism who had participated in the program entered the program emitting verbalizations. Yet 82 percent left the program verbalizing meaningful words. Seventy-one percent of the toddlers with autism also showed improvement in the amount of time spent in close proximity to their nondisabled peers. Improvements were also evidenced regarding verbal interactions with parents, size of vocabulary, engagement in toy play, and independent self-care skills. McGee et al. (1999) concluded that more funds should be devoted to such programs and that these types of programs be made more cost-effective so that more toddlers can attend and benefit from them.

Flexer, Simmons, and Tankersley (1997) used a program evaluation design to describe a program in which master's-level students gain unique experiences and training as part of their special education teacher training. In this program, participants earn certificates in supported employment by providing case management and on-the-job support services such as job coaching, job training, and social skills training to transition-age youths with developmental disabilities. Doctoral students in the fields of special education and rehabilitation counseling oversee and supervise the master's students. The students with development disabilities are recruited from local high schools and are employed in jobs throughout the university (e.g., food service, grounds keeping, mail delivery, custodial work, clerical positions). The authors reported a number of benefits associated with the program. Youths with developmental disabilities gain "real world" job experience, as well as individualized instruction regarding social skills, problem-solving, and task completion. The master's-level students gain valuable and unique training regarding job development and placement, employer-educator relations, career counseling, personal futures planning, and case management. Doctoral students furthered their skills in budgeting, supervision, program evaluation, and advocacy on behalf of students with disabilities and their families.

Historical/Archival Research

In many cases, the impact of a program, policy, or intervention is not readily apparent by observing phenomena as they occur or by conducting follow-up studies shortly after the program has been completed. Historical/archival studies are retrospective in nature and involve analysis of data that were previously collected. Primarily, historical/archival studies in special education have involved examinations of legislation, social trends, and large-scale programs designed to meet the needs of students with disabilities.

For example, McLeskey, Henry, and Axelrod (1999) examined data compiled in annual Reports to Congress to investigate placement trends for students with learning disabilities (LD). These reports are prepared for Congress by the U.S. Department of Education, Office of Special Education Programs (OSEP) to indicate the degree to which the IDEA is being implemented throughout the nation. The reports represent "the most reliable national data base regarding the identification and placement of students with disabilities" (McLeskey et al., 1999, p. 56). The six most recent Reports to Congress, representing the school years from 1988/1989 to 1994/1995, were analyzed in this investigation. Results indicated that students with LD have increasingly been placed in less restrictive settings. The cumulative placement rate for students with LD in general education classes increased dramatically over the six-year time span, whereas students with LD were placed in resource rooms and separate schools with decreasing frequency. However, the cumulative placement rate for students with LD in separate classes (in public schools) has actually increased during these same years. The authors noted that this general trend toward greater inclusion has implications for the roles, responsibilities, and training of both general and special educators.

Fujiura and Yamaki (2000) also used a historical/archival design to investigate their contention that as social and economic dynamics—as well as the numbers of individuals with disabilities—have changed in recent years, the relationship between poverty and disability status has also changed. The authors analyzed statistical summaries of the National Health Interview Surveys from 1983 to 1996. Independent variables were poverty (i.e., family above or below poverty level, living in a single-parent home) and being from a minority group. The dependent variable was being a child with a disability. The results of a regression analysis indicated that living in a single-parent home was significantly related to having a childhood disability in both 1983 and 1996. A child was 55 percent more likely to have a disability when being raised in a single-parent household (in comparison to a two-parent home) in

1983, and 88 percent more likely in 1996. After controlling for poverty and family status (being raised in a single- or two-parent household), minority status did not significantly relate to disability status in 1983 or 1996. Poverty did not significantly relate to disability status in 1983, but it did in 1996. A child was 86 percent more likely to have a disability when being raised in an impoverished household at this time. Results were interpreted to suggest "an exacerbation of the link between poverty and disability" (Fujiura & Yamaki, 2000, p. 196). The authors recommended that special education become less isolated and be considered in conjunction with related social health issues.

Longitudinal Studies

Whereas historical/archival investigations track participants over an extended period of time that has already elapsed, longitudinal studies actively track the sample by collecting data on participants at a point in time and then following them into the future, making periodic "checks" at specified intervals (McMillan & Schumacher, 1997). These studies typically involve large samples of participants with a set of common characteristics (e.g., a particular disability) and the researchers monitor participants' progress over time as a means of framing life activities, experiences, and outcomes in a developmental context. Longitudinal studies enable the researcher to make comparisons between participants' initial responses and the experiences that they record at each subsequent point of data collection. Longitudinal techniques are frequently used in educational research to gauge children's academic and intellectual development (McMillan & Schumacher, 1997).

Miller, Brownell, and Smith (1999) used a longitudinal design to investigate why teachers stay in or leave special education. Given special education teacher shortages and increasing numbers of students with disabilities, a great deal of attention has been given to understanding the high rates at which special education teachers leave the profession of teaching or transfer into general education. Miller et al. (1999) surveyed 1,576 Florida special education teachers regarding a number of factors that they believed to contribute to staying, leaving, or transferring out of the special education classroom. Two years later, the status of the teachers surveyed was ascertained (i.e., still teaching in special education, teaching in general education, or not teaching). Four variables were found to significantly distinguish those who stayed, left, or transferred two years later. Teachers who stayed in special education were most likely to hold current certification, whereas those who left teaching held the fewest certifications. "Stayers" also indicated that they were significantly less stressed about their jobs than were "transfers" and "leavers." Likewise, stayers perceived the climate of their schools as being significantly more positive compared with transfers and leavers. Finally, those who stayed in special education were significantly older than those who transferred to general education. The authors discussed strategies for improving special education teacher retention related to the four variables identified earlier.

Forgan and Vaughn (2000) also used a longitudinal design to compare changes in outcomes over a two-year transition period (i.e., sixth and seventh grade) for seven included students with LD to outcome changes for seven nondisabled students. The transition from elementary to middle school can be problematic for all students, but it is generally thought to be particularly difficult for students with disabilities. Students in the two groups were from the same sixth-grade classroom and were matched on ethnicity and gender. The outcomes examined included reading performance, quality of students' friendships, and global and academic self-concept. Data on these outcomes were collected at the beginning and end of sixth grade (the last year of elementary school), and at the middle and end of the seventh grade (the first year of middle school).

Although students with LD made substantial progress in reading performance in the sixth grade, their reading performance actually decreased slightly from the middle to the end of the seventh grade. Nondisabled students made small gains in reading performance in both the sixth and seventh grades. Students with LD made very large gains in the quality of their friendships in the sixth grade. However, quality of friendships decreased slightly after entering middle school, and it increased only very slightly from the middle to the end of the seventh grade. Nondisabled students' quality of friendships increased slightly during the sixth grade, increased on attending junior high school, and then decreased slightly during the seventh grade. Reflective of their academic performance and quality of friendships, both the global and academic self-concept of students with LD both increased during the sixth grade, was significantly lower after entering middle school and increased slightly from the middle to the end of the seventh grade (although both aspects of self-concept remained lower at the end of the seventh grade than at the end of the sixth grade). The global self-concept of nondisabled students rose in the sixth grade, stayed relatively constant after entering middle school, and then declined slightly during the seventh grade. The academic self-concept of these students increased slightly during the sixth grade, remained the same after entering middle school, and then declined drastically from the middle to the end of the seventh grade. Forgan and Vaughn (2000) summarized that there were "no obvious differences regarding how students with LD and NLD [not learning disabled] students make the transition to middle school" (p. 38). Given that the only outcome on which students with LD decreased during the seventh grade was reading performance, it was suggested that academics, and social/emotional outcomes be the focus of special concern for students with LD during this period of transition.

Empirical Literature Reviews

Empirical literature reviews involve the creation, codification, and analysis of numerical data on the basis of specific aspects (e.g., themes, topics, authors, and methods) of existing special education literature. It is the numerical expression of data that distinguishes the empirical literature review from the synthetic literature reviews described in Chapter 8 (see Bellini & Rumrill, 1999). Special education researchers often use numerical expressions of data generated from the literature to answer questions such as "What institutions are most frequently represented in the professional literature?" and "What types of studies have been done in particular areas of inquiry?"

Waller, Armstrong, McGrath, and Sullivan (1999) used an empirical literature review for another purpose, to investigate how students with autism are described in published research. The definition of and diagnostic criteria for autism have undergone substantial changes over the past decades. The most common diagnostic criteria now used are likely to refer to a heterogeneous group of individuals. Thus, it is important that researchers adequately describe individuals with autism who have participated in their studies so that readers can appropriately interpret and generalize findings. The authors reviewed all empirical articles that included participants with autism published in the *Journal of Autism and Developmental Disorders* from February 1993 to April 1997. Of the 152 studies reviewed, 77 percent reported the gender of participants, 18 percent described their sample as autistic but included participants who were not diagnosed with autism, 55 percent were not clear regarding the source of the diagnosis, and 79 percent did not specify whether students with dual diagnoses (in which the participant was diagnosed with autism and one or more other disabilities) could be included in the sample. The authors concluded that researchers need to more carefully denote the characteristics of the participants with autism in their studies to avoid frustrating or even misleading those who "read about techniques applied to subjects who are not described in sufficient detail ..." (Waller et al., 1999, p. 488).

Sileo and Prater (1998) also used an empirical literature review to examine the most recent editions of 10 textbooks typically used in college and university courses designed to prepare educators to work with parents and families of students with disabilities for the books' multicultural content. The authors proposed that special educators should acquire "the knowledge, skills, attitudes, and strategies necessary for effective interactions with students and families from diverse heritage" (Sileo & Prater, 1998, p. 513) to optimally involve the parents and families of students with disabilities. Empirical examination of these textbooks involved determining (a) the percentage of content allocated to cultural diversity, (b) the number of mentions of specific cultural groups, and (c) the amount of coverage devoted to each of 15 expert-validated topics regarding cultural diversity.

Content coverage in the texts varied greatly, from 0 percent to 55 percent of the text allocated to cultural diversity. Five of the ten texts had at least one full chapter devoted to the subject. Hispanic groups were mentioned most frequently in textbooks, followed by African-Americans, Asian-Americans, and American Indians/Alaska natives. Pacific Islanders were mentioned least frequently. Among the topics associated with cultural diversity mentioned most frequently in the texts were need for teachers to develop sensitivity to cultural diversity, issues and strategies for working with diverse families and parents, characteristics of various cultural groups, identification and assessment issues, and overrepresentation of culturally diverse groups in special education. Among the topics least frequently mentioned were identification and teaching of culturally diverse learning styles, appropriate instructional strategies for students from culturally diverse groups, representation of culturally diverse groups in curricular materials, and underrepresentation of culturally diverse students in gifted programs. The authors recommended that, depending on which textbook is being used, teacher educators should consider supplementing the use of textbooks with experiences working with parents and families of students with disabilities from diverse cultural backgrounds.

Meta-Analyses

Rather than analyzing or interpreting the actual data contained in existing articles, the empirical literature review (as described earlier) creates data from the researcher's examination of the literature. This approach often yields important summary information, but it can also lead to readers drawing erroneous conclusions. Suppose that a researcher conducts an empirical literature review of 10 studies that examined the effects of intervention A and intervention B on behavior of students with autism. The researcher finds that six of the studies reported a greater impact on behavior with intervention A, whereas four studies indicated superior effects associated with Intervention B. On the basis of these findings, it may appear evident that intervention A is more effective and should be adopted in classrooms with students with autism. However, that conclusion cannot be reached with any real certainty without an examination of such factors as the relative effect sizes of the studies reviewed, the number of participants in each investigation, and the specific circumstances of each intervention trial. It is possible that most studies favoring intervention A involved very small samples of students and also frequently showed positive effects of intervention B. Alternatively, many of the investigations that reported that intervention B was more effective may have used very large samples and showed no positive effect for intervention A. Despite the fact that more studies showed intervention A to be more effective, intervention B may be more efficacious.

Meta-analyses go several steps further than empirical literature reviews in examining the aggregate findings of related studies. Meta-analyses involve the analysis of the actual findings of a number of published research studies. Essentially, meta-analyses calculate the average effect of an intervention or of group membership across a number of studies and participants. Meta-analyses can provide an in-depth description of research findings (Glass, 1976, 1977) and can also serve an explanatory function, because findings observed across numerous related investigations bring with them a deeper level of understanding that may explain the interrelationships of variables (Cook, Cooper, Cordray, Hartman, Hedges, Light, Louis, & Mosteller, 1992).

To conduct a meta-analysis, there must be a common measure for expressing results across many studies. This common measure is known as effect size, which expresses the strength or magnitude of a relationship between two variables (Cohen, 1988). It is a standard score that reflects the mean of one group or condition in relation to another group or condition. The basic formula for calculating an effect size for any reported relationship is as follows (Glass & Hopkins, 1996, p. 290):

$$ES = \frac{X_e - X_c}{SD_c}$$

where

X_e = the mean (arithmetic average) of the ***experimental*** group;

X_c = the mean score for the ***control*** group; and

SD_c = the standard deviation of the scores for the ***control*** group.

Although this formula seems to imply that meta-analyses can only consider or include data from experimental designs, any studies in which two or more different treatment groups or conditions are observed can be included (Hunter & Schmidt, 1990; Lirgg, 1991).

The equation for calculating effect sizes indicates that a mean derived for one group or condition is compared with a standard or baseline (i.e., the other group or condition) to determine how much it deviates from that standard. The result is then evaluated in terms of the amount of variability present in the baseline condition or comparison group. The primary advantage of a meta-analysis is that a multitude of studies can be effectively summarized into a few relatively simple statistics. The effect size statistic, as calculated by the preciding formula, is expressed as a positive or negative decimal number, between positive 1 and negative 1 in most cases. A positive number indicates that the experimental or treatment group performed better than the control group or comparison condition. Alternatively, a negative number indicates that the comparison condition yielded higher performance on the outcome measure than did the treatment condition. Larger numbers, either positive or negative, represent greater between-group or between-condition differences. For example, an effect size of +1 indicates that the treatment group in a particular study outperformed the control group, on average, by one standard deviation.

Meta-analyses are becoming increasingly common in the special education literature as special educators seek a method for objectively determining practices that are more effective than others (see Landrum, Tankersley, & Cook, 1999). For example, given the rapid increase in the numbers of children identified as having LD, it appears critically important to determine which teaching methods are effective with this population of students. Swanson and Hoskyn (1998) conducted a meta-analysis to investigate the effectiveness of different types of interventions in different domains of schooling for students with LD. Articles or reports were selected for the meta-analysis that (a) were published between 1963 and 1997, (b) involved an experimental design with a comparison or control condition, (c) provided sufficient information for computing effect sizes, (d) administered a treatment to students with LD that was over and above what they would have received in a typical classroom, and (e) were published in English. The dependent measures in the 180 identified studies were grouped into 17 general categories (e.g., word recognition, reading comprehension, memory, mathematics, affective/self-concept, intelligence, social skills, language). Twenty clusters of instructional components were found to be present in the treatments in the studies (e.g., drill repetition and practice review, individualization and small group, strategy modeling and attribution training, segmentation, advance organizers, one-to-one instruction, control difficulty or processing demands of task, technology). From these twenty clusters, four general groups of interventions were constructed: direct instruction (lessons delivered in small groups of students who are given several opportunities to respond and receive feedback about accuracy and responses), strategy instruction (instruction involving advance organizers, organization, elaboration, summarization, general study strategies, metacognition, attributions, and/or evaluation of a strategy), combined direct and strategy instruction, and neither direct nor strategy instruction.

Two of the main findings of the meta-analysis are summarized here. First, although treatments in some areas tend to be more effective than those in other areas, no outcomes appeared to be resistant to change. However, large effects ($> + 0.70$) were evidenced for the studies that targeted outcomes in reading comprehension, vocabulary, and creativity. Relatively smaller effect sizes ($< + 0.55$) were associated with outcomes in spelling, mathematics, general reading, social skills, perceptual processes (handwriting), and language processes (listening comprehension). Second, some types of treatments were more effective than others. Studies that combined direct and strategy instruction were significantly more effective than when treatments consisted of either type of instruction in isolation or neither type of instruction. Moreover, only a few instructional components—sequencing, drill-repetition-practice, controlling task difficulty, segmentation of information, technology, small interactive groups, augmentation of teacher instruction, directed questioning/responding, and strategy cueing—were found to optimally predict high effect sizes. Practitioners may use the results of this meta-analysis to direct their efforts and maximize their effectiveness when making decisions regarding which instructional interventions to use with students with LD.

Elbaum, Vaughn, Hughes, and Moody (1999) also used a meta-analysis to investigate the relationship between reading outcomes for students with disabilities and grouping format (i.e., student pairs, small groups, and mixed formats). The authors identified 20 studies that met the researchers' criteria for inclusion in the analysis (e.g., participants included students with disabilities, intervention occurred in area of language arts, study was reported between 1975 and 1995, data reported were sufficient to compute an effect size). The mean weighted effect sizes for small groups, pairs, and multiple group formats were, respectively, $+ 1.61$, $+ 0.40$, and $+ 0.36$. The effect sizes for small groups and pairs, but not for multiple group formats, were reported to be statistically significant. Further analysis indicated that in cross-age pairings, a high positive effect size ($+ 0.86$) was associated with students with disabilities being tutors, but a nonsignificant negative effect size ($- 0.07$) was associated with students with disabilities being tutees (those receiving tutoring). Results indicated that alternate grouping, particularly small groups and pairs, should be a "preferred approach to reading instruction" (Elbaum et al., 1999, p. 411). The authors also suggested, "whenever possible, students with disabilities should be given the opportunity to tutor students who are at least one grade level lower than they are" (p. 411).

SUMMARY

Researchers in special education apply a wide variety of quantitative techniques to answer a vast array of questions. Quantitative research has provided the foundation of scientific inquiry in the field of special education and has influenced policy and practice since the inception of our profession. Each type of study described in this chapter features distinct methods, analytical techniques, the use (or nonuse) of inferential statistics, levels and types of control or manipulation that are exercised on the independent variable, and strength of the warrant for new knowledge that is yielded. For all of the features that distinguish categories of quantitative designs, they all translate observations into numbers and focus on summarizing or aggregating these numbers to bring meaning to the research findings.

As readers move from this chapter and begin to examine qualitative research in Chapter 7, we caution against dichotomizing quantitative and qualitative method. Although quantitative and qualitative modes of inquiry originated from different, sometimes competing, schools of thought, we believe that it is the researcher's questions, not his or her ideological persuasion, that should be the primary factor in determining the scientific methods that he or she selects. Despite the many specific differences between quantitative and qualitative research that will become apparent as readers examine the next chapter and compare it with the methods discussed here, effective quantitative and qualitative research can both generate new knowledge by answering the theory-based inquiries of special education researchers.

Chapter 7

QUALITATIVE RESEARCH DESIGNS

Connie J. McReynolds,
Lynn C. Koch,
Phillip D. Rumrill, Jr.
Melody J. Tankersley,
Megen E. Ware, and
Mary L. Hennessey

INTRODUCTION

THE QUALITATIVE PARADIGM consists of a wide variety of research designs used to investigate phenomena that have not been previously studied or for which limited information is available (Bellini & Rumrill, 1999; Creswell, 1994; Hagner & Helm, 1994). As with all other research, the selection of a methodological approach for a specific qualitative study is guided by the nature of the problem and the world view and psychological attributes of the researcher (Creswell, 1994). Qualitative research is conducted with a focus on the perspectives of people who are most directly affected by the phenomena under study. Data are collected in the field rather than in laboratories or other contrived settings (Conrad, Neumann, Haworth, & Scott, 1993).

Data collection for qualitative research is comprised of procedures such as in-depth interviews and extended observations that enable the researcher to acquire "rich" or "thick" descriptions of the meanings that research participants ascribe to their experiences (Bogdan & Biklen, 1992; Denzin & Lincoln, 1994; Strauss & Corbin, 1990). Data are analyzed using nonmathematical procedures. Thus, the units of analysis in qualitative research are words, sentences, pictures, and phrases rather than numbers (Polkinghorne, 1991).

Rooted in anthropology and sociology, qualitative research is conducted in social and behavioral science disciplines such as education, counseling, psychology, and organizational management to garner a greater understanding of discipline-specific phenomena (Conrad et al., 1993; Hagner & Helm,

1994; Polkinghorne, 1991). Although less widely applied in special education research, qualitative inquiry has enhanced our understanding of important issues in the lives of people with disabilities. The purpose of this chapter is to provide an overview of qualitative procedures and to discuss their application to special education research. In the following sections, we examine (a) the researcher's role in qualitative inquiry, (b) major assumptions of qualitative research, (c) types of qualitative designs, (d) methodological issues, (e) communication of qualitative findings, and (f) examples of qualitative research in the fields of special education and disability studies.

RESEARCHER'S ROLE

In qualitative inquiry, the researcher is viewed as the instrument of data collection (Polkinghorne, 1991). The accuracy of research findings depends largely on his or her skills, experience, and rigor. An effective qualitative researcher is an expert on the topic of interest and can make quick decisions about what information to seek, what questions to ask, and what observations to make. The qualitative researcher is trained in listening, interviewing, observing, and writing. In addition to these skills, the researcher must possess a keen understanding of human interactions (Lincoln & Guba, 1985).

Because qualitative researchers interact directly with their data sources (i.e., research participants) they must also be aware of how their own experiences and personal characteristics can serve to influence or bias the interpretation of results. Some researchers conduct a self-interview to initiate the data collection process as a means of clarifying their assumptions and expectations. Qualitative researchers are also responsible for explicitly stating their biases in reporting research results (Creswell, 1994). For example, if a researcher believes that inclusive educational settings are the best option for all students with disabilities, he or she should describe how such a belief might influence his or her interpretation of data collected when answering research questions pertaining to inclusion. Safeguards such as triangulation, member checks, and multiple researchers (see section on Credibility of Findings) are often built into the design and methodology of qualitative projects to minimize researcher bias.

MAJOR ASSUMPTIONS OF QUALITATIVE RESEARCH

In addition to the researcher being the primary instrument of data collection, qualitative research has other characteristics that distinguish it from quantitative research. The following is a list of major assumptions about qualitative research (Creswell, 1994; Hagner & Helm, 1994; Lincoln & Guba, 1985):

1. Qualitative research is conducted in natural settings where people live, work, and play.
2. Categories or themes are discovered from repeated comparisons of the data rather than "overlaid like a template on the participants or their situation" (Hagner & Helm, 1994, p. 291); hypotheses evolve from the data collected.
3. The data that emerge from a qualitative study are descriptive and reported in words or pictures rather than in numbers.
4. Data analysis occurs through induction rather than deduction; theory or hypotheses are not established before the investigation begins.
5. Understanding occurs as a result of engaging in an in-depth study of the phenomena of interest; researchers are as interested in the process that is occurring as they are in the outcome.
6. Qualitative researchers make ideographic interpretations of the research findings; they are more interested in understanding the total picture of the focus of inquiry than they are in making generalizations of that focus to other situations.
7. Meanings and interpretations of research findings are negotiated with participants, because it is their perceptions or realities that the researcher seeks to understand.
8. The criteria for judging the empirical soundness of qualitative studies emphasize coherence, insight, instrumental usefulness, and trustworthiness rather than reliability and validity.

QUALITATIVE RESEARCH DESIGNS

Qualitative research is conducted for purposes of (a) *exploring,* (b) *explaining,* or (c) *describing* certain phenomena. From this framework, the researcher considers various qualitative research designs in pursuit of the best match for the research question or problem being addressed.

Exploratory studies are conducted when the researcher is investigating phenomena that are not well understood, when variables need to be identified or discovered, or when the research purpose is to generate hypotheses for further investigation. Sample research questions are as follows: What is happening in this particular setting? What are the salient themes, patterns, or categories that the participants view as important? How are certain patterns linked together? The case study or grounded theory approach (see discussions in the following section) are appropriate designs for exploratory studies. A qualitative study of the school-to-work transition needs of adolescents with spina bifida, for example, would most likely be exploratory in nature, because it has been only recently that children with this condition have been surviving into early adulthood.

Explanatory studies are conducted when an understanding of the impetus behind the research phenomenon is needed or when the researcher wants to identify plausible factors associated with the phenomenon (Marshall & Rossman, 1989). Multisite studies or ethnographic designs are applicable to explanatory research studies.

A researcher who applied quantitative methods to document a significant, positive relationship between family socioeconomic status and academic achievement among middle school students with learning disabilities might follow up that study with an explanatory qualitative investigation to unearth some of the factors and issues that underlie that relationship. Several high-achieving students with learning disabilities might be selected to examine in greater depth how their parents' means and resources have contributed to the students' academic success. Not only would this approach add insight to the observed correlation between socioeconomic status and academic achievement, it might also bring to light factors associated with achievement that are not related to socioeconomic status (e.g., number of hours spent studying per week, quality of instruction received at school, social acceptance by peers).

Descriptive studies are those in which the researcher is interested in documenting the salient features (e.g., behaviors, events, processes, attitudes, beliefs) of the phenomenon of interest. Case studies or ethnographic designs typically constitute descriptive qualitative studies (Marshall & Rossman, 1989). For example, a researcher seeking a school principal's perspective on inclusion might conduct an in-depth case study of one principal in an effort to document and describe that administrator's experiences with students with disabilities, actions in implementing the Individuals with Disabilities Education Act, interactions with other administrators related to disability issues, reports from classroom teachers regarding students with disabilities, and knowledge of inclusion from economic and philosophical vantage points.

As in quantitative research, the particular qualitative research design is selected after the purpose of the study has been determined. Within the qualitative paradigm lies a number of potential research designs as eluded to in the previous paragraphs. For the purpose of this chapter, discussion will focus on the following designs: (a) ethnography, (b) case study, (c) multisite study, and (d) grounded theory.

Ethnography

The term "ethnography" has been used by sociologists and anthropologists to describe observations of and participation in various cultures (Bogdan & Biklen, 1992; Crowson, 1993). Ethnography provides an approach to understanding people in their natural settings, and it is concerned with exploring the complex cultural phenomena that characterize human interactions. Ethnographers seek to understand the broad cultural dynamics of a society as conceptualized by their research participants.

Ethnographic data are obtained through natural activities such as talking, listening, and observing human behaviors (Guba, 1978). Information gathered by these means provides a mechanism for identifying cultural symbols (e.g., special education labels). The relationships among cultural symbols are explored and used to provide the researcher with an enhanced understanding of the culture (Marshall & Rossman, 1989). Bogdan and Biklen (1992) provided the following description of ethnography:

> When culture is examined from this perspective, the ethnographer is faced with a series of interpretations of life, common-sense understandings that are complex and difficult to separate from each other. The ethnographer's goals are to share in the meanings that the cultural participants take for granted and then to depict the new understanding for the reader and for outsiders. (p. 39)

Case Study

Case studies are in-depth explorations of a single subject or setting, a particular event or circumstance, or even a single set of documents (Merriam, 1988). The qualitative case study design provides a means of exploring, characterizing, or chronicling events for the purpose of "revealing the properties of the class to which the instance being studied belongs" (Guba & Lincoln, 1981, p. 371). Qualitative case studies may take three primary forms: (a) historical organizational, (b) observational, and (c) life history (Bogdan & Biklen, 1992).

HISTORICAL ORGANIZATIONAL. Historical organizational case studies focus on a specific organization, considering its development over a certain period of time. Sources of information may include people who were involved in the organization since its inception, written records and other types of documentation, and observations of the present organization. For example, a qualitative researcher might be interested in understanding how the Council for Exceptional Children began and evolved into the primary organization for the education of children and youth with disabilities. Historical organizational case studies would be an appropriate method for conducting this inquiry.

OBSERVATIONAL. Observational case studies concentrate on a specific aspect of the organization (e.g., a particular place, a specific group of people, a distinct activity) framed in present-tense terms (Bogdan & Biklen, 1992). Participant observation serves as the main technique used for data collection. Participant observation involves the researcher in systematic, but unobtrusive, data collection in the natural settings of the participants. The researcher collects data through (a) observing what the participants say and do, and/or (b) conducting in-depth interviews that are often unstructured and open ended. To understand the day-to-day lives of special education classroom teachers, an investigator might spend months observing several classrooms and interviewing several teachers to obtain data.

LIFE HISTORY. Life histories consist of collecting a first-person narrative of one person, obtained through extensive interviewing (Helling, 1988). This type of case study may be used to depict a famous person's life or to understand human behavior from that individual's perspective. Extensive life histories may produce hundreds or even thousands of pages of transcripts. Other life history case studies may include more limited data on a particular topic or a certain period of a person's life. For an excellent example of life history case studies, see McMahon and Shaw's (1999) *Enabling Lives*, a collection of biographies of prominent Americans with disabilities.

Multisite Study

When using the multisite study design, the researcher's orientation is toward developing or extending theory. As the term "multisite" implies, multiple sites or sources of information are used in this type of design. The two most popular approaches used with the multisite study design are modified analytic induction and the constant comparative method. Modified analytic induction involves collecting and analyzing data to develop a theoretical model describing all of the variations of a particular phenomenon (Bogdan & Biklen, 1992). The following steps are involved in the modified analytic induction method (Bogdan & Biklen, 1992; Robinson, 1951):

1. Develop a rough definition and explanation of the particular phenomenon early in the research process.
2. Compare the definition and explanation to the data as the data are collected.
3. Modify the definition and explanation as data are encountered that do not fit the existing definition/explanation.
4. Actively seek data that may not fit into the existing formulation.

5. Redefine the phenomenon and formulations until a universal relationship is achieved.

The constant comparative method (Glaser & Strauss, 1967; Strauss & Corbin 1990) is similar to the modified analytic induction method in that data analysis is conducted throughout the data collection process. However, it differs in that the researcher is seeking to define the themes and categories as the data collection process unfolds, rather than establishing an *a priori* definition against which to compare observed data. Because of its fluid, unassuming approach, the constant comparative method is more generally accepted and used in current qualitative research than the modified analytic induction method. The following steps are performed throughout the research process with a constant interplay back and forth (Bogdan & Biklen, 1992; Glaser, 1978):

1. Start collecting data.
2. Begin to identify key issues or recurrent events that will be developed into categories.
3. Collect data that further support the categories and develop an understanding of the variations within each of the categories.
4. Describe and account for all variations within the data and continue to search for additional incidents.
5. Describe basic social processes and relationships as you see them emerging in the model.
6. Explore the core categories through sampling and coding.

Grounded Theory

In the grounded theory approach, the researcher does not begin with a specific theory and then seek to prove it. Rather, the researcher begins with an area of interest and, through the process of gathering data, analyzing the data, and forming concepts and themes, the researcher develops a theoretical formulation from which a framework for action emerges (Strauss & Corbin, 1990). Grounded theory evolves throughout the course of data collection and analysis as concepts, and the relationships among them are identified and then conditionally tested throughout the analysis of data (Denzin & Lincoln, 1994). As a scientific method, grounded theory is rigorous in data analysis, interpretation, and validation (Creswell, 1994; Denzin & Lincoln, 1994; Glaser & Strauss, 1967; Strauss & Corbin, 1990).

Glaser and Strauss (1967) identified the following criteria used to determine the applicability of a theory as it is grounded to a central phenomenon:

fit, understanding, and generality. Fit is achieved if the theory is considered to reflect the everyday reality of the area being studied. If the theory is carefully induced from diverse data, the theory should be understandable to the individuals who participated in the research project and to research consumers (Strauss & Corbin, 1990). In achieving generality, the interpretations must be conceptual in nature, broad enough to display an abstractable quality, and reflective of the various contexts in which the phenomenon occurs in real world situations. For more in depth discussion on these concepts, see Glaser and Strauss (1967) or Strauss and Corbin (1990).

METHODOLOGICAL ISSUES

The methodology in qualitative research consists of a variety of procedures used in the collection, analysis, and reporting of data (Creswell, 1994). Although precise agreement among qualitative writers and researchers regarding specific procedures does not exist, we will address the following methodological issues in this section: (a) the literature review, (b) research questions, (c) sampling, (d) data collection procedures, (e) data management – recording procedures, (f) data analysis procedures, (g) credibility of qualitative findings, and (h) limitations of qualitative research.

The Literature Review

Many qualitative researchers (like quantitative researchers) begin their investigations with a review of literature in the topic area of interest. By beginning the investigation with a literature review, researchers are able to examine how other scientists have approached the topic of interest and to "refine" their own research design (Glesne & Peshkin, 1992; Polkinghorne, 1991).

In qualitative research, the literature review continues beyond the outset of the project into the data collection and analysis phases of the study. Themes emerging from the data often require a review of previously unexamined literature (Glesne & Peshkin, 1992; Strauss & Corbin, 1990), because the findings of previous studies (both qualitative and quantitative) are viewed as tentative or inconclusive. In that regard, the literature review becomes part of the data that are analyzed (Creswell, 1994; Polkinghorne, 1991).

Because qualitative studies are exploratory, explanatory, or descriptive in nature, the literature related to the topic of interest is used inductively so that it does not direct the researcher's questions or suppress the development of new theoretical formulations (Creswell, 1994; Strauss & Corbin, 1990). The amount of literature reviewed varies depending on the qualitative design. For example, in theoretically oriented qualitative studies such as ethnographies, the literature review may be quite extensive; on the other hand, in grounded theory and case studies, the literature review may be much more restricted (Creswell, 1994).

The literature review in both quantitative and qualitative research informs readers about the results of related studies, relates the current study to prior studies, and provides a rationale for the current study (Creswell, 1994; Strauss & Corbin, 1990). In some written qualitative reports, a brief literature review is included in the introduction to frame the problem of interest. In others, a more extensive literature review is provided in a separate section. In most studies, the literature is also compared and contrasted with the researcher's current findings at the end of the report (Creswell, 1994). Chapter 9 of this book provides thorough descriptions of the sections and composition of a research article.

Research Questions

In qualitative inquiry, preliminary research questions are formulated to provide a framework within which to focus the research design and guide the data collection process (Glesne & Peshkin, 1992). Research questions are not static, nor are they tested like quantitative hypotheses (Strauss & Corbin, 1990). Rather, they are continuously reformulated throughout the data collection and analysis processes. This flexibility enables the researcher to follow the lead of research participants rather than impose his or her perspectives on those who are affected by the phenomena under study. In this manner, the researcher obtains information relevant to the participant's own experiences. Qualitative researchers in special education and disability studies often use in-depth interviews to answer their research questions because interviews provide the latitude necessary to probe for specific details concerning the information offered by participants (Bogdan & Biklen, 1992; Glesne & Peshkin, 1992; Marshall & Rossman, 1989). Research participants are encouraged to reflect on and elaborate the details of their experiences. Interviews are conducted over a period of anywhere from thirty minutes to several hours, and participants are sometimes interviewed more than once.

Although qualitative researchers often use interview protocols, it is the research participant who ultimately guides the interview. Thus, interview protocols are designed to be flexible enough to incorporate modifications and changes as the data collection process continues (Denzin & Lincoln, 1994; Glesne & Peshkin, 1992). Focus groups or expert panels may review the questions and make specific recommendations for changes or additional questions when an interview protocol is developed. Members of these focus groups or expert panels typically consist of individuals with characteristics similar to those of targeted research participants, other qualitative researchers, and/or people with expertise in the phenomena under study.

Sampling

Sampling procedures in qualitative research are quite different from those used in quantitative research. The most important considerations in qualitative sampling decisions are related to who will be included as research participants, identifying the research settings, and determining appropriate sampling times. Decisions regarding these issues have a significant impact on the results because of the subjective nature of the sampling variables and must be carefully deliberated before the initiation of the study (Maxwell, 1996). Because it is generally not possible to interview everyone or to observe everything related to the phenomenon of interest, a sampling strategy is used to determine which participants, sites, and times to include (Glesne & Peshkin, 1992). Therefore, the sampling strategy used in qualitative research is referred to as "purposeful" (Maxwell, 1996, p. 70), because participants are chosen on the basis of their perceived ability to facilitate the understanding of the phenomenon investigated, in the places most convenient to observe the phenomenon, and at a time when the most information can be gathered.

Purposeful sampling in qualitative research has also been defined as "criterion based selection" (LeCompte & Preissle, 1993, p. 69). The purposeful sampling technique is used in the deliberate selection of persons, settings, and events to provide answers to the research questions. It is also used when the number of individuals being studied is relatively small and when the use of random sampling could prohibit the inclusion of the very participants about whom the researcher is attempting to learn (Maxwell, 1996). The goals of purposeful sampling include (a) identifying similarities and differences in the population being studied, (b) examining specific conditions of a particular phenomenon, and/or (c) establishing controlled comparisons.

For some research questions or problems, access to research participants may be difficult to achieve (e.g., accessing parents of children with highly stigmatizing disability labels). In those cases, researchers often use a strategy commonly referred to as "convenience sampling." Convenience sampling permits the specific selection of research participants who are known and available and therefore convenient to the researcher (Weiss, 1994). Finding a convenience sample can often lead to other sampling techniques such as "snowballing" (Patton, 1990). Snowballing involves asking the first person interviewed to recommend others who possess the quality of interest and following suit with subsequent participants. Snowballing, then, provides the researcher access to participants who might otherwise not be discovered.

PARTICIPANTS. The selection of participants in qualitative research "rests on the multiple purposes of illuminating, interpreting, and understanding" (Glesne & Peshkin, 1992, p. 27) their perspectives. In most qualitative situations, the researcher is unable to interview all potential participants or observe everything. Therefore, participants are selected on the basis of the type of information they can provide in answering the research questions. If the researcher is more interested in developing an in-depth understanding of the participants' situation, extended periods of time will be spent with a small number of participants. However, if the researcher wants to gather a broader perspective, a larger number of participants are interviewed in a less intensive manner (Creswell, 1994).

SITES. Although some research questions are global and do not require an actual site or setting for conducting the research, many research questions need to be answered within the context of a specific site. This might be particularly true in special education where phenomena of interest often involve questions related to teaching and learning, thereby requiring observation in the classroom setting. According to Marshall and Rossman (1989), the following four issues require consideration in selecting the appropriate sampling site(s): (a) physical access to the site, (b) variety of data sources available within the site, (c) amount of time access to the participants and data can be granted within the site, and (d) quality and credibility of the data provided within the site.

TIMING. The timing surrounding the research can influence the type and quality of data collected. The availability of participants may dictate the length of interviews or observations. If, for example, teachers are interviewed during their lunch break, the researcher is limited by the actual time constraint of the break and must compete with the time the teachers need to eat. In addition, the time periods represented by the data could also influence the findings. For example, if documents reviewed are not current, inconsistencies with other data sources might occur. The researcher will need to consider each decision regarding timing by asking questions related to the effect the decision will ultimately have on quality of data gathered. The more aware the researcher is about the potential ramifications of decisions of timing, the wiser the final decisions are likely to be (Bogdan & Biklen, 1992).

Data Collection and Recording Procedures

In qualitative research, data emerge from the interactions of researchers with their data sources (Polkinghorne, 1991). The selection of data sources is conducted on theoretical grounds rather than probability theory. The data collected in qualitative research are often described as "thick," because they consist of vivid and rich descriptions of the phenomena under study.

Qualitative data collection efforts can generate hundreds of pages of information. Typical sources of data include field notes (e.g., observations, interviews, memos documenting the researcher's own experiences, transcripts from taped interviews, photographs, descriptive statistics (quantitative data), and documents (personal and official). Personal documents may include diaries, letters, and autobiographies. Official documents may include newsletters, policy documents, codes of ethics, statements of philosophy, minutes from meetings, student records, and personnel files.

Before the initiation of data collection, the researcher considers what data will be recorded and how they will be gathered. A protocol form is often used to document observations in the field such as descriptive notes (e.g., accounts of particular events and activities, a reconstruction of the dialogue, characteristics of the research participants, reflective notes (e.g., personal thoughts, impressions, ideas, problems, prejudices), and demographic information (Bogdan & Biklen, 1992; Creswell, 1994).

During the data collection and recording process, the qualitative researcher must consider methods to ensure accuracy of the information being obtained (see Credibility of Research Findings). As Dexter (1970) pointed out:

> No one should plan or finance an entire study in advance with the expectation of relying chiefly upon interviews for data unless the interviewers have enough relevant background to be sure that they can make sense out of interview conversations or unless there is a reasonable hope of being able to hang around or in some way observe so as to learn what it is meaningful and significant to ask. (p. 17)

Data Management Procedures

As previously mentioned, a great deal of data is often generated during a qualitative research project. Because data management and analysis are integrally related, the data must be organized to facilitate easy retrieval. Levine (1985) outlined five main principles in the management of qualitative data:

1. *Formatting.* Include consistent information in the field notes (e.g., name of the researcher, the site, the participant(s), the date). Maintain the notes in a notebook, file folder, or other like container.
2. *Cross-referral.* Reference information from one file to another to permit ease of data retrieval.

3. *Coding.* The coding system can either be prestructured or evolve during the research project. It includes identifying and organizing categories as they emerge from the data (see Data Analysis section for more detailed explanation).

4. *Abstracting.* Condense lengthy material into summaries while retaining a clear link back to the original field notations.

5. *Locators.* Use unique numbers or letters to serve as identification markers for specific materials in field notes (see Levine, 1985 for a more in depth discussion).

Qualitative data management can be a daunting task. However, advances in technology have added substantial efficiency to the management of qualitative data. Computer software packages (e.g., ATLAS, NUDIST, AQUAD, QUALPRO, Metamorph, HyperQual) have been developed to provide efficient methods for sorting and coding qualitative data.

Data Analysis Procedures

The researcher is involved in multiple tasks throughout the research process, including data collection, analysis, and writing (Creswell, 1994). Qualitative designs are built on a back-and-forth movement from data gathering to analysis, then back to more data gathering. Research categories are developed through the use of the modified analytic induction or constant comparative methods (Glaser & Strauss, 1967; Glaser, 1978; Strauss & Corbin, 1990). Data analysis is comprised of the identification of words and phrases in a series of coding processes known as open, axial, and selective coding (Strauss & Corbin, 1990).

Open coding involves breaking down data or "tak[ing] apart the story" (Haworth & Conrad, 1997) for the purpose of examining, comparing, conceptualizing, and categorizing the data. Conceptual labels (i.e., themes) are constructed for specific happenings, events, or other phenomena. As similarities are discovered within the various concepts, they are grouped together in a new, more abstract unit called a category (Strauss & Corbin, 1990).

Axial coding is used to integrate the data, or emerging themes, in new ways by making connections between categories. Potentially causal conditions such as events, incidents, and happenings that lead to the occurrence or development of a specific type of situation or phenomenon are explored as they lead to an emerging theory (Haworth & Conrad, 1997).

Selective coding provides a means for integrating information, and it produces a higher level of systematic analysis through a series of steps that are not necessarily linear. The first step involves the conceptualization of the "story line," (i.e., the core or primary category) identified in the previous stages of coding (i.e., open and axial). The next steps consist of relating similar categories to the core or primary category and testing those relationships by referring back to the data for corroboration (Strauss & Corbin, 1990).

Initial categories or themes are tested by deliberately searching for contradictory evidence. If contradictory evidence is discovered, the initial categories are revised to incorporate the new evidence. This process is repeated over and over until thematic categories are sufficient to include *all* the various pieces of evidence; at that point, the data collection is ceased.

In grounded theory, theoretical saturation is sought. Theoretical saturation occurs when new or relevant data no longer seem to be emerging from the data, when the categories or themes have been well developed, and when the relationship among categories or themes has been clearly established without any overlapping categories (Strauss & Corbin, 1990).

Credibility of Qualitative Findings

Because the intent of qualitative research is to uncover meaning rather than verify causal relationships between variables or generalize findings to other settings and populations, the terms "reliability" and "validity" have a different meaning in qualitative research than they do in quantitative research (Creswell, 1994; Glesne & Peshkin, 1992; Lincoln & Guba, 1985; Maxwell, 1996; McReynolds & Koch, 1999). In fact, many qualitative researchers use terms such as "credibility," "trustworthiness," and "authenticity" in lieu of reliability and validity, which are often expressed numerically in quantitative studies.

Established techniques are used to ensure the credibility of qualitative research findings. These techniques include (a) audit trails, (b) field notes, (c) memos, (d) triangulation, (e) discrepant data, (f) member checks, and (g) peer debriefers.

AUDIT TRAIL. The audit trail provides a mechanism for subsequent reviews by other researchers and has been identified as the "single most important trustworthiness technique" (Lincoln & Guba, 1985, p. 283). An audit trail consists of (a) raw data, including audiotapes, interview notes, and memos; (b) products of data reduction and analysis, including coding procedures; (c) products of data reconstruction and synthesis; and (d) process notes (Lincoln & Guba, 1985).

FIELD NOTES. Maintaining field notes entails the recording of comprehensive and detailed information, sometimes referred to as "thick descriptions" (Geertz, 1983). The use of field notes ensures that important information from the researcher's personal experiences in the study are incorporated into the process of analysis. In addition, field notes provide the qualitative researcher with useful examples and direct quotations from participants.

Qualitative researchers are careful to maintain a distinction between interpretive information and actual descriptions of fact. Interpretive information is generated by the researcher and is based on his or her understanding (or interpretation) of the situation. Actual descriptions of fact are based on specific events, activities, or actions that are either observed or accurately documented.

MEMOS. Memos are used throughout the qualitative research process to record personal biases, assumptions, and feelings (Bogdan & Biklen, 1992). This approach serves to record the researcher's thoughts, perspectives, intuitions, and preliminary ideas regarding the ongoing investigation. Recording the researcher's preliminary ideas safeguards against the loss of important ideas during the research process (Glesne & Peshkin, 1992). Memos are also used by peer reviewers to gain additional perspective on the data.

TRIANGULATION. Triangulation is defined as the researcher's effort to collect information from a diverse range of individuals and settings, using a variety of methods in order to construct appropriate explanations of the phenomena being investigated (Denzin, 1970). Information collected from a variety of sources is compared and contrasted and serves to protect the accuracy of data interpretation (Denzin & Lincoln, 1994). Triangulation, then, provides a means of cross-referencing interpretations made during data analysis. It further minimizes the possibility of arriving at erroneous interpretations and conclusions. Triangulation of data can include comparisons to the researcher's own experiences and results from literature reviews and use of multiple researchers and multiple sources of data.

The active participation of multiple researchers in qualitative research projects provides several advantages. The first is the ability to evaluate multiple sites during the same time frame. In addition, multiple researchers bring different skills, attributes, and perspectives to the evaluation process (McReynolds & Koch, 1999; Wax, 1979). Such differences reduce the possibility of personal biases or preconceptions influencing the findings (Hagner & Helm, 1994). In situations in which a researcher is working alone, alternative methods are available to enhance the credibility of findings (see Peer Debriefers).

Qualitative research findings are the result of a compilation of data obtained from a wide range of sources. Sources can include interviews, observations, documents, and visual images (Creswell, 1994). For example, data obtained from interviews could include audio/visual recordings, notes, and observations of research participants. Observations may include descriptions of the physical surroundings, the reactions of research participants, and any other information relevant to the topic under study. Data can further be obtained through the review of various types of documents (e.g., official memos, minutes, archival material including visual images such as photographs). Multiple sources of data enhance credibility by providing additional references for triangulation.

DISCREPANT DATA. Occasionally, data obtained during the course of a study may not support the researcher's preliminary conclusions. Discrepant data must be rigorously examined, along with supporting data, to determine whether the research findings (i.e., categories, themes) are to be retained or modified. The qualitative researcher must be diligent in the examination of discrepant data to avoid prematurely dismissing relevant data that do not fit with existing conclusions (Maxwell, 1996).

MEMBER CHECKS. Participant feedback is considered critically important in establishing the accuracy of data interpretations in qualitative studies (Creswell, 1994; Denzin & Lincoln, 1994). In that spirit, research participants are often given the opportunity to comment on the preliminary conclusions reached by the researchers. This process is called member checks. Member checks provide an additional level of credibility regarding the accuracy of emerging themes and categories. This involves asking research participants to provide feedback to the researchers concerning data interpretations (Fielding & Fielding, 1986). The feedback situation also provides a checkpoint in protecting any confidential information or the identities of research participants.

PEER DEBRIEFERS. Peer debriefers are used as a means of testing the researcher's ideas against those of a peer or peers who have not been involved in the research project. The use of peer debriefers provides an opportunity to obtain alternative perspectives regarding the interpretation of the data, thereby enhancing the credibility of the research findings (Lincoln & Guba, 1985). Debriefing can occur any time during the research process and requires involving a peer in clarifying interpretation of the data.

The use of peer debriefing helps to reduce the influence of two additional threats to qualitative research credibility and trustworthiness: researcher bias and reactivity (Maxwell, 1996). Researcher bias can occur when the interpretation of data corresponds with the researcher's preconceived notions (Miles & Huberman, 1994). Researcher bias can be guarded against through the use of member checks and peer debriefers (Creswell, 1994; Denzin & Lincoln, 1994). Reactivity refers to the potential effect of the researcher on the setting or individuals being researched. The goal in qualitative research is to understand reactivity and to use it productively instead of attempting to eliminate it from the study (Maxwell, 1996). Because it is impossible to completely prevent reactivity in an interview or other procedure that actively engages the researcher with participants, care must be taken in understanding how the researcher may be influencing the response of the participant. The researcher's use of reflective statements and open-ended questions, avoidance of leading questions, and restatement of the participant's comments are effective strategies in managing reactivity throughout the interview process (Maxwell, 1996).

Limitations of Qualitative Research

When judged against the criteria used to evaluate the empirical soundness of quantitative research, qualitative procedures may appear to lack rigor (Polkinghorne, 1991). However, on closer inspection of the procedures, strategies, and methods used in qualitative research, this is far from the truth. Readers must keep in mind that the objective of qualitative research is fundamentally different from that of quantitative research. In qualitative research, the purpose is to understand the subjective meaning that people ascribe to their world, not to make inductive generalizations and verify causal relationships between or among variables (Maxwell, 1996). Thus, the notion of empirical soundness (i.e., research validity) takes on a different meaning in qualitative research. Scientific rigor and credibility are no less of a concern to qualitative researchers than they are to quantitative researchers. In fact, qualitative researchers adhere to well-established procedures as detailed in the preceding sections of this chapter to ensure the accuracy of their research findings.

This is not to imply that qualitative research is without limitations. Some of the data collected in qualitative studies, for example, are in the form of self-reports. Self-reports can introduce error into a study because they rely on individuals' memories to reconstruct their experiences with the phenomena of interest (Polkinghorne, 1991). How we remember our past experiences is often influenced by our current experiences and perceptions, and our memories are not always 100 percent accurate.

Qualitative researchers, as the instruments of data collection, also can introduce additional limitations to a study. Researchers must be cognizant of how their role is perceived by participants and how they influence the manner in which participants communicate with them (e.g., what information is shared and what information is withheld). In addition, as previously mentioned, the researcher's own biases may lead to misinterpretations of meaning (Creswell, 1994). Therefore, researchers must be aware of the potential influence of their preconceptions on the selection and interpretation of observations (Murphy & Salomone, 1983).

Finally, the intent of qualitative research is for researchers to develop a unique interpretation rather than to generalize findings, as is the objective of quantitative research. However, generalizability can be discussed from a limited perspective as it relates to categories or themes that emerge from qualitative data analysis. The researcher can address the central assumptions, the selection of participants, data collection procedures, and biases—thereby enhancing the possibility of replicating the study in another setting (Creswell, 1994; Yin, 1989).

QUALITATIVE RESEARCH IN SPECIAL EDUCATION

Historically, the research surrounding people with disabilities has focused primarily on quantitative methods. More recently, however, researchers have called for greater use of qualitative procedures to enhance our understanding of important issues in special education and other disability studies disciplines (Ferguson, 1993; Ferguson & Halle, 1995; Hagner & Helm, 1994; McPhail, 1995; McReynolds & Koch, 1999; Miller, 1990). Along the same line, the National Institute on Disability and Rehabilitation Research (NIDRR) has emphasized the need for participatory action research (PAR) that directly involves people with disabilities in developing, conducting, evaluating, and disseminating special education and rehabilitation research (Walker, 1993).

Because the real experts on disability are people with disabilities and their significant others (Freedman & Fesko, 1996; Wright, 1983), it is critical that special education researchers and practitioners acquire a thorough understanding of the perspectives and concerns of people with disabilities. Understanding the perspectives and concerns of family members is also important because of the crucial role that families play in supporting people with disabilities to achieve their educational and life goals (Freedman & Fesko, 1996).

Although a scarcity of information on the perspectives of individuals with disabilities still exists, we have witnessed a steady increase in qualitative special education research that seeks to understand their experiences (Ferguson, 1993; Ferguson & Halle, 1995; Miller, 1990). Qualitative studies have also been executed to describe and explain processes involved in the education of students with disabilities.

Collet-Klingenberg (1998), for example, conducted a case study (within a grounded theory framework) to examine the transition-related experiences of children with disabilities in a public school setting. The school identified in the study was a small, rural high school (with an enrollment of 111 students) that served 10 students with learning disabilities. Data were obtained through (a) a review of documents and records that detailed the planning and implementation of transition services, (b) unstructured and semistructured interviews, and (c) participant observations in school and community settings. Data were analyzed using the constant comparative method with a focus on the crystallization of data to derive themes from highly individual, discrepant, and often very specific events and conversations. Although the study was not outcome-focused, issues of student learning and outcomes were considered; the study confirmed the importance of parent and student involvement in transition planning, and it also underscored the positive effect of school-based and community-based transition teams on postschool outcomes for children with learning disabilities.

In an ethnographic study, Kliewer and Landis (1999) explored teacher perceptions of the meaning of curricular individualization for preschool through primary-aged students with moderate to severe cognitive disabilities. Participants included 14 teachers and six families that had a preschool or primary-aged child with a moderate to severe disability. Data were collected through interviews, participant observations, and document analysis. Within the data, specific themes emerged and were organized into primary codes, then further divided into subcodes. The researchers found that individualizing practices appeared to originate from two disparate sources of understanding: institutional and local. In institutional understanding, individualization for children with disabilities often proceeds in legalistic fashion, and it corresponds to an institutionalized set of professional, cultural, and social presumptions surrounding the concept of mental retardation (Kliewer & Landis, 1999). Local understanding was found to encompass assumptions that originate in the teachers relationship with an actual child, which is surrounded by the immediate instructional context. The authors concluded that truly responsive services for children with moderate to severe disabilities must involve local understanding based on the teacher's relationship with the child and the child's family.

In another example, Vaughn, Moody, and Schumm (1998) conducted a qualitative study to examine reading instruction and grouping practices for students with learning disabilities used by special education teachers in a resource room. Fourteen special educators representing 13 schools were observed three times over the course of a one-year period and interviewed at the beginning and end of the school year. Eighty-two students, of whom 77 were identified as learning disabled and five were identified as developmentally or orthopedically disabled, were also observed. According to the researchers, results showed that teacher-student interactions were characterized by broken promises. The most obvious of these was the broken promise to the student and his or her parent that an individualized reading program would be provided to meet each student's specific needs. Respondent teachers found it extremely difficult to provide individualized reading programs when they were responsible for teaching eight or more students at one time.

In another qualitative investigation, Kliewer (1998) examined the development of literacy among of 10 students with Down syndrome over a two-year period. Traditionally, children with Down syndrome have been excluded from literacy opportunities because: (a) reading is often viewed as a curricular end-product requiring students to master a set of isolated subskills in an age-normed, linear sequence and (b) children with Down syndrome are believed to lack the cognitive capacity necessary to master literacy subskills at an age-normed pace (Kliewer, 1998). Data were collected from 45 observations and 12 interviews that were conducted and transcribed in 1,300 pages of field notes. A variety of settings were chosen to observe participants, including both regular and special education classrooms. Seven themes were identified from the data: (a) direct classroom-imposed illiteracy, (b) indirect classroom-imposed illiteracy, (c) interpreting behavior as illiterate, (d) direct support of literacy acquisition, (e) indirect support of literacy acquisition, (f) assumption of literacy in student behavior, and (g) literacy as a negotiation tool. Results indicated that teachers actively connected children with Down syndrome to the literate community only when students were involved as full participants in the regular routines and general lessons of classrooms made up of children with and without disabilities.

The results of several qualitative studies on the same topic can also be synthesized and analyzed. For example, Klingner and Vaughn (1999) wrote a synthesis article reviewing 20 qualitative studies that investigated the perceptions of a total of 4,659 students in kindergarten through 12th grade on instructional procedures in general education classrooms that included students with high-incidence disabilities. Studies were selected by conducting an extensive search to ensure that all of the existing research in this area was located. The researchers used five major modes of searching: (a) searches in subject indexes, (b) citation searches, (c) footnote chasing, (d) consultation, and (e) browsing. Once the set of articles was assembled, the next step was to read and code each study using the following categories: purpose of the study, participants, data sources, and applicable findings. Next, the researchers applied an analytical method that synthesized and summarized the results of each study. Thirteen of the studies used individually administered interviews; one study used focus group interviews; and eleven studies used written surveys, questionnaires, or scales (several studies used more than one of those methods). A cross-study analysis generated seven categories of findings: grading practices, homework, assignment routines, helping practices, instructional practices, grouping arrangements, and adaptations. One of the most important findings from this synthesis was that most students did not perceive instructional adaptations and accommodations to meet the special needs of selected students (with and without disabilities) as problematic (Klingner & Vaughn, 1999).

SUMMARY

The purpose of qualitative research is to explore, explain, or describe phenomena from the perspective of research participants. Exploratory studies are initiated when the researcher wishes to investigate phenomena that are not well understood, when variables need to be identified or discovered, or to generate hypotheses for further research. Explanatory studies are conducted to define the impetus behind the phenomenon being studied or to identify plausible factors related to the phenomenon. Descriptive studies are used to document the features of the phenomenon of interest. The strength of the qualitative paradigm lies in its search for unknown variables. Qualitative studies often formulate a basis for additional research, including quantitative investigations.

Qualitative research provides a mechanism for conveying information through the use of "rich" and "thick" descriptions, thereby permitting a deeper understanding of the research participant's experience and point of view. In asking individuals to describe their worlds and their experiences with disability, special education researchers can gain a better understanding of the perspectives of people with disabilities and those who interact with them.

In this and the preceding chapter, we have attempted to provide the reader with an overview of quantitative and qualitative research designs. Our hope is that the merits of each will be given due consideration. The field of special education stands to gain immensely from the appropriate application of research designs, a process that is always driven by the researcher's curiosity and the research question that he or she asks.

Chapter 8

SYNTHETIC LITERATURE REVIEWS

Phillip D. Rumrill, Jr.

INTRODUCTION

Chapters 6 and 7 of this book describe the quantitative and qualitative methods that special education researchers use to conduct investigations involving original or extant data. Much of the text of this or any other introductory research book is devoted to the design, execution, analysis, and reporting of empirically based research. However, a discussion of empirical research designs in special education does not fully capture the range of techniques that scholars use in building the professional literature. A considerable proportion (more than half in some journals) of the articles that appear in the special education literature is comprised of works whose purpose is to synthesize existing information in a way that contributes new knowledge to the profession.

Known as synthetic literature reviews (Bellini & Rumrill, 1999; Bolton, 1979), these articles make an important contribution to our field. They serve to postulate or advance new theories and models, examine important and/or controversial topics in the lives of special education teachers and students, present "how to" tips and strategies to improve best practices, and explain new developments in educational and disability policy (e.g., laws and their effects, administrative regulations). In so doing, synthetic literature reviews frame current issues that must be addressed in future services and research. They describe the current state of both art (practice) and science (research) in focused areas of inquiry, add new insights and applications, and provide critical analyses of other published works. By including this chapter, we want to emphasize that the concept of scholarship encompasses much more than the numerous empirical designs described to this point in the book; scholarship also includes thoughtful, systematic examinations of the impact, implications, and applications that researchers derive from reading the work of others.

As in the companion text on research in rehabilitation counseling (Bellini & Rumrill, 1999), we have organized this chapter around categories reflecting the overarching purposes of selected synthetic literature review articles. We do not categorize articles by topic area, although the works that we summarize and review herein were purposively chosen to represent the wide range of subject matter that is embodied in the contemporary special education literature. With that in mind, this chapter describes synthetic literature reviews of four types: theory or model-building articles, treatises on complicated or controversial issues, informational reports and "how to" strategies to enhance professional practice, and explanations of emerging and important issues.

THEORY OR MODEL-BUILDING

One of the recurring and most important themes of this book is that theory both prompts and results from scientific inquiry. Theory provides the conceptual basis on which investigators deduce the specific relationships among variables or propositions that are evaluated by use of empirical observations drawn from particular samples. In many cases, the results of scientific efforts to test theory-based propositions lead researchers to suggest modifications in existing theories, thereby adding new knowledge that transcends the findings of a particular investigation. Theory also serves to bridge the "qualitative vs. quantitative" dichotomy; theory is, by definition, grounded in a qualitative understanding of human phenomena. It is dynamic, subjective, and based in the theorist's individual reality–but its evaluation depend on objective (quantitative) and replicable methods that are used to test propositions under the most stringent knowledge-generating warrants.

The field of special education, like the social sciences in general, does not have a unifying theoretical base on which student services, teachers' professional identities, and preservice training are founded. It is our impression that the many social scientific theories that have been postulated and tested over the past 100 years provide a "menu" of sorts from which special educators choose in applying their individual practices to broader explanations of human behavior. Indeed, we believe that there is no need for the field of special education to develop an overarching explanatory framework for the profession. We do believe that it is imperative for our field to become more aware of the use and application of theory as it applies to both practice and research. With that in mind, we will highlight in the forthcoming paragraphs several recent articles that have advanced theories or models to explain phenomena bearing on the lives of people with disabilities.

Sands and Doll (1996) advanced a theoretical model for fostering self-determination in children with disabilities. Historically, the concept of self-determination has been viewed as a higher order process of integrating meta-cognition, self-perception, social problem solving, and autonomous decision making. Therefore, efforts to enhance self-determination in students with disabilities have tended to center on transition-age youths who are seeking to move from school settings into the world of work and/or community living situations. The model of self determination proposed by Sands and Doll incorporates elements of this important developmental process into service planning during children's early elementary years. In this way, strategies for enhancing self-determination are given a "head start" in the early grades, which makes students more likely to adopt self-determination skills as they enter the school-to-work or school-to-school transition phase of their educational programs.

Speaking of transition, Gartin, Rumrill, and Serebreni (1996) introduced what they referred to as the Higher Education Transition Model in a recent synthetic literature review article. They made the point that most formalized transition initiatives emphasize the needs of students with severe disabilities in making the transition from school to work. At the same time, disappointing postsecondary educational retention rates have indicated for years that students with disabilities who plan to attend college after high school need more assistance than is currently available with the significant life adjustment that invariably accompanies enrollment in higher education. The Higher Education Transition Model provides guidelines for special education teachers whose students may be interested in attending college after high school graduation, and specific transition services identified by the authors for college-bound students were clustered into three domains: orientation to the college and community, psychosocial adjustment, and academic development. Perhaps the most important element of services related to the transition into higher education was described as the collaboration among secondary special education teachers, school-based transition coordinators, rehabilitation professionals, and student services professionals at the college or university level.

In another theory/model-building article, Eber, Nelson, and Miles (1997) described an innovative approach to school-based wraparound planning for extending educational services to students with emotional and behavioral disorders. Wraparound planning is part of a system of care that features a community-based approach to providing comprehensive, integrated services through multiple agencies and professionals, always in close collaboration with the student's family. A wraparound plan includes descriptions of multidisciplinary services, blended across agencies, that address the student's needs in more than one life domain. These domains include residence, family, social, emotional/psychological, educational/vocational, safety, legal, medical, spiritual, cultural, behavioral, and financial. The most important contribution of the article authored by Eber et al. (1997) is that it provides a framework for extending school-based services into the student's other endeavors and for extending the student's other endeavors into the school curriculum. Wraparound planning offers a formalized mechanism for true interdisciplinary collaboration, a concept that has been widely written about but disappointingly underactualized in special education practice.

Mallory (1995) drew an important connection between theory and social policy in his examination of the cultural, ecological, and familial aspects of life-cycle transitions for people with disabilities. He pointed out that one of the challenges inherent in smoothing life-cycle transitions for people with disabilities is that social policy in the United States tends to be intervention-ist rather than preventive or anticipatory. He maintained that the policies that extend services to people with disabilities take effect only after the per-son's family and other support systems have failed to provide for his or her needs. Mallory (1995) suggested that periods of life-cycle transition, marked by movement from one stage or setting to another, render the person with a disability particularly vulnerable to falling through the proverbial cracks in the American service delivery system, because people in transition both (a) need more assistance than at other times and (b) must drop below a mini-mum threshold of self-reliance before becoming eligible for needed services. Accordingly, his model of life-cycle transitions provides a view of the devel-opmental needs of people with disabilities within a broad sociopolitical con-text, incorporating elements of the individual, his or her cultural orientation, resources available in the local community, and the policies that either facil-itate or impede his or her pursuit of important life goals.

TREATISES ON COMPLICATED OR CONTROVERSIAL TOPICS

Another important role of the synthetic literature review in special educa-tion research is to identify, explain, and provide persuasive perspectives on complicated or controversial issues in the lives of children with disabilities and special education professionals. Typically, these treatises begin by trac-ing the history of the issue, then proceed with a description of the concern's current status and its implications for policy and practice. Finally, the author concludes with recommendations regarding how to best address the issue, often accompanied by a "call to action" for policymakers, practitioners, par-ents, advocates, and/or people with disabilities themselves.

For example, Kauffman (1999) issued a commentary on the current status and future directions of the field of special education. He characterized the profession as having an identity crisis, and he cast perceptions of special education on the part of society at large within the context of implications regarding the continued viability of the profession. According to Kauffman, the prevailing view of special education is that it is (a) ignorant of history, (b) apologetic for its very existence, (c) overconcerned with image, (d) proceeding without direction, (e) unrealistic in its expectations for children with disabilities, (f) focused on issues other than teaching and learning, (g) oblivious to sociopolitical changes in society, (h) "mesmerized by postmodernist/deconstructionist inanities" (Kauffman, 1999, p. 244), (i) susceptible to "scam artists" who put self-promotion above the needs of children with disabilities, and (j) immobilized by anticipation of sweeping reforms in the American public educational system. Not surprisingly, Kauffman's primary theme was the need for changes in virtually every aspect of special education - changes in the way that special educators are trained, changes in state and federal laws to allow for the provision of more effective services, changes in the pursuit of a scientific knowledge base, and changes in the way that practitioners interact with all stakeholders (e.g., children with disabilities, non-disabled children, parents, other teachers, school personnel, health care providers). As these changes are made, Kauffman urged researchers in the field to conduct scientifically sound empirical research as a means of maintaining and, in many cases, rebuilding the profession's knowledge base.

Schriner, Rumrill, and Parlin (1995) identified the issue of equity in disability policy as a potentially problematic concept in the current era of inclusion, civil rights, and independent living. They noted that equity in services for people with disabilities usually means providing supports for people with disabilities that are not available to nondisabled people in universalized settings, which is precisely the case with special education services. The authors suggested that the very nature of special education and rehabilitation services, which are specialized by design, perpetuates the perception on the part of society in general that people with disabilities are so "different" that they require assistance and protection not available to nondisabled citizens as a means of participating actively in contemporary society. They also made the point that such a perception is antithetical to most disability advocates' support for fair and equal treatment without concessions or special provisions.

More specifically, Schriner et al. (1995) attributed some of the problems associated with the "Are people with disabilities just like everyone else, or are they so different that they require 'special' considerations?" controversy to the fragmentary allocation of services, whereby people with some types of disabilities have access to benefits that are not available to other disability groups. Applying the example of preferential services for people who are blind in a number of settings, they recommended a system of educational and social services based on the needs of individuals not on categorical affiliation with specific disability groups. This "universalized" approach to human services is controversial, because many people believe that it undermines professions such as special education and rehabilitation counseling, which are rooted in the necessity for people with disabilities to be served by experts who possess specific knowledge about their unique (i.e., special, needs).

Related to the issues of equity and human difference, Artiles (1998) examined the always controversial phenomenon of racial and ethnic minorities being disproportionally represented in special education programs. He noted that the simple fact that there is a higher incidence of disabilities among certain groups of individuals (e.g., African-Americans, hispanic/latinos) does not fully account for the vast overenrollment of minority children in special education. Artiles contended that a more explanatory factor could lie in a more complex issue that resides at the very heart of American social policy, namely, how people viewed as "different" are treated. The fact that minority children with disabilities, who are identified as "different" in two ways, are singled out for different (i.e., special) treatment by the school system (as mandated by federal law) could serve to isolate; separate; and, some would say, render them "different" to a greater extent than would be the case were they not provided with differential treatment in the form of special education services. On the other hand, how do we provide for the needs of individuals whose characteristics of "differentness" place them at significant disadvantages in our perpetually less than-perfect society? Typically, this is achieved by offering specialized services that address the unique needs of designated individuals or groups, always with the underlying assumption that those needs are so unique or different that they necessitate differential treatment. In a field with finite resources, special education professionals are involved in making exceedingly difficult decisions concerning who will receive services and what those services will entail. In making those determinations, it is important to place day-to-day practices into a broader context of society's treatment of people on the basis of differentiating characteristics. This wide-angle view, couched in political and philosophical terms, is the most important contribution of Artiles' synthetic literature review article.

Thomas and Rapport (1998) examined the current status of federal court decisions related to the least restrictive environment (LRE) provisions of the Individuals with Disabilities Education Act (IDEA) of 1990. Intimately connected with the controversy surrounding inclusion of children with disabilities in public school programs, LRE is one of the most commonly contested issues when parents and public schools disagree as to the most suitable educational placement for a child. Thomas and Rapport addressed this controversial issue within the context of changing standards for what constitutes LRE by virtue of recent court verdicts. They also presented a comprehensive

LRE standard on the basis of case law modifications to the original provisions set forth in the IDEA. By distilling this complicated topic into its present-day interpretations on the part of judges and juries, the authors offered an important work that will stand to benefit parents and school personnel alike with a clearer understanding of how sweeping legal provisions are operationalized, contested, adjudicated, and modified.

Drasgow (1998) presented a compelling treatise on the role of American Sign Language (ASL) in the development of linguistic competence for children who are deaf. He asserted that ASL should be viewed as the first or primary language for deaf children who acquire that language at an early age, and that English should be taught as a second language for those children in both private schools for the deaf and public school special education programs. Drasgow's philosophical rationale for considering ASL a first language had three tenets: (a) that ASL is a natural language for people who cannot hear or vocalize words, (b) that children learn ASL in a predictable and developmental pattern, and (c) that deafness should be viewed as a cultural difference rather than a medically based disability. He also pointed to empirical evidence that deaf children who are fluent in ASL perform better on virtually every educational and life outcome measure than do deaf children who do not know ASL. Funneling the ASL controversy into practical applications for special education teachers, Drasgow concluded his article with programming guidelines to aid educators and curriculum specialists in teaching English as a second language to deaf children whose primary language is ASL.

INFORMATIONAL REPORTS AND "HOW TO" STRATEGIES

One of the most fundamental roles of special education literature is to provide information that can assist educators and practitioners in advancing contemporary standards of best practice. To that end, recent journals in our field are packed with a wealth of "how to" strategies to improve educational programs and services for people with disabilities.

For example, Carnine (1997) addressed the gap that is often found between research and practice in education. Some researchers argue that the gap exists because their research is not designed to make a practical difference and that practitioners do not appreciate the implications of research findings vis a vis educational services. On the other hand, many practitioners believe that too much research addresses esoteric topics with limited anchoring in the real world and that teachers should be more actively involved in designing meaningful, applied research. Carnine discussed three important factors related to evaluating research: trustworthiness, usability, and accessibility. The author explained that improving these dimensions in special education research could enable investigators to report more relevant findings and, thereby, bridge the research practice gap. Some of Carnine's recommendations included describing participants and interventions more clearly to facilitate replication and generalizability; aligning dependent measures more closely with research objectives to maintain internal consistency; focusing on interventions that are efficient and manageable to implement; collaborating with practitioners to establish the feasibility of intended research projects; deciding what types of information should be more widely distributed; and altering current methods of dissemination.

Kamps and Tankersley (1996) examined the current trends and research issues associated with the prevention of behavioral and conduct disorders in children. They identified several themes in existing research on this subject, including early intervention and prevention services that focus on family dynamics; school-based prevention programs including effective teaching practices, peer mediation, social skills intervention, self-management, and classroom management; and within- and across-setting collaboration. The authors also presented a number of guidelines for improving research on behavioral and conduct disorders, such as increased attention to the impact of universal programs for at-risk youth, continued investigation of teacher and parent support systems, evaluation of prevention programs, and increased commitment to funding empirical investigations.

In another article, Bailey, McWilliam, Darkes, Hebbeler, Simeonsson, Spiker, and Wagner (1998) provided guidelines to assess family outcomes in early intervention programs. Most evaluations into the effectiveness of early intervention have focused on the outcomes of children, but the impact of early intervention on family life is also an important consideration. Accordingly, Bailey et al. developed a list of questions that can be used to help assess family outcomes in two areas, subjective family perceptions of the early intervention experience and the objective impact on the family. The authors noted that considering family outcomes provides researchers and practitioners with a broader view of how critical early intervention services are implemented and received.

Osborne, DiMattia, and Russo (1998) examined legal considerations involved in providing special education services in parochial schools. Their article addresses two important questions: (1) "Must private school students with disabilities be provided with the same level of services as their public school peers?" and (2) "Are school districts required to provide parochial school students with on-site special education services?" The authors cited numerous court cases that identify instances in which students with disabilities have received special education services while attending parochial schools. The 1997 amendments to the IDEA clearly state that a school district may provide special education and related services on the premises of a private school, including a parochial school. The amendments also indicate that school districts do not need to spend more money on a parochial school child than a public school child for the same services. Furthermore, school districts are given some discretion regarding where and how those services will be provided. Therefore, the authors of this article offered important guidelines to aid school districts in determining whether and what services will be provided to students with disabilities who choose to attend parochial schools.

Many other articles have presented strategies and guidelines for special education practitioners to expand their assessment and intervention repertoires. Storey and Certo (1996) reviewed the supported employment literature and proposed guidelines to special educators and rehabilitation counselors for enhancing supported employees' use of natural supports in the workplace. Steere, Gregory, Heiny, and Butterworth (1995) advocated for more widespread adoption of services related to lifestyle planning for young adults with disabilities, a model that includes vocational issues but is not limited to them. Bellini and Royce-Davis (1999) suggested collaborative guidelines for transition team members who are working with secondary students with disabilities. Baer, Martonyi, Simmons, Flexer, and Goebel (1994) advanced a trilateral group process model to facilitate employer relations in school-to-work transition services. Chalmers and Faliede (1996) offered guidelines to facilitate the inclusion of children with mild and moderate disabilities in rural school settings. Rockwell and Gluetzloe (1996) described a number of innovative strategies to assist special educators in devising group instructional activities for children with emotional and behavioral disorders. Marn and Koch (1999) delineated several "how to" strategies for addressing the developmental and educational needs of adolescents with cerebral palsy.

EXPLANATIONS OF EMERGING AND IMPORTANT ISSUES

A final category of articles that synthesize existing literature and present new perspectives pertains to the important and emerging issues facing the special education field at the beginning of the twenty-first century. These articles address such issues as the roles and functions of special education professionals, new developments in the policies that govern special education, and the changing needs of people with disabilities in a technologically advanced information age.

Speaking of technology, Parette and Angelo (1996) examined the importance of family involvement in the selection and monitoring of

Augmentative and Alternative Communication (AAC) strategies. The article focuses on three main issues: (a) the prescription of appropriate AAC devices, (b) implementation of AAC across multiple contexts, and (c) maintenance of AAC use and anticipation of transition needs. Regarding the prescription of AAC devices, the authors stressed that the AAC device must be related to specific and clearly defined goals that result in greater independence for the child, the device should be compatible with practical constraints such as the available resources or amount of training required for the child and professionals to use the device, and it should result in the student achieving desirable and sufficient communication outcomes. In the section concerning the implementation of AAC devices, the authors emphasized the importance of family support and the impact that the AAC device will have on each member of the family. Finally, the authors provided strategies for teachers and families to educate the community about AAC, especially during the child's transition experiences.

Hanson and Carta (1995) addressed the emerging challenges involved in providing special education services for families with multiple risks. Specifically, they discussed the changing structure and characteristics of the American family and the increased influence of several societal concerns, including poverty, substance abuse, and exposure to violence. The effects of these problems on children and their development are the key focus of the article, and the authors offered three strategies for outreach to multiple-risk families: (1) providing a wide range of educational, health, and social services at the school; (2) using family associates and paraprofessionals who assist families in gaining access to services; and (3) employing home visitors to enhance contact with children's parents and caregivers. It is important to recognize that families with multiple risks may require assistance in numerous nonschool areas before they can make use of other interventions that address their children's specific educational needs.

In another article, Katsiyannis and Maag (1997) discussed emerging remedies for ensuring appropriate educational experiences for children with disabilities, the current state of special education litigation, compensation for children and parents, and other legal considerations. The purpose of the article was threefold: (a) to provide an overview of traditional remedies afforded to parents of children with disabilities; (b) to address issues associated with the provision of compensatory education; and (c) to investigate the potential of monetary damages within the legal parameters of the IDEA and Section 504 of the Rehabilitation Act of 1973. Traditionally, courts have granted relief under IDEA that includes orders to reimburse parents for their expenditures on private school education for a child if such a placement is the only way to appropriately meet the child's educational needs. These decisions have given rise in recent years to compensatory educational strategies as a means of providing a free and appropriate public education. Types of compensation have included extra assistance in the form of tutoring, summer school services, extended residential placements, and allied health services such as occupational and physical therapy. When courts have ruled that compensatory education is not appropriate, reasons have included students' waiting too long after graduation to make their complaints, inadequate substantive evidence of alleged violations on the part of the school district, and students' failure to make any progress despite appropriate programming. Given the increased incidence of disabling conditions in many American school districts, and the constantly escalating costs of providing appropriate educational services for students with disabilities, the issue of compensatory education is likely to be an important one for parents and educators alike for many years to come.

Cook and Rumrill (2000) identified the need for the field of special education to reconcile the concepts of inclusion and transition in providing quality services for youths with disabilities. They noted that the move toward full inclusion of students with disabilities is predicated on the assumption that generalized educational programming is the best way to meet the needs of most students (with and without disabilities), which flies in the face of specialized service initiatives such as transition. They encouraged researchers, practitioners, and policymakers to consider the implications of this paradox, and especially how it affects students with disabilities during adolescence, one of the most important developmental periods in their lives.

SUMMARY

Synthetic literature reviews make significant contributions to the theory and practice of special education. The entirety of works that bring forth new perspectives from comprehensive analyses of existing research in areas such as those discussed in this chapter has helped the special education profession to:

1. Build theoretical models on which to base practices;
2. Analyze and, in some cases, reconcile controversial issues in the lives of children with disabilities;
3. Develop important skills related to the delivery of responsive, effective services; and
4. Stay abreast of emerging issues in our dynamic field.

As readers move from reading this text to incorporating research utilization strategies into their own practices as special education professionals, they will be well served to remember the important contributions that synthetic literature reviews make to the advancement of knowledge and enhancement of practice in special education.

Chapter 9

GUIDELINES FOR COMPOSING AND EVALUATING RESEARCH ARTICLES

Phillip D. Rumrill, Jr.
Mary L. Hennessey, and
Bryan G. Cook

INTRODUCTION

IN THIS CHAPTER, we examine the sections of a research article and provide guidelines for conducting critical analyses of published works. Drawn from the American Psychological Association's (1994) *Publication Manual* and related descriptions in other research design texts (Bellini & Rumrill, 1999; Heppner et al., 1992; 1999; Kazdin, 1998; McMillan & Schumacher, 1997), general descriptions of each component of a research article are followed, section-by-section, by a reprinted article from the special education literature. We conclude the chapter with a framework that university instructors, graduate students, and special education practitioners can use in critiquing research articles on the basis of their scientific merits and practical use.

Before we move into descriptions of the sections of a research article, we want to briefly address the concept of technical writing as it applies to the composition of academic manuscripts. Journals adhering to the American Psychological Association's (1994) publication guidelines favor manuscripts that are written in direct, uncomplicated sentences. Editors prefer that text be written in the active voice; whenever possible, sentences should begin with their subjects and follow with verbs and objects (e.g., "The researcher conducted an experiment." rather than "An experiment was conducted by the researcher.") In the name of concise communication, extraneous phrases and clauses that add words to the sentence without enhancing the overall statement should be avoided (e.g., In order to..., For purposes of..., As far as...is concerned....") Technical writing is also marked by the sparing use of adverbs (e.g., very, somewhat, strikingly) and adjectives that do not serve to further define or specify the terms that they are modifying (e.g., interesting, important, good, noteworthy).

Organization is another critical element of an effectively composed journal article, with multilevel headings serving to guide the flow of text and the reader's attention. For authoritative information regarding the style and formatting guidelines for submitting manuscripts to most journals in social science fields, readers should consult the American Psychological Association's (1994) *Publication Manual.*

For a more literary perspective on technical writing, readers should consider the following composition guidelines that were first presented in George Orwell's (1946) *Politics and the English Language*:

1. Never use a metaphor, simile, or other figure of speech that you are used to seeing in print.
2. Never use a long word where a short one will do.
3. If it is possible to cut a word out, always cut it out.
4. Never use the passive (voice) where you can use the active.
5. Never use a foreign phrase, a scientific word, or a jargon word if you can think of an everyday English equivalent.
6. Break any of these rules sooner than say anything outright barbarous (p. 170).

SECTIONS OF A RESEARCH ARTICLE

The American Psychological Association (1994) presented guidelines for authors to follow in composing manuscripts for publication in professional journals. Most journals in disability studies and special education adhere to those style and formatting guidelines. In the paragraphs to follow, descriptions of each section of a standard research article are presented: Title, Abstract, Method, Results, Discussion, and References. After our generalized descriptions of each section, we have reprinted (with the kind permission of Pro-Ed Publishers) verbatim sections of a recent empirical article by Cook, Semmel, and Gerber (1999) which was published in *Remedial and Special Education.*

Title

As with other kinds of literature, the title of a journal article is an important feature. At the risk of contravening the "You can't judge a book by its cover" maxim, many articles in special education journals are either read or not read on the basis of the prospective reader's consideration of the title. Hence, a clear, concise title that provides the articles key concepts, hypotheses, methods, and variables under study is critical. A standard-length title for a journal article in the social sciences is 12 to 15 words, including a subtitle if appropriate. Social science indexing systems, which track and categorize journal articles by topic area, rely heavily on titles in their codification systems. Therefore, if authors want other scholars to be directed to their works, they must carefully compose a title that reflects the article without distractive or irrelevant descriptors. Cook et al. (1999, p. 199) presented the following title: *Attitudes of Principals and Special Education Teachers Toward the Inclusion of Students with Mild Disabilities: Critical Differences of Opinion.*

Abstract

Next to the title, the abstract is the most widely read section of a journal article (Bellini & Rumrill, 1999). In an empirical article, the abstract should be a succinct, 100 to 150 word summary of the investigation's key features, including the research problem, objectives, research questions/hypotheses, sample, scientific procedures, independent and dependent variables, and relevant results. Results of the study should be summarized in full in the abstract; authors should describe both significant and nonsignificant findings, not only those that upheld their hypotheses or expectations. The American Psychological Association (1994) also recommends that abstracts note the primary conclusions that can be drawn from reported findings.

The abstract serves as an advance organizer for the article, and it should include every important premise, method, and finding of the investigation. Like the Preface that commonly introduces readers to full-length textbooks, the abstract provides a thorough, albeit summary, glimpse of the contents of the article. In most instances, the title is what determines whether a reader will read the abstract; the abstract determines whether the reader will read the body of the article. Cook et al. (1999, p. 199) prefaced their article with the following abstract:

Attitudes of 49 principals and 64 special education teachers regarding the inclusion of students with mild disabilities were investigated. Results of a discriminant analysis indicated that principals and special educators were separated into groups with 76 percent accuracy according to their responses to items drawn from the Regular Education Initiative Teacher Survey (Semmel, Abernathy, Butera, & Lesar, 1991). Items measuring attitudes toward the efficacy of included placements with consultative services, the academic outcomes associated with included placements, and the protection of resources devoted to students with mild disabilities correlated most highly with the discriminant function. Findings are discussed in relation to their implications for the implementation of inclusion reforms and the educational opportunities of students with mild disabilities.

Introduction

Immediately after the abstract, the introductory section of the article sets the stage for the study on which the article was based. It orients the reader to the problem or issue being addressed, develops the logic and rationale for conducting the investigation, and expresses the empirical hypotheses or research questions. Heppner et al. (1999) suggested that the introduction should answer questions such as why the topic is an important one to study, what previous work bears on the topic, how existing work logically connects to the authors research questions and/or hypotheses, how the question will be researched, and what predictions can be made.

To answer these questions, authors typically address three major elements in the introductory section of an article: (1) the research problem, (2) the framework for the study, and (3) the research questions and hypotheses (Heppner et al., 1992; 1999; McMillan & Schumacher, 1997). Although we will describe each introductory element in discrete, linear fashion in this text, it is important to point out that many (if not most) authors blend these considerations to fit the flow and logic of their respective manuscripts.

THE RESEARCH PROBLEM. The very first sentences of an empirical journal article should draw the readers attention to the scope, impact, and current status of the problem or issue being investigated. This initial orientation is most effectively achieved by applying the broadest possible perspective to the concern. A study of postsecondary employment rates among special education students who took part in a particular transition program might be introduced by citing national statistics concerning the postschool outcomes of children with disabilities across the United States. An article describing the effects of a model classroom management program for third graders with multiple disabilities might begin with a review of existing literature concerning the impact of students' behavior on academic achievement in the early grades.

THE FRAMEWORK FOR THE STUDY. The specific theoretical and empirical framework for the particular investigation is the second part of the Introduction. Authors review existing literature related to the identified problem, then build a logical rationale for a study that addresses gaps or inconsistencies in the literature. The author should present the theoretical or conceptual model that drove the investigation, as well as provide enough background to enable the reader to comprehend the rationale for the current study. This framework highlights the purpose of the current study (e.g., to evaluate the effectiveness of a classroom management program for children with disabilities) which is then operationalized in the research questions or hypotheses.

THE RESEARCH QUESTIONS AND HYPOTHESES. The Introduction section of a research article often concludes with a statement of the research questions and/or hypotheses that served to guide the study. A more speculative research question tends to be used in descriptive research designs (e.g., surveys, program evaluations, empirical literature reviews) (see Chapter 6), or in qualitative studies (see Chapter 7). Examples of speculative research questions related to special education could include: "What concerns do parents of children with disabilities have regarding inclusion?," "What themes are evident in the psycholinguistic development of deaf preschool students?," and "What steps are special education and general education teachers taking to meet the LRE mandate of the Individuals with Disabilities Education Act?"

Hypotheses, on the other hand, are predictive by design (see Chapter 2). Their specificity depends on the theory underlying them or previous research, but they should include the direction of the anticipated results whenever possible. Independent and dependent variables should be specified in the hypothesis, but they need not be fully operationalized (i.e., described in terms of how they were measured and/or manipulated) because this is typically done in the Method section. The primary purpose of the hypothesis is to articulate the expected relationship among study variables. Examples of directional hypotheses could include: "Participation in a behavior management program will decrease aggression for children with behavioral disorders;" "Anxiety, depression, and low self-esteem will be collectively, positively, and significantly related to dropout rates among adolescents with learning disabilities;" and "Special education teachers will rate students with severe disabilities as less favorable candidates for postsecondary education than similarly qualified students with mild or no disabilities."

The introduction presented by Cook et al. (1999, pp. 199–200), which effectively blends discussions of the research problem, the conceptual framework of the study, and research questions and hypotheses, is as follows:

> Advocates have suggested that the inclusion (see Note) of students with disabilities into general education classrooms is a moral imperative that does not require, and cannot wait for, empirical justification (Biklen, 1985, 1991; Stainback & Stainback, 1989; Stainback, Stainback, & Ayres, 1996). This moral advocacy stand has coincided with considerable increases in inclusive placements for students with mild disabilities. For example, Lerner (1997) noted that the nationwide prevalence of general education placements for students with learning disabilities--the largest group of students with mild disabilities--increased 95% in the 5-year span from 1987/1988 to 1992/1993. However, recent research has indicated that inclusive placements are not frequently associated with, nor conducive to, improved outcomes for students with mild disabilities (Baker & Zigmond, 1995; Ochoa & Olivarez, 1995; Zigmond & Baker, 1990; Zigmond et al., 1995). Paradoxically, it appears that inclusion reforms are being implemented with increasing frequency despite findings that have not generally documented desired or appropriate outcomes.

Kauffman, Gerber, and Semmel (1998) recommended that caution was warranted regarding inclusion due to, among other reasons, lack of support among those charged with its implementation. Positive attitudes of key school personnel were seen as critical prerequisites for successful inclusion (Horne, 1985; Semmel, 1986; Villa, Thousand, Meyers, & Nevin, 1996). In a recent review of 4 decades of attitudinal research, Scruggs and Mastropieri (1996) reported that 65% of general education teachers indicated support for the nebulous concept of inclusion. However, when items were termed more specifically, an average of only 40.5% of general education teachers conceptually agreed with inclusion. Additionally, only 38%, 29%, 28%, and 11%, respectively, reported that they had adequate material support, expertise or training, time, and personnel support for successful implementation of inclusion. These less-than-optimistic attitudes among general education teachers appear to portend difficulty in introducing and successfully implementing inclusive reforms. However, these attitudes--as well as their effects on included students--may be mitigated by positive attitudes of other influential school personnel.

The present investigation examined and compared the attitudes of school principals and special education teachers. We chose to examine the attitudes of these two groups of educators because

1. The attitudes of these educators are less frequently measured than the well-documented attitudes of general education teachers.

2. Despite the relative scarcity of research on these educators, their attitudes appear to be critical determinants of the success of inclusion reforms.

3. The examination provides a unique comparison of those who determine school policy and school-level resource allocation (i.e., principals) and those with the most training and experience regarding the instruction and management of students with mild disabilities (i.e., special education teachers).

The support and leadership of principals has been documented as integral for successful school change (Fullan, 1991), effective schools (Purkey & Smith, 1983), and successful inclusion (Hasazi, Johnson, Liggett, & Schattman, 1994; Sage, 1996). As school-site administrators and policy leaders, principals influence reform implementation decisions, control resource allocations, and exert a supervisory role relative to school personnel. Hence, principals attitudes toward inclusion represent a particularly powerful influence on schoolwide policy implementation and operational innovations.

Positive attitudes among special education teachers also appear to be necessary for the success of inclusion. These professionals represent certified roles dedicated to meeting the needs of students with disabilities; they have received skills necessary for effectively working with such children, and are frequently seen as knowledgeable advocates for students with disabilities. Hence, special educators are in a unique position to shape schoolwide attitudes toward inclusion. Indeed, Fox and Ysseldyke (1997) reported that special education teachers are relied on to sell inclusion to general education teachers. Special education teachers also directly influence the outcomes associated with inclusion by delivering instruction in inclusive classrooms and providing guidance to other direct service providers in inclusive settings through consultation and collaboration. Given the lack of requisite expertise, training, and resources reported by general education teachers (Scruggs & Mastropieri, 1996), special education teachers are often sought as experts to take responsibility for and lead the day-to-day implementation of inclusion reforms (Fox & Ysseldyke, 1997). Therefore, although the support of principals appears necessary for inclusion reforms to be introduced and supported with appropriate resources, successful implementation may depend on support among special education teachers.

It is theorized that attitudes toward inclusion vary as a function of proximity to the implementation of inclusion policies (Jamieson, 1984; Semmel, Abernathy, Butera, & Lesar, 1991). Principals are relatively distal to the practice of inclusion and are thus predicted to hold positive attitudes toward the reform movement. Positive attitudes among principals may help to explain recent increases in inclusive placements. Alternatively, special education teachers--who, unlike principals, are directly involved in implementing inclusion--are predicted to be unsupportive. The relative lack of support among special educators is hypothesized to both reflect and exacerbate deleterious effects of inclusion reforms on many students with mild disabilities. These conflicting attitudes among principals and special education teachers, may, then, explain the paradoxical simultaneous expansion and disappointment associated with inclusion reforms.

The present study sought to extend and clarify the existing literature base indicating that principals and other administrators hold positive attitudes toward inclusion (Davis & Maheady, 1991; Gavar-Pinhas & Schmelkin, 1989; Gickling & Theobald, 1975; MacMillan, Jones, & Meyer, 1976) and that special education teachers are either unsupportive (Gickling & Theobald, 1975; Semmel et al., 1991), ambivalent or slightly positive regarding inclusion (Davis & Maheady, 1991; Garvar-Pinhas & Schmelkin, 1989; Moore & Fine, 1978; Schmelkin, 1981). The investigation also expands on existing direct comparisons of teachers and administrators (see Davis & Maheady, 1991; Garvar-Pinhas & Schmelkin, 1989; Gickling & Theobald, 1975) by examining attitudes toward allocation of resources in inclusive schools. In the context of recent demands for accountability and high-stakes testing, administrators may view inclusion as a means to redirect special education resources to higher-achieving students who are more likely to positively affect mean test scores (see Cook, Gerber, & Semmel, 1997). The relative separation of principals from the implementation of inclusion may also make them less likely to recognize the resource hungry nature of inclusion reforms (Fox & Ysseldyke, 1997) and exacerbate tendencies not to protect resources committed to included students with mild disabilities. It is therefore predicted that although principals are relatively more supportive of the concept and potential benefits of inclusion, they are less committed to safeguarding instructional resources specifically designated for included students.

Method

The Method section specifies how the research questions were addressed and/or how the hypotheses were tested. It should provide the reader with sufficient information so that one could replicate the investigation. Because the Method section is the primary source for determining the validity of the study (see Chapter 5), the quality and clarity of this section is generally regarded as the strongest determinant of whether an empirically based manuscript will be accepted for publication (Heppner et al., 1999; Munley, Sharking, & Gelso, 1988).

Although the type and order of subsections found in the Method section of a research article vary depending on the design of the study and the authors judgment related to the flow of text, most articles include descriptions of the study's subjects or participants; instruments, measures, and variables; materials; design; and procedures.

SUBJECTS OR PARTICIPANTS. According to Heppner et al. (1992; 1999), the Method section should include (a) the total number of subjects and numbers assigned to groups, if applicable; (b) how subjects were selected and/or assigned; and (c) demographic and other characteristics of the sample relevant to the studys purpose. Some authors also include a description of the population from which the study sample was drawn, an indication of the representativeness of the sample vis a vis the broader population, the circumstances under which subjects participated (e.g., whether they were compensated or what risks they assumed), statistical power analyses, and response rates (if applicable).

INSTRUMENTS, MEASURES, AND VARIABLES. The Method section must include a detailed description of how all study variables were operationalized, measured, scored, and interpreted. All instruments or measures that were used in sampling, conducting the study, and evaluating results should be specified in terms of content (e.g., number of items, item formats, response sets), how measures were administered, scoring procedures, relationship to study variables, and psychometric properties (e.g., reliability, standardization, validity). Authors should also include a rationale for selecting each instrument, that is, why that instrument was the best choice for measuring a particular construct.

MATERIALS. Researchers should also include a description of any materials that were used to carry out the investigation. Written guides for participants, instructional manuals, media or technology, and scientific apparatus or equipment should be noted in detail. Examples of equipment and technology that might be described in a Materials subsection include a stopwatch, computers or software programs, and assistive devices such as electronic speech boards.

DESIGN. One of the most important features of the Method section is a clear description of the design of the study. This is essential because the design serves as the link among the research questions/hypotheses, the scientific procedures used in carrying out the study, the findings of the study, and how results are interpreted. Authors typically label their designs in terms of how variables were manipulated, observed, and analyzed. Thereby, the design is the unifying force in connecting the research objectives to the results and to the knowledge claim that is made. To every extent possible, a direct reference to the hypotheses should be made when authors identify the design of a particular investigation. For example, Rumrill, Roessler, and Denny (1997, p. 7) described their design as follows: "The researchers selected a three-group, posttest-only (experimental) design to assess the interventions univariate and multivariate effects on (a) self-reported attitudes (situational self-efficacy and acceptance of disability) and (b) participation in the accommodation request process."

PROCEDURES. In the Procedures subsection, authors chronologically list every step they took in developing, administering, and evaluating the study. Beginning with initial recruitment of participants, following the study through collection of the last datum, and including everything in-between, this subsection should provide the reader with a step-by-step protocol that could serve as a guide for replicating the study. Descriptions of any interventions should be provided in detail, along with summaries of the qualifications of project personnel who were instrumental in executing the investigation. Descriptions of study procedures should also include how the investigation was concluded and a statement of any debriefing or follow-up services provided to participants.

In aggregate, the Method section comprises the most important information found in a research article. Cook et al. (1999, pp. 201) captured the essence of a detailed, concisely written Method section. It follows below:

Sample

Schools. The sample was drawn from the School Environment Project (SEP; see Semmel & Gerber, 1997), a longitudinal investigation of the effects of school environments on the performance and self-esteem of students with mild disabilities who were included in general classrooms for various parts of the school day (see Cook et al., 1997). From a stratified random sample of 1,126 urban and suburban schools originally contacted in two southern California counties, 57 diverse schools (33 elementary schools and 24 junior high schools) agreed to participate in the entire project. Sample schools had implemented a wide array of inclusive practices, but all were including the majority of their students with mild disabilities for at least part of the school day. Specifically, sample schools fully included an average of 10.5% (SD = 17.8%) of their students with mild disabilities, 69.4% (SD = 29.4%) of such students for at least half of, but less than the entire, school day, and 20.1% (SD = 24.4%) for less than half of the school day or not at all.

Respondents. Of the 57 participating school principals, 49 completed and returned the portion of the SEP questionnaire asking respondents to rank their agreement with statements regarding inclusion (85.96% return rate). Questionnaires were also given to special education teachers in participating schools. In the elementary sample, questionnaires were given to 1 randomly selected special education teacher within each school. Twenty-nine elementary special education teachers completed and returned the instrument (87.7% return rate). In each junior high school 2 special education teachers were randomly selected to receive the survey. Thirty-five junior high school special education teachers returned questionnaires (72.91% return rate). The return rate for the entire sample was 81.88%. See Appendix E for demographic information on survey respondents.

Instrumentation

One section of the SEP questionnaire directs respondents to provide a rating of their personal opinion on 21 statements regarding the inclusion of students with mild disabilities. These 21 statements were drawn from the Regular Education Initiative Teacher Survey (REITS; see Semmel et al., 1991). The REITS was developed as a confirmatory factor analytic tool to investigate the attitudes of teachers to the primary components of proposed inclusion models. Semmel et al. (1991) reported a mean item reliability coefficient of .87 (range .86 to .88) for the 61 items on the survey and a mean Cronbach coefficient alpha of .82 (range .79 to .83) for the 14 derived factors. The 21 statements on the SEP questionnaire included the highest-loading items from seven of the orthogonal factors. These highest-loading items were selected for the present investigation because they parsimoniously represent a wide breadth of information regarding attitudes toward inclusion. See Appendix F for the items used, their corresponding REITS factors, and factor loadings. Response options on the SEP questionnaire include ratings of 1 (strongly disagree), 2 (disagree), 3 (undecided), 4 (agree), and 5 (strongly agree) on a Likert-type scale. Two items (7 and 18) are phrased negatively. Throughout the analyses, responses to these items were flipped, or rearranged to reflect the most positive response as the highest value, in accordance with the other items.

Procedure

SEP field associates distributed questionnaires to respondents when they visited participating schools to conduct student testing. Questionnaires were returned in self-addressed stamped envelopes (see Semmel & Gerber, 1997, for a detailed description of project procedures).

Analysis

Missing data, representing 1.32% of the total data set, were conservatively replaced with mean item values derived from the entire sample. Univariate means and standard deviations for each item were used to describe the reported attitudes of respondents. Nonparametric bivariate procedures (Mann-Whitney U tests) were then used to analyze the differences between principals and special educators attitudes on the seven specific items. A multivariate discriminant function was used to determine whether principals and special education teachers were reliably differentiated on the basis of their responses on the seven items.

Results

The Results section of a research article should include a complete inventory of all relevant findings observed by the investigators. In articles that report quantitative studies (see Chapter 6), results are typically presented in two parts--summary, or descriptive, statistics related to participants performance on whatever measures were taken (e.g., means, standard deviations, frequencies, percentages) (see Chapter 3), and statistical analyses related to the specific hypotheses of the study (e.g., analysis of variance, multiple regression, factor analysis) (see Chapter 3). We believe that all analyses conducted as part of the investigation should be reported in full, not only those that yielded statistically significant results. The *Publication Manual* of the American Psychological Association (1994) provides considerable guidance related to **how** statistics should be presented in the Results section, but it does not provide adequate guidelines regarding **what** statistical information should be included. Heppner et al. (1999, pp. 525-526) identified a pattern in recent social science literature whereby researchers tend to err on the side of providing too little statistical information:

> The trend has been to report less; for example, one rarely sees analysis of variance source tables anymore. More disturbing is the tendency not to report important information (such as size of test statistic and probability levels) when results are non-significant. This minimalist point of view puts the emphasis on statistical significance and ignores concepts such as effect size, estimation, and power.

A quantitative Results section should be limited to the findings obtained by the researcher(s) in the current investigation. Speculation concerning what those findings mean in a larger context is reserved for the Discussion section.

The Results sections of qualitatively oriented articles display much more variety in the content and manner of presentation than is found in quantitative articles. Because the researchers subjective interpretations help to shape the processes and outcomes of qualitative investigations (see Chapter 7), results are often framed in broad, interpretive contexts. In that regard, the lines between the Results and Discussion sections are often blurred in qualitative research.

Researchers (qualitative and quantitative) commonly use tables and figures to summarize and/or graphically depict their results. There is wide variability in terms of the content and presentation of tables and figures, with the most important universal requirement being easy interpretability for the reader.

Cook et al. (1999, pp. 202-203) presented their results as follows:

Descriptive Results

Means and standard deviations for principals' and special education teachers' responses to each item are presented in Appendix G. The mean value of principals responses exceeded a score of 4 (agree) only on Item 1 (special education teachers should assist with the instruction of all students experiencing learning difficulties in general classrooms). The mean response of special education teachers was above a score of 4 only on Item 11 (currently mandated resources for students with mild disabilities must be protected regardless of the setting of services). General agreement with an item may alternatively be indicated by more than half of a given group responding with agree or strongly agree. The majority of both principals and special education teachers agreed with Item 1 (87.75% and 76.56% agreed, respectively). The majority of principals also expressed agreement with the statement that the general education classroom with consultant services is the most effective educational environment for students with mild disabilities (Item 20; 63.26% of principals agreed; only 26.98% of special education teachers agreed).

Mean response values of principals and special education teachers were above 2 (disagreement) on all items. However, the majority of both principals and special education teachers disagreed with Item 14 (teachers have the instructional skills to teach all students, including those with mild disabilities; 51.02% and 69.35% disagreed, respectively), and agreed with negatively phrased Items 18 (time devoted to state and curriculum goals would be reduced under inclusion; 55.10% and 56.45% agreed, respectively) and 7 (teachers cannot meet the needs of students with mild disabilities in general education classrooms; 69.38% and 57.81% agreed, respectively). Two-thirds of special education teachers also expressed disagreement with the statement that inclusion would increase the achievement levels of students with mild disabilities (Item 19); alternatively, only 22.44% of principals disagreed.

Bivariate Analyses

Mann-Whitney U tests indicated statistically significant differences ($p < .05$) between the opinion of principals and special education teachers on five of the seven items (see Table 3). Principals expressed significantly greater agreement with statements that special education teachers should assist with the instruction of all students experiencing learning difficulties in general classrooms (Item 1), $Z = 2.17$, $p = .02$; that teachers have the instructional skill to teach all students, including those with mild disabilities (Item 14), $Z = 2.41$, $p = .01$; that the achievement levels of students with mild disabilities would increase if students were placed in general classrooms (Item 19), $Z = 3.69$, $p = .0002$; and that the general classroom with consultant services is the most effective environment for students with mild disabilities (Item 20), $Z = 4.14$, $p < .0001$. Special education teachers reported significantly higher agreement with Item 11, that currently mandated resources for students with mild disabilities must be protected regardless of the setting of services, $Z = -3.38$, $p = .0007$. It should be noted that the p values associated with Item 1 and 14 do not exceed an alpha level conservatively adjusted for conducting seven comparisons ($.05/7 = .007$).

Multivariate Discriminant Function Analysis

A discriminant function analysis separated principals and special education teachers according to a multivariate combination of the seven items. Given two groups, only one discriminant function can be produced. The discriminant function yielded a canonical correlation of .52 indicating that there were significant differences between the attitudes of principals and special education teachers on the seven items, $L = .72$, $X^2(7) = 33.90$, $p < .0001$. Meaningful correlations of individual items with the discriminant function were established at $r > .50$ (this is analogous to item loadings in factor or principal components analysis). Item 20 ($r = .71$), Item 19 ($r = .56$), and Item 11 ($r = -.55$) were the primary predictors of the discriminant function.

It is expected that approximately 57.48 respondents ($48[48/102] + 57[57/102]$), or 50.86% of the sample, would be classified correctly by chance. The discriminant function successfully classified 86 of the 113 respondents into their proper grouping (76.11%). Thirty-four of the 49 principals (69.38%) were classified correctly on the basis of the discriminant function. The multivariate combination of the seven items correctly classified 52 of the 64 special education teachers (81.25%).

Discussion

The Discussion section provides the researcher with a forum to go beyond the current investigation and examine the contributions of the study findings to existing literature, theory, policy, and professional practices. The first part of a thoughtful Discussion is typically an analysis of the study's results vis a vis the research questions and hypotheses. Researchers often begin with a discussion of whether the hypotheses were upheld, posit possible explanations for those outcomes, and draw implications from the findings back to the research problem that was identified in the Introduction. If the results provide a warrant for modifying or retesting the conceptual framework on which the investigation was based, the Discussion section is the place to suggest a reformulation of the underlying theory. Researchers should also include a statement of the scientific limitations of the current study, along with specific recommendations for future research. Finally, the researcher ends the article with a cogent summary of the conclusions, in the most general sense, that can be drawn from the methods and findings of the current study. Some authors use a separate Conclusion section for this purpose.

In their Discussion section, Cook et al. (1999, pp. 203-206) framed both the results of the study and the major discussion points within the context of the conceptual framework for the investigation (which was presented in the Introduction). It is presented below, along with the article's Conclusion (p. 206).

> Results indicated that principals and special education teachers hold significant differences of opinion regarding inclusion, replicating the results of Garvar-Pinhas and Schmelkin (1989). Discussion of these attitudinal differences focuses on implications for the implementation and outcomes of inclusive reforms.

Divergent Attitudes with Critical Consequences

Two of the items that significantly correlated with the discriminant function, and thus distinguished special education teachers from principals, represent the vision of many inclusion advocates. It is frequently argued that students with mild disabilities improve their academic achievement (Item 19) when placed in the optimally effective environments of a general education classroom with consultant services (Item 20; see Reynolds, Wang, & Walberg, 1987; Will, 1986). Principals supported these sentiments to a significantly greater degree than did special education teachers. This finding is undoubtedly favorable to those who desire the implementation of inclusion policies. However, findings indicating a lack of support for these ideals among special educators--those with the most training and experience regarding the education of students with mild disabilities who are expected to lead the implementation of inclusion--appear to warrant grave concerns for the educational opportunities of students with mild disabilities.

Policy mandates circumscribe the activities of those who are charged with executing policy as part of their daily activities. There exists little control or direct supervision of teachers in schools. Rather than adminstrative mandates, teachers' attitudes, experiences, and pragmatic realities most directly determine the myriad of complex and instantaneous classroom decisions that determine the effect of policy on students. Ultimately, then, it is these "street-level bureaucrats [who] are the policy-makers in their respective work arenas" (Weatherley & Lipsky, 1977, p. 172). Public schools have been described as "decoupled" or "loosely coupled" institutions because of the propensity for policies decreed at an administrative level to be transformed by direct service providers (see Gamoran & Dreeben, 1986; Meyer & Rowan, 1977). We hypothesize that the significantly less optimistic attitudes of special educators may result in inclusion, when mandated in a top-down fashion, being co-opted by teachers who do not see it as effective or appropriate.

The remaining item that significantly correlated with the discriminant function deals with resource allocation and further indicates the potential damage that inclusion may bring to the educational opportunities of students with mild disabilities. Whereas 75.51% of special educators indicated strong agreement (the highest available rating) with the statement that mandated resources should be protected for students with mild disabilities regardless of setting, only 32.65% of principals reported a similarly high rating. Thus, although principals were significantly more supportive of the general efficacy and academic outcomes of inclusion, the majority was not in strong agreement that resources mandated for the instruction of students with mild disabilities warrant protection. These attitudes suggest that principals may see inclusion, at least in part, as a cost-saving measure, which may further explain both the expansion of inclusion and the often less-than-desired outcomes associated with the reform. If participating principals have acted on their reported attitudes, many schools may be implementing inclusion reforms without requisite resources (or supportive direct care providers). Without these resources, included students with mild disabilities are less likely to fall within the "instructional tolerance" boundaries of general education teachers and receive instruction geared to their unique needs in inclusive classes (see Gerber, 1988). The dangers of including students without the support of special education teachers is, then, greatly exacerbated when the resources identified as necessary for an appropriate education for students with mild disabilities are not protected.

Desirability Versus Feasibility

The most positive attitudes were generally found in response to items stating desired goals (that resources for students with mild disabilities must be protected, and that special education teachers should assist in the instruction of all experiencing academic difficulties). The high response agreement to these items may reflect their desirable or rhetorical nature. It is noteworthy that similar levels of support were not associated with statements regarding the readiness, feasibility, or benefits associated with inclusion. These results concur with Schumm and Vaughn's (1991) finding that although teachers consistently rated adaptations associated with inclusion as desirable, they found them to be significantly less feasible.

Politically Correct Policymaking?

The majority of principals and special educators indicated that teachers do not have the instructional skills to meet the academic needs of students with mild disabilities in general classrooms. These findings are consistent with previous reports of general educators' own perceptions of their ability to successfully implement inclusion (Semmel et al., 1991). Given these concerns, it is somewhat curious that the majority of principals agreed that inclusion (with consultant services) is the most effective placement option for students with mild disabilities. Given their views on teacher readiness, it is perhaps also inconsistent that the majority of principals did not disagree (as the majority of special education teachers did) that the achievement of students with mild disabilities would increase when the students are included. These findings appear to support the conjecture of Garvar-Pinhas and Schmelkin (1989), that "principals appear to respond in a more socially appropriate manner than may actually be the case in reality" (p. 42).

Implications and Recommendations

Special education teachers play direct and influential roles in the implementation of inclusion reforms but are relatively unconvinced of the efficacy of inclusion. They may, then, be less likely to enthusiastically address the impediments that typically occur during the implementation of educational reforms such as inclusion, engender support for inclusion among other direct service providers, and implement inclusion reforms with fidelity. All these factors may help to explain previous reports documenting the frequently disappointing outcomes associated with inclusion (e.g., Baker & Zigmond, 1995). It is therefore recommended that reformers take direct measures to secure the support of special educators and other direct service providers before implementing inclusion. Without this support, the efforts and costs associated with implementing inclusion reforms may produce more frustrations than benefits. Strategies for garnering support may include involving direct service providers in a more bottom-up method of generating and implementing policy, as well as providing the conditions, resources, and time to make successful inclusion seem to be a feasible outcome that warrants the commitment of those charged with its implementation.

On the other hand, principals held generally optimistic views regarding the benefits of inclusion. Yet it should be recognized that although principals' positive attitudes may influence whether and how schools adopt inclusion policies, they do not guarantee that such policies are successful. Indeed, principals' attitudes often contrast with available emprirical evidence. For example, their belief that inclusion results in improved academic achievement is contrary to the recent findings of Baker and Zigmond (1995) and Zigmond et al. (1995). Similarly, although principals felt that inclusive classrooms with consultative services are the most appropriate placement option for students with mild disabilities, it has been reported that serious impediments to traditional consultative services exist in inclusive environments, which often result in ineffective outcomes (see Johnson, Pugach, & Hammitte, 1988).

Wolfensberger (1994) posited that recent educational reforms are increasingly based on "what feels good, what one wants, [and] the way one wants the world and life to be" (p. 25). If school-level policies regarding inclusion are based on political correctness and what principals desire and feel good about--rather than what has been shown to be feasible and effective, and what is supported by those who teach students with mild disabilities--it is little wonder that inclusion has met with limited success. It is therefore recommended that administrators solicit the input of influential and knowledgeable school personnel, such as special education teachers, and consult available empirical evidence on the efficacy of specific reform initiatives and associated strategies. Special educators should also, to the maximum extent possible, make their views known and actively participate in the decision-making process to balance the attitudes and aspirations of administrators in the process of determining school policy.

Exacerbating the previously discussed attitudinal discrepancies is the relatively low commitment among principals to protect resources for students with mild disabilities in included settings. These attitudes may suggest that principals see inclusion, at least in part, as a cost-saving measure; this may further explain recent increases in implementation of inclusion. However, special educators are almost unanimous in their agreement that the current level of resource support be protected. If inclusion is implemented with fewer resources devoted to included students with mild disabilities, the worst-case scenario of "dumping" students into included classes to compete with nondisabled students may be increasingly realized. Given the recent press in general education to produce academic excellence, teachers of inclusive classes may, if operating without constraints, choose to focus their instructional resources on higher achievers who are more likely to positively affect mean test scores. Such an allocation of limited resources decreases the educational opportunities of included students with mild disabilities who were initially referred out of general education because they did not respond well to instruction focused on students with typical or accelerated learning needs (see Cook et al., 1997). It is therefore recommended that teachers, parents, and other advocates require that their resource needs in inclusive environments be secured as a prerequisite of agreeing to an inclusive placement.

We hypothesize that the negative attitudes of key personnel--such as special education teachers--toward inclusion are, at least in part, based on negative experiences regarding the outcomes of inclusion or the conviction that inclusion will not produce appropriate outcomes. Perhaps the best way to improve special educators' attitudes toward inclusion, then, is to improve the likelihood that it will result in successful outcomes. Many of the recommendations put forth by the National Commission on Teaching and America's Future (Darling-Hammond, 1996) to improve the U.S. educational system would appear to also improve outcomes associated with inclusion. For example, the report calls for improved and extended pre-professional training; for professional development opportunities that go beyond the "unproductive 'hit-and-run' workshops" (Darling-Hammond, 1996, p. 195); for reducing teacher isolation by providing regularly scheduled collegial work and planning time; for blurring the distinctions between traditional roles such as general educator, special educator, and principal; for a greater proportion of school personnel, including principals, to be directly involved in delivering instruction; for streamlining resource allocation to classroom learning; and for giving teachers greater collective responsibility for student learning.

Perhaps in a school system that has implemented these recommendations, inclusion would be more likely to result in appropriate outcomes. Such conditions and outcomes would also appear to engender improved attitudes toward the implementation of inclusion among special (and general) education teachers, which would further improve the prospect of successful inclusion. Alternatively, these recommendations would also enable principals to directly familiarize themselves with the obstacles and resource-hungry nature of inclusion as well as the attitudes of direct care providers to any number of reform initiatives, because part of their typical day would be spent working in a variety of classrooms. This involvement may cause the attitudes of principals toward inclusion to be more closely aligned with those of special education teachers and empirical findings. This grounded vantage, when coupled with the prescribed shared decision making and obfuscation of traditional roles, may curtail the frequency of inclusion being implemented without requisite resources or support, therefore greatly improving its chances for success.

Limitations and Suggested Future Research

A number of limitations to the current research should be recognized to delimit the results and their implications. The research involved principals and special education teachers from elementary and junior high schools in one region and thus may not generalize to other educators, areas, or levels of schooling. However, the schools involved represent a wide array of settings, sizes, socioeconomic statuses, and degrees of inclusion (see Semmel & Gerber, 1997). Additionally, this research involved attitudes toward the inclusion of only students with mild disabilities. Further research is warranted regarding attitudes toward inclusion of students with severe disabilities. However, initial evidence appears to support an extension of these findings to the concept of full inclusion. For example, Downing, Eichinger, and Williams (1997) reported that approximately half of the general and special educators, but no principals, felt that the general education classroom was not the best environment for students with severe disabilities.

Research utilizing direct observation relating the attitudes of school personnel to their behavior is also necessary to validate the proposed relationship between divergent attitudes of school personnel and the paradoxical expansion and lack of success associated with inclusive reforms. Reported attitudes do not necessarily correspond with the actions in which the individual engages. However, significant correlations between teacher beliefs and practices regarding inclusion have been documented (Schumm, Vaughn, Gordon, & Rothlein, 1994). Finally, although the items used in this study appear to have high face validity, it is recognized that the limited number of items used may pose a threat to construct validity.

Further research may also fruitfully extend this analysis by examining the attitudes of general education teachers. Previous literature has been relatively consistent in documenting that general education teachers are relatively less supportive of inclusion than special education teachers (Davis & Maheady, 1991; Garvar-Pinhas & Schmelkin, 1989; Schmelkin, 1981). However, they may have recently developed more positive attitudes, which would be significant given their role in the implementation of inclusion. Reasons for the negative attitudes among special education teachers should also be explored to offer further insight on how to improve their attitudes and the potential success of inclusion reforms. Indeed, one possible explanation of the negative attitudes of special educators is that they are protecting their jobs and the status quo of educational practices. However, such explanations do not invalidate the attitudes or their influence.

Conclusion

Principals and special education teachers were separated into groups with 76% accuracy based on their attitudes toward seven items regarding integration.

Special education teachers and principals disagreed most strongly on items stating that the achievement of students with mild disabilities increases when they are included (principals expressed greater agreement), and that the resources devoted to students with mild disabilities must be protected regardless of setting (special education teachers expressed greater agreement). Given their roles regarding the implementation of inclusion reforms in schools, we conjecture that the significant attitudinal discrepancies of principals and special education teachers may pose a possible explanation for inclusion policies being increasingly implemented and not generally producing improved outcomes. It is recommended that the attitudes of special education teachers be considered in the decision-making process regarding the implementation of inclusion, principals temper their optimistic attitudes of significant school personnel when making policy decisions, and a wide range of systemic school reforms be implemented to enhance the efficacy of inclusion. The probability of appropriate outcomes may improve attitudes of special education teachers toward inclusion, which may, in turn, improve the efficacy of inclusion reforms.

References

The final section of a research article is always a listing of the references that were cited in the body of the text. References are listed in alphabetical order, according to authors' last names. Most special education and disability studies journals require adherence to the American Psychological Association's (1994) guidelines regarding the composition of the References page. The works cited by Cook et al. (1999, pp. 207, 256) appear in the References section of this book.

GUIDELINES FOR CRITIQUING RESEARCH ARTICLES

It is our hope that understanding the components, organization, and composition of a research article, by means of the descriptions and examples provided to this point in the chapter, will make special educators better informed consumers as they read the professional literature. As readers digest the contents of research articles and apply them to their practices, the anatomy of empirical reports can serve as a useful rubric for critically analyzing the quality, content, and practical significance of published research. Appendix H presents guidelines and specific questions for conducting a section-by-section critique of a special education research article. College and university course instructors are encouraged to modify this framework to meet their students specific needs in research design use and classes.

SUMMARY

Chapters 6, 7, and 8 of this book document the numerous ways to conduct scholarly research and make valuable contributions to the knowledge base of special education. When composing research reports, it is important for special education scholars to exercise creativity in their scientific endeavors within the context of prevailing publication guidelines set forth by the American Psychological Association (1994). Specifically, research articles published in most social science journals share in common clear and descriptive titles; 100 to 150 word abstracts; introductory sections including the research problem, the conceptual framework of the study, and research questions/hypotheses; method sections describing the sample, instruments, materials, design, and procedures; full reports of relevant results; discussions of the limitations of the study and implications for future research; and references presented in accordance with the American Psychological Associations style guidelines.

Understanding the sections of a research article helps readers to make decisions regarding the quality and practical significance of research investigations published in the special education literature. By delineating the contents of a research article and providing a framework for critiquing research reports, we hope that this chapter has prepared readers to assimilate contemporary special education literature into their professional development and continuing education activities.

Appendix E

SUMMARY OF DEMOGRAPHIC INFORMATION FOR SURVEY RESPONDENTS

Characteristic	*Principals*		*Special education teachers*	
	M	SD	M	SD
Years in current role	7.30	6.32	6.55	4.31
Years at current school	5.42	4.33	5.27	4.31
Years of teaching experience	15.29	7.90	14.87	6.69
Years of general education teaching experience	14.93	7.91	5.28	5.89
Years of special education teaching experience	1.06	3.50	9.76	5.29
	n	%	*n*	%
Highest Degree Attained				
Bachelors	0	0.00	19	29.69
Masters	39	79.59	39	60.94
Doctorate	10	20.41	5	7.81
Unreported	0	0.00	1	1.56

Note. From "Attitudes of Principals and Special Education Teachers Toward the Inclusion of Students with Mild Disabilities: Critical Differences of Opinion," by B. G. Cook, M. I. Semmel, and M. M. Gerber, 1999, *Remedial and Special Education, 20*(4), p. 201. Copyright 1999 by *Remedial and Special Education.* Reprinted with permission.

Appendix F

SEP QUESTIONNAIRE ITEMS WITH CORRESPONDING REITS FACTORS AND FACTOR LOADINGS

SEP Questionnaire Item	REITS Factor	Factor Loading
1. The special education teachers should assist in the instruction of both students with mild handicaps and other students experiencing learning difficulties.	Special education teachers role	.900
7. Regular class teachers cannot meet the academic needs of students with mild handicaps currently in their classrooms.	Teacher preparedness	.714
11. If students with mild handicaps are placed full time in the regular class, then currently mandated special education resources for their instruction must be protected.	Redistribution of resources	.811
14. Regular class teachers have the instructional skills to teach both students with mild handicaps and regular students.	Generic instructional/ collaborative skills	.826
18. The time devoted to state/district curriculum goals would decrease if students with mild handicaps were placed full time in the regular classroom.	Instructional time	.566
19. Achievement levels of students with mild handicaps would increase if they were placed full time in the regular classroom.	Achievement outcomes	.798
20. The regular classroom with special education consultant services is the most effective environment to educate students with mild handicaps.	Effectiveness of consultant services model	.596

Appendix G

MEANS AND STANDARD DEVIATIONS OF PRINCIPALS' AND
SPECIAL EDUCATION TEACHERS' ATTITUDES REGARDING
INCLUSION

SEP Questionnaire Item	Principals		Special Education Teachers	
	M	SD	M	SD
1. The special education teachers should assist in the instruction of both students with mild handicaps and other students experiencing learning difficulties.	4.30*	0.89	3.84*	1.21
7. Regular class teachers cannot meet the academic needs of students with mild handicaps currently in their classrooms.	2.44	0.98	2.57	1.13
11. If students with mild handicaps are placed full time in the regular class, then currently mandated special education resources for their instruction must be protected.	3.91**	1.05	4.51**	0.73
14. Regular class teachers have the instructional skills to teach both students with mild handicaps and general students.	2.89*	1.10	2.39*	1.10
18. The time devoted to state/district curriculum goals would decrease if students with mild handicaps were placed full time in the regular classroom.	2.47	0.81	2.39	0.87
19. Achievement levels of students with mild handicaps would increase if they were placed full time in the regular classroom.	3.26**	0.97	2.53**	1.10
20. The regular classroom with special education consultant services is the most effective environment to educate students with mild handicaps.	3.77**	0.98	2.81**	1.19

Note. From "Attitudes of Principals and Special Education Teachers Toward the Inclusion of Students with Mild Disabilities: Critical Differences of Opinion," by B. G. Cook, M. I. Semmel, and M. M. Gerber, 1999, Remedial and Special Education, 20(4), p. 203. Copyright 1999 by Remedial and Special Education. Reprinted with permission.

Appendix H

GUIDELINES FOR CRITIQUING RESEARCH ARTICLES

Instructions: Answer the following questions regarding the article,
" _____ ".
Use examples from the article to support your analyses.

A. Title

1. Did the title describe the study?
2. Did the key words of the title serve as key elements of the article?
3. Was the title concise (i.e., free of distracting or extraneous phrases)?

B. Abstract

4. Did the abstract summarize the studys purpose, methods, and findings?
5. Did the abstract reveal the independent and dependent variables under study?
6. Were there any major premises or findings presented in the article that were not mentioned in the abstract?
7. Did the abstract provide you with sufficient information to determine whether you would be interested in reading the entire article?

C. Introduction

8. Was the research problem clearly identified?
9. Is the problem significant enough to warrant the study that was conducted?
10. Did the authors present a theoretical rationale for the study?
11. Is the conceptual framework of the study appropriate in light of the research problem?
12. Do the author's hypotheses and/or research questions seem logical in light of the conceptual framework and research problem?
13. Are hypotheses and research questions clearly stated?
14. Overall, does the literature review lead logically into the Method section?

D. Method

15. Is the sample clearly described, in terms of size, relevant characteristics, selection and assignment procedures, and whether any inducements were used to solicit subjects?

Note. From *Research in Rehabilitation Counseling* (p. 204), by J. Bellini and P. Rumrill, 1999, Springfield, IL: Charles C Thomas • Publisher, LTD. Copyright 1999 by Charles C Thomas • Publisher, LTD. Reprinted with permission.

16. Do the instruments described seem appropriate as measures of the variables under study?
17. Have the authors included sufficient information about the psychometric properties (e.g., reliability and validity) of the instruments?
18. Are the materials used in conducting the study or in collecting data clearly described?
19. Are the studys procedures thoroughly described in chronological order?
20. Is the design of the study identified (or made evident)?
21. Do the design and procedures seem appropriate in light of the research problem, conceptual framework, and research questions/hypotheses?
22. Overall, does the method section provide sufficient information to replicate the study?

E. Results

23. Is the Results section clearly written and well organized?
24. Are data coding and analysis appropriate in light of the studys design and hypotheses?
25. Are salient results connected directly to hypotheses?
26. Are tables and figures clearly labeled? Well organized? Necessary (non-duplicative of text)?

F. Discussion and Conclusion

27. Are the limitations of the study delineated?
28. Are findings discussed in terms of the research problem, conceptual framework, and hypotheses?
29. Are implications for future research and/or special education practice identified?
30. Are the authors general conclusions warranted in light of the results?

G. References

31. Is the reference list sufficiently current?
32. Do works cited reflect the breadth of existing literature regarding the topic of the study?
33. Are bibliographic citations used appropriately in the text?

H. General Impressions

34. Is the article well written and organized?
35. Does the study address an important problem in the lives of people with disabilities?

36. What are the most important things you learned from this article?
37. What do you see as the most compelling strengths of this study?
38. How might this study be improved?

Chapter 10

THE FUTURE OF
SPECIAL EDUCATION RESEARCH

Phillip D. Rumrill, Jr. and
Bryan G. Cook

INTRODUCTION

T O THIS POINT IN THE BOOK, we have attempted to establish a historical
foundation for special education research and have endeavored to provide readers with an overview of selected articles from the special education
literature, primarily organized around the research designs and methods that
investigators use to answer their research questions. With this grounding set
in the past and present of special education research, our aim in this, the
final, chapter is to look ahead to the future, to discuss emerging issues for
special education researchers, research consumers, and children with disabilities as we enter the twent-first century.

The perspectives we offer in this chapter are based chiefly on our own
experiences and perspectives as researchers, educators, service providers,
and research consumers. We frame what we think will be new developments
in special education in sociopolitical, regulatory, heuristic, and (we hope)
practical contexts. Content in this chapter focuses on (a) the role of theory in
contemporary and future special education research, (b) the role of research
in contemporary and future special education practice, (c) the topic areas that
we regard as most fertile for future inquiry, and (d) the research approaches
and strategies that investigators are likely to draw on in addressing those topics.

THE ROLE OF THEORY IN SPECIAL EDUCATION RESEARCH

Theory plays an important role in the generation of research ideas and in
the development of a profession's knowledge base. Throughout history, the

advancement of scientific knowledge has depended on the development of theory, empirical evaluation of theoretical propositions, and refinement of theory and knowledge on the basis of the findings of systematic research studies. Without the guidance of theory, research investigations are conducted in isolation and without an articulated rationale. In that case, they are difficult to relate to one another and apply to practice. Thus, to advance our knowledge of special education, we need to devote more of our time and energy to theory-driven research rather than to theory-free investigations. For example, most contemporary disability studies scholars (e.g., Artiles, 1998; Cook & Rumrill, 2000; Kauffman, 1999; Wehman, 1996) frame educational services for children with disabilities as a complex interaction of personal, environmental, and systems variables. These theories and models serve to organize and explain hypothesized relationships among personal, environmental, and experiential phenomena in the lives of people with disabilities, their family members, their teachers, and other stakeholders. Despite this, few empirical investigations address, either wholly or in part, propositions rooted in contemporary special education theories and models. To optimally use theory toward the end of improving educational opportunities for students with disabilities, special education scholars must develop specific, theory-based propositions that follow from contemporary theories and models—theories and models that have been refined through rigorous empirical research. Theory provides the necessary framework for the advancement of scientific knowledge, but knowledge can only be verified incrementally through successive, individual studies that are relatively narrow in scope (Bellini & Rumrill, 1999).

THE ROLE OF RESEARCH IN
SPECIAL EDUCATION PRACTICE

Turning attention to the role of research in special education practice, it is important to point out that research findings are often not directly applicable to professional practice (Serlin, 1989); that is, research rarely tells practitioners exactly what to do in specific situations. Rather, research contributes to effective practice through the testing, confirmation or disconfirmation, and refinement of causal explanations, which specify what variables are related; how they are related; the nature of the processes that are involved; and the extent to which variable relationships can be generalized across populations, settings, and conditions (Bellini & Rumrill, 1999). In the absence of theory-driven research in special education, theory and model-building become academic exercises that have minimal relevance to practitioners and little impact on special education practices. Therefore, we urge special education scholars to develop stronger theoretical bases for their empirical work. Research, especially applied research, can and should be grounded in theory, and we hope to see a "back to basics" movement in special education research, whereby theoretical propositions are generated from conceptual frameworks and results are then used to refine these frameworks and theories. Such a movement will provide scientists with stronger warrants for new knowledge claims than is the case in many existing atheoretical investigations. Also of great importance, it will more rapidly bridge the gap between the profession's need for and use of new knowledge–thereby allowing research to keep up with field practice (and, hopefully, vice versa).

Specific research areas in special education that are likely to benefit most from application of contemporary social science theories include educational processes and outcomes, family issues in the adjustment to and acceptance of disability, the reciprocal impact of self-perceptions and the perceptions of others in formulating personal responses to disability, peer acceptance and interactions, and other specific interactions of personal and contextual factors that influence the success and failures of children with disabilities in all aspects of education. Moreover, the development and testing of theory-based educational and psychosocial interventions have the potential to yield valuable information for both scholars and practitioners regarding *what* facilitates the achievement of valued outcomes for children with disabilities and *why*. Finally, the ways in which we identify and categorize the children with whom we work help form the basis for our thinking about and relationships with our students. As such, systematic, theory-based research should also evaluate the relative usefulness of different conceptions of disability (e.g., minority group model, individual difference/human variation model, medical model) within a theoretical context.

EMERGING TOPIC AREAS IN
SPECIAL EDUCATION RESEARCH

The existing knowledge base in special education has been built in small increments, with successive studies serving to extend the ones before them along specific lines of inquiry. As we look ahead to the future, we recognize that the current subject matter of empirical work in our field will be expanded by new research initiatives designed to build on what we already know. The progressive, linear approach to developing valid knowledge (Bellini & Rumrill, 1999) serves many useful purposes, but it also requires vigilance on the part of scientists to avoid merely "recycling" what has already been done and, thereby, thwarting the expansion of our knowledge.

Many research topics in special education (e.g., teachers' attitudes toward the concept of inclusion, litigation patterns under IDEA) represent second-order investigations, one (or more) step removed from the primary foci of special education research, which are (a) the interests, skills, values, and experiences of children with disabilities; and (b) how the special education process facilitates participation of children with disabilities in all social roles. In fairness, these lines of inquiry have served and will continue to serve important descriptive and evaluative functions for the profession. Still, a peril is inherent in devoting so much energy to secondary issues (to the exclusion of primary topics). Special education research may be viewed as irrelevant to its primary beneficiaries (i.e., people with disabilities and their families). We need to place the focus of our efforts to generate new knowledge where it has always belonged—on our students. Perhaps if we better understood their needs, we could better meet their needs. In so doing, the field might not have to struggle so ardently with its identity—nor would it have to labor under the current perception of other professionals that special education is primarily a reactive subdiscipline; that is, we often spend more time reacting to policies that are effectuated by other stakeholders than we do understanding the educational experiences of students with disabilities.

Teaching Strategies

A number of areas of scientific inquiry are particularly important to the immediate future of special education. One such area is teaching strategies. Nothing is more elemental in the delivery of special education services than the manner and content of instruction provided to children with disabilities, and the literature in our field is replete with thoughtful and comprehensive treatises on innovative teaching, what works and does not work, and curriculum design. Unfortunately, there is a scarcity of empirical evidence to support the effectiveness of most particular teaching strategies with particular student populations. The result is that teaching strategies comprise one of the most widely written-about topics in our field but also one of the most underresearched subjects. This discrepancy between the respective volumes of expert opinion and empirical evidence renders this all-important subject area highly susceptible to politically charged rhetoric, entrepreneurial marketing, and untested interventions that could yield harmful results for children who deserve scientifically validated educational services. The only way to correct this troubling trend is to refocus the study of teaching strategies into systematic, controlled, intervention-based studies that compare various teaching strategies for their effectiveness with clearly defined samples of students with disabilities. Questions like "How do children with learning disabilities most effectively learn to read?," "How can children with visual impairments most effectively learn algebra?," and "How do community-based instructional techniques benefit children with behavioral disorders?" can only be answered by applying and reapplying experimental and quasi-experimental principles such as those outlined in Chapter 6 of this book. It is time to empirically test the "models," "guidelines," "frameworks," and "calls to action" that have dominated the literature in this most basic area of our field but that have also gone largely unvalidated by several generations of special education researchers.

Policy Research

The knowledge base in special education also requires systematic and comprehensive evaluations of disability and educational policy initiatives. Special education research often plays little or no role in formulating state and federal policies that affect special education students and professionals alike. Parent groups, disability advocates, and other educational profession-als have been much more effective agents of change, which often leaves researchers and practitioners in special education to lament the policies that have been officiated on the strength of efforts by other stakeholders. Policy research in special education needs to shift from asking constituency groups their opinions about existing policies to garnering a clearer understanding of political action, the manner in which broad policy initiatives are articulated into practice, and how American disability policies fit into broader sociopo-litical mechanisms (e.g., welfare, education, civil rights, workforce develop-ment, health care).

Assistive and Medical Technology

Another burgeoning area for special education and disability studies scholars in the years to come will be assistive technology. We need to follow developments in this dynamic facet of our field and systematically study the effectiveness, safety, availability, practicality, and use patterns of new devices as they come on the market, as well as student and parental satisfaction with assistive technology devices. Examples of assistive technology domains with significant growth potential include speech-to-print programs for students with hearing impairments, voice recognition software for children with mobility impairments, voice-output and large-print screen readers, and mobility aids. We also look for in-depth inquiries into the interactions between medical technology and assistive technology; in that regard, the interface among health care professionals, special educators, allied health professionals, rehabilitation engineers, children with disabilities, parents, and funding sources will be of paramount interest.

Medical science will continue to have major effects on special education practice and research. Improved prenatal and early childhood detection measures enable us to identify many disabling conditions more quickly than ever before, hence increasing the need for early intervention services. People with congenital conditions such as spina bifida can now look forward to adulthood thanks to medical advances that have vastly extended their life expectancies. This trend has significant implications for transition planning and other secondary special education services. Children with HIV/AIDS are increasingly being viewed as having a chronic, rather than terminal, disease—a classification that brings with it numerous research and service delivery implications. Children who incur traumatic brain injuries and spinal cord injuries, too often resulting from violence, will rely heavily on cooperation between professionals in the areas of medical and assistive technology as they transition into adulthood as people with severe disabilities. These are only a few examples of how technology is changing the entire landscape of our field, but they again underscore the need for special education research to keep in step with professional practice.

Transition

The processes and outcomes of several intervention strategies and professional specialty areas also need to be examined more rigorously. Among these is transition from school to adult living for young people with disabilities—a process that spans one of the most important developmental periods in people's lives. Theoretically driven, applied research is needed to assist special educators and adult service providers to collaborate more effectively in planning and providing comprehensive services to youth with disabilities who exit schools and enter the world of work, postsecondary programs, and other adult settings. More long-term follow-up data are needed to clarify (a) the service needs of transitioning youth with disabilities and (b) practices that best meet these needs. One of the most important areas for future transition research is postsecondary education. With enrollment rates of students with disabilities having more than tripled on American college and university campuses since 1978 (Henderson, 1995), more emphasis must be placed on the transition to higher education for these students—as well as transition from post-secondary programs to competitive careers and independent living.

Assessment

Another area within the field of special education that requires more rigorous empirical study is assessment. Informal assessment is a burgeoning field with many new strategies being developed by and for teachers regarding how to meet the needs of an increasingly diverse body of students in ways that formal, standardized tests cannot. Although many alternative areas of assessment have quickly become popular and are commonly used for students with and without disabilities, there is often a dearth of research evidencing the effectiveness, or the reliability and validity, of new assessment techniques. For example, authentic assessment, performance-based assessment, and portfolio assessment are frequently used to gauge the progress of students and the effectiveness of curricula and instruction, yet they may provide unreliable information. In addition, in areas of special education such as early childhood special education and the education of students with severe disabilities, a shortage of well-researched assessment instruments exists. As new instruments are developed to assess the skills and aptitudes of young children with disabilities and students with severe disabilities, research will be needed to determine whether the instruments yield reliable and valid results.

In addition to researching the reliability and validity of instruments, researchers will need to examine the degree to which students with disabilities are participating in statewide proficiency tests, what kinds of accommodations they are being provided, and how these results are being reported. IDEA 1997 mandated that students with disabilities participate in state proficiency tests. Advocates for children with disabilities fought for this mandate because proficiency tests are being used as a primary indicator of the effectiveness of schools, teachers, and instructional programming. If students with disabilities do not take these tests, as has traditionally been the case, they are left out of the process for determining what constitutes quality education. However, because of their disabilities, many students in special education cannot meaningfully participate in standard proficiency tests. Some students with disabilities therefore take the standard test with one or more accommodation (e.g., extended time, having the test read aloud to them), take an alternate test, or are exempted from (do not take) part or all of their state's proficiency test. Further research is needed regarding how to most meaningfully include students with disabilities in this process.

Perhaps the most important area of assessment in which research needs to focus is teachers' implementation of reliable and valid informal assessment in their day-to-day instructional practices. Oftentimes, teachers use assessment only to evaluate student performance and assign grades. Yet, assessment is a vital tool in effectively determining what to teach, at what level to teach, and when to change instructional strategies. Unfortunately, some teachers base these critical decisions on unsystematic observations and hunches about what is best for their students. More research is needed to determine what kind of training and supports are associated with teachers incorporating systematic and effective informal assessment practices (e.g., error analysis, criterion-reference testing, curriculum-based measurement) into their instructional routines.

Inclusion

Any discussion of the future of special education must involve inclusion. Because the inclusion of students with disabilities into general education classrooms has become a defining issue in special education, one that has a direct impact on the quality of education and life for students with disabilities, it is recommended that research be done to explore how to make inclusion more effective. Although inclusion is one of the most frequently covered topics in the professional special education literature, much of the work done on this subject does not involve empirical research at all; rather, it tends to represent authors' thoughts and opinions in the area of inclusion. In addition, much of the research that does exist on inclusion is in the form of case studies that (a) have extremely limited generalizability and (b) often describe cases purposefully selected to correspond with the authors' personal perspectives. The aggregate extant literature on inclusion, therefore, reflects advocacy stances more than the results of objective research.

One way to improve the relevance of research conducted in the area of inclusion is to focus on student outcomes. Too often, research does not involve any consideration of how children's academic and social development is affected by inclusive reforms. Because the academic performance, behavior, peer acceptance, social interactions, and self-esteem of students with disabilities comprise the focus of special education, these outcomes should be the criteria for research involving inclusion. For example, there is a vast body of literature investigating the attitudes of teachers toward the concept of inclusion. Yet, it has not been conclusively established that teachers' attitudes toward the idea of inclusion are empirically linked to the outcomes of their included students. Much of this literature, then, begs the question of whether and how teacher attitudes toward inclusion matter. By using student outcomes as the dependent variable in studies examining the issue of inclusion, the persistent problem of producing research that has little or no implications for practice could be, at least to some extent, alleviated.

It is also recommended that research on inclusion be increasingly differentiated by disability level and type. Because the characteristics and needs of included students with disabilities differ so dramatically, research that does not specify type and severity of disability may be oversimplistic and may not correspond to the realities of inclusive education. For example, teachers may feel quite differently about including students with students with severe disabilities compared with how they feel about including students with mild disabilities. Yet, attitudinal surveys routinely ask teachers to rate their agreement with a number of statements made about the practice of including students with disabilities in general. Similarly, researchers must be careful to specify the disability categories and other relevant characteristics of included students participating in their studies. In this way, readers of the published study know the specific population to which the results apply—and, just as importantly, to whom the findings do not apply. For example, it stands to reason that peers interact with included students with multiple disabilities differently than they do with included students with learning disabilities. Therefore, strategies that have been empirically demonstrated to increase the quality and quantity of peer interactions for included students with learning disabilities may not be effective in improving the same outcomes for students with multiple disabilities.

It is also recommended that research on inclusion increasingly focus on school, classroom, and teacher variables that are relatively easy to manipulate, and, therefore, relatively easy to translate into changes in practice. Although student-related variables are important foci of special education research, they may prove less amenable to change. For example, if it is demonstrated that students with behavioral disorders are less accepted by their peers than are included students with mental retardation, educators cannot simply change the characteristics or labels of the students with behavioral disorders as a means of improving their peer acceptance. Alternatively, if increased teacher training (e.g., number of college courses taken in the area of special education) is empirically demonstrated to correspond with improved outcomes for included students with disabilities, a specific strategy that educators can implement to improve inclusive educational outcomes is revealed (i.e., provide inclusive teachers with more formal training in special education).

Collaboration

Special education researchers must increase their efforts to investigate the issue of collaboration between teachers. Although special education teachers have long interacted with a variety of school personnel (e.g., speech therapists adaptive physical educators), the advent of inclusion has required special and general education teachers to more regularly and directly work together in the delivery of services and instruction for students with disabilities. In an inclusive environment, special and general educators may teach together for all or part of the school day, divide the class and teach their groups separately for parts of the day, or take turns delivering aspects of lessons while the other works with individual students. Even when special education teachers are not physically present in inclusive classrooms, they collaborate with general education teachers outside of class regarding the content, structure, and instructional methods and adaptations to be implemented. Most scholars agree that successful collaboration between special and general education teachers is a critical element of service delivery for students with disabilities to attain appropriate outcomes in inclusive classrooms. In spite of this, extremely little is known about what kinds of personal characteristics, experiences, interaction styles, and supports are associated with successful collaboration. The literature is replete with anecdotal stories about successful collaboration between teachers. However, many collaborative efforts are ineffective and even counterproductive when they involve individuals who have different instructional approaches or who simply do not get along. Systematic research is needed to identify variables that contribute to making collaborative teaching work. This will elevate the status of the term "collaboration" from hopeful rhetoric to a viable aspect of the professional knowledge base.

EMERGING RESEARCH DESIGNS AND METHODS

As special education researchers apply scientific methods to address those emerging issues discussed to this point in the chapter (and many other topics), it is important to note that they way research is conducted is likely to change just as dramatically as the topics under study will. This section examines a number of trends that we anticipate for the forseeable future in terms of how science is applied in special education research.

Using Experimental and Quasi-Experimental Research Designs

First and perhaps most basically, there is a need to strengthen the scientific properties of research designs so as to better assess the effects of educational interventions for students with disabilities. The most common ways to assess specific interventions in special education appear to be causal comparative and single-subject studies, both of which present major limitations to the warrant for new knowledge that is derived from research findings. For example, a researcher wishing to test a particular way of teaching reading skills to children with learning disabilities would likely deliver the intervention to an intact group of students with learning disabilities, who were placed in one or several classrooms. The researcher might compare this group's acquisition of reading skills with the skill acquisition of a group of students with learning disabilities who were enrolled in classrooms that did not offer the new teaching strategy. Although students in the nonintervention group do provide a frame of reference for comparison, the researcher does not know, because of the nonrandom nature of group assignment, whether other characteristics of the comparison group might differentiate those students' abilities to develop reading skills irrespective of the teaching strategy. The internal validity of this study is compromised because there is no way to know whether differences in reading skills are attributable to the intervention or to factors related to the educational placement of participating students.

Another researcher seeking to test a particular classroom management strategy with children who have behavioral disorders might use a single-subject approach wherein two or three students are selected and systematically tracked while various aspects of the intervention are introduced. These investigations are usually tightly controlled, but the problem of external validity (i.e., generalizability) presents itself because there is no way to determine how representative the two or three students taking part in the study are vis á vis the broader population of children with behavioral disorders.

Without question, the field of special education needs more experimental studies in which moderate to large numbers of participants are scientifically drawn form constituent populations, randomly assigned to treatment and control groups, and examined before and after particular interventions have been applied. Although there are inherent ethical and practical challenges involved in conducting true experiments in "in vivo" settings such as the classroom (see Chapter 4), we must strengthen the scientific conviction with which we claim that certain teaching, classroom management, and student planning strategies impact the lives of our students.

Appropriate Use of Qualitative Research

We have recently begun to see the broad applicability of qualitative research methods in special education. As a means of investigating phenomena that have not been previously examined, identifying variables for theory-building purposes, and providing understanding of the lived experience of a student with disabilities that is not possible using quantitative methods, qualitative research will play a vital role in expanding our profession's knowledge base. Within the qualitative realm, we hope to see a movement toward prolonged engagements with research participants within their natural environments and the application of more rigorous research methods to enhance the credibility of qualitative findings. The grounded theory method of qualitative research (Strauss & Corbin, 1991)–whereby theoretical propositions are developed on the basis of observation and then tested, revised, and refined through prolonged engagement and systematic data analysis–is well suited to contribute to the theoretical foundation of our profession.

Multivariate Analyses

For special education researchers who use quantitative research methods, we believe that multivariate analyses that take into account the various levels of influence that have an impact on the outcomes of students with disabilities are necessary. For example, when examining student outcomes (e.g., academic performance, peer acceptance, self-esteem) special education researchers must not only look at the effect of instructional variables, they must also realize that variables such as peer group composition, teachers' experience and expertise, parental support, and school culture all have an indirect but important effect on the school experiences and educational opportunities of students. This is particularly true for students with disabilities, whose educational outcomes depend on specialized supports and services and whose schooling experiences vary tremendously within and among schools and classrooms. If we ignore the role of these contextualizing variables in the analysis of student outcomes, it is likely that the real effects of instructional variables will be obfuscated by the unmeasured impact of the teacher, classroom, school, and community. Analyses that enable researchers to evaluate the combined effects of a number of independent variables on a number of dependent variables such as multivariate analysis of variance and canonical correlations are most sensitive to the intricate interrelationships among school-, class-, and student-level variables. It is also important that statistical analysis be sufficiently sophisticated to reflect the "nested" nature of these variables. In other words, school-level variables (e.g., principal support, staff cohesiveness) affect all classrooms within that school. Variables related to the classroom (e.g., class size) and teacher (e.g., years of teaching experience) similarly affect all students clustered within a particular classroom. Therefore, we also encourage special education researchers to use emerging multivariate methods of analysis such as hierarchical linear modeling (HLM) so that the multiple layers of students' educational experiences can be more fully and realistically considered when attempting to explain the educational outcomes of students with disabilities.

SUMMARY

In an applied social science field such as special education, policy, practice, and scientific inquiry are shaped through an ongoing, reciprocal process of identifying and answering research questions. Thus, many of the impending changes in special education research that we have forecast in this chapter stem from changes in disability in educational policy that have an impact on the profession and practice of special education.

Today's special educators are subject to new regulations and policy shifts, increasing legal responsibilities, heightened certification and licensure standards, demands to collaborate with other professionals, and pressures to function as both generalists and specialists (to name just a few current trends). The rapidly changing landscape of our field places heavy demands on special educators to update their knowledge to continue to provide quality services for children with disabilities. In the same vein, special education researchers must keep current with respect to new developments in the field if the contributions that they make to the knowledge base are to be considered meaningful by policymakers, administrators, teachers, parents, and people with disabilities.

This chapter provides a brief summary of changes that we anticipate and/or desire in the special education research enterprise over the next five to ten years. It reflects our own experiences as disability studies researchers and educators, as well as the syntheses of the current research scene that we attempted to achieve in the first nine chapters of this book. In total, we hope that this text has provided an overview of the past, present, and possible future of special education research–as well as a meaningful examination of the role of scientific inquiry in all aspects of special education practice.

BIBLIOGRAPHY

Alber, S.R., Heward, W.L., & Hippler, B.J. (1999). Teaching middle school students with learning disabilities to recruit positive teacher attention. *Exceptional Children, 65*, 253-270.

Alberto, P.A., & Troutman, A.C. (1999). *Applied behavior ananlysis for teachers* (5th ed.). Upper Saddle, NJ: Merrill.

American Counseling Association (1995). *Code of ethics and standards of practice.* Alexandria, VA: Author.

American Educational Research Association, American Psychological Association, & Council on Measurement in Education (1985). *Joint technical standards for educational and psychological testing.* Washington, DC: American Psychological Association.

American Psychological Association (1992). Ethical principles of psychologists and code of conduct. *American Psychologist, 47*, 1597-1611.

American Psychological Association. (1994). *Publication manual of the American Psychological Association* (4th ed.). Washington, DC: Author.

American Psychological Association Ethics Committee (1983). *Authorship guidelines for dissertation supervision.* Washington, DC: Author.

Angoff, W. H. (1988). Validity: An evolving concept. In H. Wainer, & H. I. Braun (Eds.), *Test validity,* (pp. 19-32). Hillsdale, NJ: Erlbaum.

Artiles, A. (1998). The dilemma of difference: Enriching the disproportionality discourse with theory and context. *Journal of Special Education, 32*(1), 32-36.

Ary, D., Jacobs, L., & Razavieh A. (1985). *Introduction to research in education.* New York: CBS College Publishing.

Asher, S., Parkhurst, J., Hymel, S., & Williams, G. (1990). Peer rejection and loneliness in childhood. In S. Asher & J. Coie (Eds.), *Peer rejection in childhood* (pp. 253-273). New York: Cambridge University Press.

Babbie, E. (1995). *The practice of social research.* New York: Wadsworth.

Baer, R., Martonyi, E., Simmons, T., Flexer, R., & Goebel, G. (1994). Employer collaboration: A tri-lateral group process model. *Journal of Rehabilitation Administration, 18*(3), 151-163.

Bailey, D. B., McWilliam, R. A., Darkes, L. A., Hebeler, K., Simeonsson, R. J., Spiker, D., & Wagner, M. (1998). Family outcomes in early intervention: A framework for program evaluation and efficacy research. *Exceptional Children, 64*, 313-328.

Bak, J. J., & Siperstein, G.N. (1987). Similarity as a factor effecting change in children's attitudes toward mentally retarded peers. *American Journal of Mental Deficiency, 91*, 524-531.

Baker, J.M., & Zigmond, N. (1995). The meaning and practice of inclusion for students with learning disabilities: Themes and implications from the five cases. *The Journal of Special Education, 29*, 163-180.

Baranek, G.T. (1999). Autism during infancy: A retrospective video analysis of sensory motor and social behaviors at 9-12 months. *Journal of Autism and Developmental Disorders, 29*, 213-224.

Barlow, D.H., & Hersen, M. (1984). *Single case experimental designs: Strategies for studying behavior change* (2nd ed.). Elmsford, NY: Pergamon Press.

Beauchamp, T.L., & Childress, J.F. (1979). *Principles in biomedical ethics.* Oxford: Oxford University Press.

Bellini, J. (1998). Equity and Order of Selection: Issues in implementation and evaluation of the mandate to serve individuals with the most severe disabilities. *Journal of Disability Policy Studies, 9*(1), 107-124.

Bellini, J., Bolton, B., & Neath, J. (1998). Rehabilitation counselors assessments of applicants functional limitations as predictors of rehabilitation services provided. *Rehabilitation Counseling Bulletin, 41*(4), 242-258.

Bellini, J., & Royce-Davis, J. (1999). Order of selection in vocational rehabilitation: Implications for the transition from school to adult outcomes for youths with learning disabilities. *Work, 13*(1), 3-12.

Bellini, J., & Rumrill, P. (1999). *Research in rehabilitation counseling.* Springfield, IL: Charles C. Thomas.

Biklen, D. P. (1991). Social policy, social systems, and educational practice. In L. H. Meyer, C. A. Peck, & L. Brown (Eds.), *Critical issues in the lives of people with severe disabilities* (pp. 387-390). Baltimore: Paul H. Brookes.

Biklen, D. (Ed.) (1985). *Achieving the complete school: Strategies for effective mainstreaming.* New York: Teacher's College, Columbia University.

Bogdan, R.C. & Biklen, S.K. (1992). *Qualitative research for education.* Boston: Allyn and Bacon.

Bolton, B. (1979). *Rehabilitation counseling research.* Baltimore: University Park Press.

Bolton, B., & Parker, R. M. (1998). Research in rehabilitation counseling. In R. M. Parker & E. M. Szymanski (Eds.), *Rehabilitation counseling: Basics and beyond* (3rd ed; pp. 437-470). Austin, TX: Pro-Ed.

Borg, W. R., & Gall, M. D. (1983). *Educational research.* New York: Longman.

Borg, W. R., Gall, J. P., & Gall, M. D. (1993). *Applying educational research: A practical guide* (3rd ed.). New York: Longman.

Bottge, B.A. (1999). Effects of contextualized math instruction on problem solving of average and below-average achieving students. *The Journal of Special Education, 33*, 81-92.

Campbell, D. T., & Fiske, D. W. (1959). Convergent and discriminant validation by the multitrait multimethod matrix. *Psychological Bulletin, 56*(2), 81-105.

Carnine, D. (1997). Bridging the research-to-practice gap. *Exceptional Children, 63*, 513-521.

Carnine, D. (1995). Trustworthiness, useability, and accessibility of educaitonal research. *Journal of Behavioral Education, 5*, 251-258.

Carr, E.G., Newsom, C.D., & Binkoff, J.A. (1980). Escape as a factor in the aggressive behavior of two retarded children. *Journal of Applied Behavior Analysis, 13*, 101-117.

Chalmers, L., & Faliede, T. (1996). Successful inclusion of students with mild/moderate disabilities in rural school settings. *Teaching Exceptional Children, 29*(1), 22-25.

Cohen, J. (1988). *Statistical power analysis for the behavioral sciences* (2nd ed). Hillsdale, NJ: Lawrence Erlbaum Associates.

Cohen, J. (1990). Things I have learned (so far). *American Psychologist, 45*, 1304-1312.

Collet-Klingenberg, L. L. (1998). The reality of best practices in transition: A case study. *Exceptional Children, 65*(1), 67-78.

Conrad, C., Neumann, A., Haworth, J.G., & Scott, P. (1993). *Qualitative research in higher education: Experiencing alternative perspective and approaches.* Needham Heights, MA: Ginn Press.

Cook, B., Gerber, M., & Semmel, M. (1997). Are effective school reforms effective for all students? The implications of joint outcome production for school reform. *Exceptionality, 7*, 77-95.

Cook, B.G., & Landrum, T.J. (2000). Teachers' views of community-based job training and inclusion as predictors of employability. Paper presented at Annual Conference of the Council for Exceptional Children. Vancouver, British Columbia.

Cook, B.G., & Rumrill, P. (1999). Inclusion and transition in special education: Partners in progress or policy paradox? *Work, 13*, 13-21.

Cook, B.G., Semmel, M.I., & Gerber, M.M. (1999). Attitudes of principals and special education teachers toward the inclusion of students with mild disabilities: Critical differences of opinion. *Remedial and Special Education, 20*(4), 199-207.

Cook, B.G., Tankersley, M., Cook, L., & Landrum, T.J. (2000). Teachers' attitudes toward their included students with disabilities. *Exceptional Children, 67*, 115-135.

Cook, T. D., & Campbell, D. T. (1979). *Quasi-experimentation: Design and analysis issues for field settings.* Chicago: Rand McNally.

Cook, T., Cooper, H., Cordray, D., Hartman, H., Hedges, L., Light, R., Louis, T., & Mosteller, F. (1992). *Meta-analysis for explanation: A case book.* Newbury Park, CA: Sage.

Corey, G., Corey, M., & Callanan, P. (1998). *Issues and ethics in the helping professions* (5th Edition). Pacific Grove, CA: Brooks/Cole.

Council for Exceptional Children. (1997, July 24). *CEC Standards for Professional Practice, professionals in relation to persons with exceptionalities and their families: Instructional responsibilities.* Reston, VA: Author. Retrieved September 2, 2000 from World Wide Web: http://www.cec.sped.org/ps/code.htm#3.

Council for Exceptional Children. (1997, July 24). *CEC Standards for Professional Practice, Professionals in relation to the profession and to other professionals: To the profession.* Reston, VA: Author. Retrieved September 2, 2000 from World Wide Web: http://www.cec.sped.org/ps/code/htm#13.

Council for Exceptional Children (1999). *Code of ethics and standards of practice.* Alexandria, VA: Author.

Creswell, J.W. (1994). *Research design: Qualitative and quantitative approaches.* Thousand Oaks, CA: Sage.

Cronbach, L. (1988). Five perspectives on the validity argument. In H. Wainer, & H. I. Braun (Eds.), *Test validity.* Hillsdale, NJ: Erlbaum.

Cronbach, L. (1990). *Essentials of psychological testing* (5th ed.). New York: Harper & Row.

Cronbach, L., & Meehl, P. (1955). Construct validity in psychological tests. *Psychological Bulletin, 52*(4), 281-302.

Crowson, R.L. (1993). Qualitative research design methods in higher education. In C.

Conrad, A. Neuman, J.G. Haworth, P. Scot (Eds.), *Qualitative research in higher education: Experiencing alternative perspectives and approaches.* Ashe Reader Series. Needham Heights, MA: Ginn Press.

Darling-Hammond, L. (1996). What matters most: A competent teacher for every child. *Phi Delta Kappan, 78*, 193-200.

Davis, J. & Maheady, L. (1991). The Regular Education Initiative: What do three groups of education professionals think? *Teacher Education and Special Education, 14*, 211-220.

Deno, S.L., Foegen, A., Robinson, S., & Espin, C. (1996). Commentary: Facing the realities of inclusion for students with mild disabilities. *The Journal of Special Education, 30*, 345-357.

Denzin, N.K. (1970). *The research act.* Chicago: Aldine.

Denzin, N.K. & Lincoln, Y.S. (1994). *Handbook of qualitative research.* Thousand Oaks, CA: Sage.

Dexter, L.A. (1970). Elite and specialized interviewing. Evanston, IL: Northwestern University Press.

Diener, E., & Crandall, R. (1978). *Ethics in social and behavioral research.* Chicago: University of Chicago Press.

Downing, J., Eichinger, J., & Williams, L. (1997). Inclusive education for students with severe disabilities: Comparative views of prinicpals and educators at different levels of implementation. *Remedial and Special Education, 18,* 133-142.

Drasgow, E. (1998). American Sign Language as a pathway to linguistic competence. *Exceptional Children, 64*(3), 329-342.

Drew, C. F. (1980). *Introduction to designing and conducting research* (2nd ed.). St. Louis: C. V. Mosby.

Drummond, R. (1996). *Appraisal procedures for counselors and helping professionals* (3rd ed.). Englewood Cliffs, NJ: Prentice-Hall, Inc.

Eber, L., Nelson, C., & Miles, P. (1997). School-based wraparound for children with emotional and behavioral challenges. *Exceptional Children, 63*(4), 539-555.

Eisner, E.W. (1997). The promise and perils of alternative forms of data representation. *Educational Researcher, 26*(6), 4-10.

Elbaum, B., Vaughn, S., Hughes, M., & Moody, S.W. (1999). Grouping practices and reading outcomes for students with disabilities. *Exceptional Children, 65,* 399-415.

Espin, C., Deno, S. & Albayrak-Kaymak, D. (1998). Individualized education programs in resource and inclusive settings: How "individualized" are they? *The Journal of Special Education, 32*(3), 164-174.

Espin, C., Shin, J., & Busch, T. (2000). *Current practice alerts: Focusing on formative evaluation.* Reston, VA: CEC-Division for Learning Disabilities and CEC-Division for Research.

Ferguson, D. (1993). Something a little out of the ordinary: Reflections on becoming an interpretivist researcher in special education. *Remedial and Special Education, 14*(4), 35-43, 51.

Ferguson, D., & Halle, J. (1995). Considerations for readers of qualitative research (Editorial). *Journal of the Association for Persons with Severe Handicaps, 20*(1), 1-2.

Fielding, N.G., & Fielding, J.L. (1986). *Linking data.* Newbury Park, CA: Sage.

Flexer, R., Simmons, T., & Tankersley, M. (1997). Graduate interdisciplinary training at Kent State University. *Journal of Vocational Rehabilitation, 8,* 183-195.

Forgan, J.W., & Vaughn, S. (2000). Adolescents with and without LD make the transition to middle school. *Journal of Learning Disabilities, 33,* 33-43.

Forness, S. R., Kavale, K., Blum, S., & Lloyd J. W. (1997). Mega-analysis of meta-analyses: What works in special education and related services. *Teaching Exceptional Children, 29,* 4-9.

Fox, N. & Ysseldyke, J. (1997). Implementing inclusion at the middle school level: Lessons for a negative example. *Exceptional Children, 64,* 81-98.

Freedman, R.I., & Fesko, S.L. (1996). The meaning of work in the lives of people with significant disabilities: Consumer and family perspectives. *Journal of Rehabilitation, 62,* 49-55.

Fujiura, G.T., & Yamaki, K. (2000). Trends in demography of childhood poverty and disability. *Exceptional Children, 66,* 187-199.

Fullan, M. (1991). *The new meaning of educational change.* New York: Teacher's College Press.

Gamoran, A., & Dreeben R. (1986). Coupling and control in educational organizations. *Administrative Science Quarterly, 31,* 612-632.

Gartin, B., Rumrill, P., & Serebreni, R. (1996). The higher education transition model: Guidelines for facilitating college transition among college-bound students with disabilities. *Teaching Exceptional Children, 29*(1), 30-33.

Garvar-Pinahas, A., & Schmelkin, L. (1989). Administrators' and teachers' attitudes toward mainstreaming. *Remedial and Special Education, 10,* 38-43.

Geertz, C. (1983). Thick description: Toward an interpretive theory of culture. In R. Emerson (Ed.), *Contemporary field research: A collection of readings* (pp.37-59). Boston: Little, Brown.

Gerber, M. (1988). Tolerance and technology of instruction: Implications for special education reform. *Exceptional Children, 54,* 309-314.

Gickling, E., & Theobald, J. (1975). Mainstreaming: Affect or effect. *The Journal of Special Education, 9,* 317-328.

Glaser, B.G. (1978). *Theoretical sensitivity.* Mill Valley, CA: Sociology Press.

Glaser, B., & Strauss, A. (1967). *The discovery of grounded theory: Strategies for qualitative research.* Chicago, IL: Aldine.

Glass, G. (1976). Primary, secondary, and meta-analysis of research. *Educational Researcher, 5,* 3-8.

Glass, G. (1977). Integrating findings: The meta-analysis of research. In L. Shulman (Ed.), *Review of research in education.* Itasca, IL: Peacock Publishers.

Glass, G., & Hopkins, K. (1996). *Statistical methods in education and psychology* (3rd Edition). Needham Heights, MA: Allyn & Bacon.

Glesne, C. & Peshkin, A. (1992). Becoming qualitative researchers: An introduction. White Plains, NY: Longman Publishing.

Guba, E.G. (1978). *Toward a methodology of naturalistic inquiry in educational evaluation.* CSE Monograph Series in Evaluation, 8. Los Angeles: Center for the Study of Evaluation, University of California.

Guba, E.G., & Lincoln, Y. (1981). *Effective evaluation: Improving the usefulness of evaluation results through responsive and naturalistic approaches.* San Francisco: Jossey-Bass.

Hagner, D.C., & Helm, D.T. (1994). Qualitative methods in rehabilitation research. *Rehabilitation Counseling Bulletin, 37,* 290-303.

Hallahan, D.P., & Kauffman, J.M. (2000). *Exceptional learners: Introduction to special education* (8th ed.). Needham Heights, MA: Allyn and Bacon.

Hanson, M. J., & Carta, J. J. (1995). Addressing the challenges of families with multiple risks. *Exceptional Children, 62,* 201-212.

Harris, R. J. (1985). *A primer of multivariate statistics* (2nd ed.). New York: Academic Press.

Hasazi, S., Johnston, A., Liggett, A., & Schattman, R. (1994). A qualitative policy study of the Least Restrictive Environment provision of the Individuals with Disabilities Education Act. *Exceptional Children, 60,* 491-507.

Haworth, J.G., & Conrad, C.F. (1997). *Emblems of quality in higher education: Developing and sustaining high-quality programs.* Boston: Allyn and Bacon.

Hays, W. (1988). *Statistics* (4th ed.). New York: Holt, Rinehart, & Winston.

Heiman, T. & Margalit, M. (1998). Loneliness, depression, and social skills among students with mild mental retardation in different educational settings. *The Journal of Special Education, 32*(3), 154-163.

Heller, K.W., Fredrick, L.D., Best, S., Dykes, M.K., & Cohen, E.T. (2000). Specialized health care procedures in the schools: Training and service delivery. *Exceptional Children, 66,* 173-186.

Helling, I.K. (1988). The life history method. In N.K. Denzin (Ed.), *Studies in symbolic interaction.* Greenwich, CT: JAI.

Henderson, C. (1995). *College freshmen with disabilities: A triennial statistical profile.* Washington, DC: American Council on Education: HEATH Resource Center.

Heppner, P., Kivlighan, D., & Wampold, B. (1992). *Research design in counseling.* Pacific Grove, CA: Brooks/Cole.

Heppner, P., Kivlighan, D., & Wampold, B. (1999). *Research design in counseling* (2nd ed). Pacific Grove, CA: Brooks/Cole.

Hinkle, D., Wiersma, W., & Jurs, S. (1998). *Applied statistics for the behavioral sciences.* Boston: Houghton Mifflin.

Hollenbeck, K., Tindal, G., & Almond, P. (1998). Teachers' knowledge of accommodations as a validity issue in high-stakes testing. *Journal of Special Education, 32,* 175 183.

Hood, A., & Johnson, R. (1997). *Assessment in counseling: A guide to the use of psychological assessment procedures* (2nd ed.). Alexandria, VA: American Counseling Association.

Horne, M. D. (1985). *Attitudes toward handicapped peers: Professional, peer and parent reaction.* Hillsdale, NJ: Lawrence Erlbaum. remedies, litigation, compensation, and other legal considerations. *Exceptional Children, 63,* 451-462.

Howie, J., Gatens-Robinson, E., & Rubin, S. (1992). Applying ethical principles in rehabilitation counseling. *Rehabilitation Education, 6,* 41-55.

Hulme, P. (1995). *Historical overview of nonstandard treatments.* Disabilities and Gifted Education Clearinghouse. (Eric Document Reproduction Service No. 384 156).

Hunter, J., & Schmidt, F. (1990). *Methods of meta-analysis.* Newbury Park, CA: Sage.

Impara, J. C., & Plake, B. S. (Eds.) (1998). *The thirteenth mental measurements yearbook.* Lincoln, NE: Buros Institute of the University of Nebraska. Buros Institute of Mental Measurements: University of Nebraska Press.

Jamieson, J. (1984). Attitudes of educators toward the handicapped. In R.L. Jones (Ed.), *Attitudes and attitude change in special education: Theory and practice* (pp. 206-222). Reston, VA: Council for Exceptional Children.

Johnson, L., Pugach, M, & Hammitte, D. (1988). Barriers to effective special education consultation. *Remedial and Special Education, 9,* 41-47.

Kalton, G. (1983). *Introduction to survey sampling.* Newbury Park, CA: Sage.

Kamps, D., & Tankersley, M. (1996). Prevention of behavioral and conduct disorders: Trends and research issues. *Behavioral Disorders, 22*(1), 41-48.

Kauffman, J.M. (1999). The role of science in behavioral disorders. *Behavioral Disorders, 24,* 265-272.

Kauffman, J.M. (1999). Commentary: Today's special education and its messages for tomorrow. *Journal of Special Education, 32*(4), 244-254.

Kauffman, J.M., Gerber, M.M., & Semmel, M.I. (1988). Arguable assumptions underlying the Regular Education Initiative. *Journal of Learning Disabilities, 21,* 6-12.

Kazdin, A.E. (1982). Single-case research designs. New York: Oxford University Press.

Kazdin, A. (1992). *Research design in clinical psychology* (2nd ed.). Needham Heights, MA: Allyn & Bacon.

Kazdin, A. (1998). *Research design in clinical psychology* (2nd ed.). Needham Heights, MA: Allyn & Bacon.

Kitchner, K. (1984). Intuition, critical evaluation, and ethical principles: The foundation for ethical decision in counseling psychology. *The Counseling Psychologist, 12*(3), 43-55.

Kliewer, C. (1998). Citizenship in the literate community: An ethnography of children with down syndrome and the written word. *Exceptional Children, 64*(2), 167-180.

Kliewer, C. & Landis, D. (1999). Individualizing literacy instruction for young children with moderate to severe disabilities. *Exceptional Children, 66*(1), 85-100.

Klingner, J. K., & Vaughn, S. (1999). Students' perceptions of instruction in inclusion classrooms: Implications for students with learning disabilities. *Exceptional Children, 66*(1), 23 37.

Kosciulek, J. F., & Szymanski, E. M. (1993). Statistical power analysis of rehabilitation counseling research. *Rehabilitation Counseling Bulletin, 36,* 212-219.

Krathwohl, D. R. (1993). *Methods of educational and social science research: An integrated approach.* White Plains, NY: Longman.

Lago-Delello, E. (1998). Classroom dynamics and the development of serious emotional disturbance. *Exceptional Children, 64*(4), , 479-492.

Landrum, T.J., & Tankersley, M. (1999). Emotional and behavioral disorders in the new millenium: The future is now. *Behavioral Disorders, 24,* 319-330.

Landrum, T.J., Tankersley, M., & Cook, B.G. (1999). *Deciding what works in special education: Three perspectives on research to practice issues.* Division on Research's Showcase Presentation. Annual Meeting of the Council for Exceptional Children, Charlotte, NC.

LeCompte, M.D., & Preissle, J. (1993). *Ethnography and qualitative design in education research* (2nd ed.). San Diego: Academic Press.

Lederer, J.M. (2000). Reciprocal teaching of social studies in inclusive elementary classrooms. *Journal of Learning Disabilities, 33*, 91-106.

Lerner, J. (1997). *Learning disabilities: Theories, diagnosis, and teaching strategies* (7th ed.). Boston: Houghton Mifflin.

Levine, H. (1985). Principles of data storage and retrieval for use in qualitative evaluations. *Educational Evaluation and Policy Analysis, 7*, 169-186.

Lin, S. (2000). Coping and adaptation in families of children with cerebral palsy. *Exceptional Children, 66*, 201-218.

Lincoln, Y., & Guba, E. (1985). *Naturalistic inquiry.* Beverly Hills, CA: Sage.

Lirgg, C. (1991). Gender differences in self-confidence in physical activity: A meta analysis of recent studies. *Journal of Sport and Exercise Psychology, 8*, 294-310.

MacMillan, D., Jones, R., & Meyer, C. (1976). Mainstreaming the mildly retarded: Some questions, cautions, and guidelines. *Mental Retardation, 14*, 3-10.

Mallory, B. (1995). The role of social policy in life-cycle transitions. *Exceptional Children, 62*(3), 213-223.

Marn, L., & Koch, L. (1999). The major tasks of adolescence: Implications for transition planning with youths with cerebral palsy. *Work, 13*(1), 51-58.

Marshall, C., & Rossman, G.B. (1989). *Designing qualitative research.* Newbury Park, CA: Sage.

Maxwell, J.A. (1996). *Qualitative research design: An interactive approach.* Thousand Oaks, CA: Sage.

Mayer, R.E. (2000). What is the place of science in educational research? *Educational Researcher, 29*, 38-40.

McGee, G.G., Morrier, M.F., & Daly, T. (1999). An incidental teaching approach to early intervention for toddlers with autism. *Journal of the Association for Persons with Severe Handicaps, 24*, 133-146.

McLeskey, J., Henry, D., & Axelrod, M.I. (1999). Inclusion of students with learning disabilities: An examination of data from Reports to Congress. *Exceptional Children, 66*, 55-66.

McMahon, B., & Shaw, L. (1999). *Enabling lives.* Boca Raton, FL: CRC Press.

McMillan, J., & Schumacher, S. (1997). *Research in education: A conceptual introduction* (4th ed.). New York: Longman.

McPhail, J. (1995). Phenomenology as philosophy and method: Applications to ways of doing special education. *Remedial and Special Education, 16*(3), 159-165, 177.

McReynolds, C., & Koch, L. (1999). Qualitative research designs. In J. Bellini & P. Rumrill, *Research in rehabilitation counseling* (pp. 151-173). Springfield, IL: Charles C Thomas Publishers.

Merriam, S.B. (1988). *The case study research in education.* San Francisco: Jossey Bass.

Merton, R. K. (1968). *Social theory and social structure.* New York : Free Press.

Messick, S. (1980). Test validity and the ethics of assessment. *American Psychologist, 35*, 1012-1027.

Messick, S. (1988). The once and future issues in validity: Assessing the meaning and consequences of measurement. In H. Wainer, & H. I. Braun (Eds.), *Test validity*, (pp. 33-45). Hillsdale, NJ: Erlbaum.

Meyer, J., & Rowan, B. (1977). Institutionalized organizations: Formal structure as myth and ceremony. *American Journal of Sociology, 83*, 340-363.

Miles, M.B. & Huberman, A.M. (1994). *Qualitative data analysis* (2nd ed.). Thousand Oaks, CA: Sage.

Miller, M. (1990). Ethnographic interviews for information about classrooms: An invitation. *Teacher Education and Special Education, 13*(3-4), 233-234.

Miller, M.D., Brownell, M.T., & Smith, S.W. (1999). Factors that predict teachers staying in, leaving, or transferring from the special education classroom. *Exceptional Children, 65,* 201-218.

Mills, P.E., Cole, K. N., Jenkins, J.R., & Dale, P.S. (1998). Effects of differing levels of inclusion on preschoolers with disabilities. *Exceptional Children, 65,* 79-90.

Moore, J., & Fine, M. (1978). Regular and special class teachers' perception of normal and exceptional children and their attitudes toward mainstreaming. *Psychology in the Schools, 15,* 253-259.

Munley, P., Sharkin, B., & Gelso, C. (1988). Reviewer ratings and agreement on manuscripts reviewed for the Journal of Counseling Psychology. *Journal of Counseling Psychology, 35,* 198-202.

Murphy, L.L., Conoley, J.C., & Impara, J.C. (Eds.) (1994). *Tests in print.* IV (Vols. 1 and 2). Lincoln, NE: Buros Institute of the University of Nebraska. Buros Institute of Mental Measurements: University of Nebraska Press.

Murphy, S.T., & Salomone, P.R. (1983). Client and counselor expectations of rehabilitation services. *Rehabilitation Counseling Bulletin, 27,* 81-93.

Nelson, J. S., Epstein, M.H., Bursuck, W.D., Jayanthi, M., & Sawyer, V. (1998). The preferences of middle school students for adatpations made by general education teachers. *Learning Disabilities Research & Practice, 13,* 109-117.

Ochoa, S., & Olivarez, A. (1995). A meta-analysis of peer rating sociometric studies of pupils with learning disabilities. *The Journal of Special Education, 29,* 1-19.

Orwell, G. (1946). Politics and the English language. In G. Orwell (Ed.), *A collection of essays* (pp. 156-171). San Diego: Harcourt, Brace, and Johanovich.

Osborne, A. G., DiMattia, P. & Russo, C. J. (1998). Legal considerations in providing special education services in parochial schools. *Exceptional Children, 64,* 385-394.

Palmer, D.S., Borthwick-Duffy, S.A., & Widaman, K. (1998). Parent perceptions of inclusive practices for their children with significant cognitive disabilities. *Exceptional Children, 64,* 271-178.

Parette, H. P., & Angelo, D. H. (1996). Augmentative and alternative communication impact on families: Trends and future directions. *The Journal of Special Education, 30,* 77-98.

Parker, R., & Szymanski, E. (1996). Editorial: Ethics and publication. *Rehabilitation Counseling Bulletin, 39*(3), 162-165.

Patton, M.Q. (1990). *Qualitative evaluation and research methods* (2nd ed.). Newbury Park, CA: Sage.

Pedazur, E. (1982). *Multiple regression in behavioral research* (2nd Ed.). New York: Harcourt Brace College Publishers.

Polkinghorne, D.E. (1991). Qualitative procedures for counseling research. In C.E. Watkins, & L.J. Schneider (Eds.), *Research in counseling* (pp.163-204). Hillsdale, NJ: Erlbaum.

Popper, K. (1959). *The logic of scientific discovery.* New York: Basic Books.

Purkey, S., & Smith, M. (1983). Effective Schools: A review. *The Elementary School Journal, 83,* 427-452.

Reynolds, M., Wang, M., & Walberg, H. (1987). The necessary restructuring of special education. *Exceptional Children, 53,* 391-398.

Robinson, W.S. (1951). The logical structure of analytic induction. *American Sociological Review, 16,* 812-818.

Rockwell, S., & Guetzloe, E. (1996). Group development for students with emotional/behavioral disorders. *Teaching Exceptional Children, 29*(1), 38-43.

Roessler, R., & Gottcent, J. (1994). The Work Experience Survey: A reasonable accommodation/career development strategy. *Journal of Applied Rehabilitation Counseling, 25*(3), 16-21.

Roessler, R., Reed, C., & Brown, P. (1998). Coping with chronic illness at work: Case studies of five successful employees. *Journal of Vocational Rehabilitation, 10*(3), 261-269.

Rosenthal, R., & Rosnow, R. L. (1969). The volunteer subject. In R. Rosenthal & R. L. Rosnow (eds.), *Artifact in behavioral research,* (pp. 61-118). New York: Academic Press.

Rosnow, R. L., & Rosenthal, R. (1989). Statistical procedures and the justification of knowledge in psychological science. *American Psychologist, 44,* 1276-1284.

Rubin, S., & Roessler, R. (1995). *Foundations of the vocational rehabilitation process.* Austin, TX: Pro-Ed.

Rumrill, P., Roessler, R., & Denny, G. (1997). Increasing confidence in the accommodation request process among persons with multiple sclerosis: A career maintenance self efficacy intervention. *Journal of Job Placement, 13*(1), 5-9.

Ryndak, D.L., Morrison, A.P. & Sommerstein, L. (1999). Literacy before and after inclusion in general education settings: A case study. *Journal of the Association for Persons with Severe Handicaps, 24,* 5-22.

Sage, D. (1996). Adminstrative strategies for achieving inclusive schooling. In S. Stainback & W. Stainback (Eds.), *Inclusion: A guide for educators* (pp. 105-116). Baltimore: Brookes.

Sands, D., & Doll, B. (1996). Fostering self-determination is a developmental task. *Journal of Special Education, 30*(1), 58-76.

Schaller, J., & Parker, R. (1997). Effect of graduate research instruction on perceived research anxiety, research utility, and confidence in research skills. *Rehabilitation Education, 11,* 273-287.

Schmelkin, L. (1981). Teachers' and non-teachers' attitudes toward mainstreaming. *Exceptional Children, 48,* 42-47.

Schriner, K., Rumrill, P., & Parlin, R. (1995). Rethinking disability policy: Equity in the ADA era and the meaning of specialized services for people with disabilities. *Journal of the Health and Human Services Administration, 17*(4), 478-500.

Schumm, J., & Vaughn, S. (1991). Making adaptations for mainstreamed students: General classroom teachers' perspectives. *Remedial and Special Education, 12,* 18-27.

Schumm, J., Vaughn, S., Gordon, J., & Rothlein, L. (1994). General education teachers' beliefs, skills, and practices in planning for mainstreamed students with learning disabilities. *Teacher Education and Special Education, 17,* 22-37.

Scruggs, T., & Mastropieri, M. (1996). Teacher perceptions of mainstreaming/inclusion, 1958-1995: A research synthesis. *Exceptional Children, 63,* 59-74.

Semmel, M.I. (1986). Special education in the year 2000 and beyond: A proposed action agenda for addressing selected ideas. In H. Prehm (Ed.), *The future of special education. Proceedings of the May 1986 CEC Symposium* (pp. 285-354). Reston, VA: The Council for Exceptional Children.

Semmel, M.I., Abernathy, T., Butera, G., & Lesar, S. (1991). Teacher perceptions of the Regular Education Initiative. *Exceptional Children, 58,* 9-24.

Semmel, M.I., Gottlieb, J., & Robinson, N. (1979). Mainstreaming: Perspectives in educating handicapped children in the public schools. In D. Berliner (Ed.), *Review of research in education* (pp. 223-279). Itaska, IL: Peacock Publishers.

Semmel, M.I., & Gerber, M.M. (1997). *The School Environment Project: Final Report.* Special Education Research Laboratory (SERL) Technical Report, University of California, Santa Barbara.

Serlin, R.C. (1987). Hypothesis testing, theory building, and the philosophy of science. *Journal of Counseling Psychology, 34,* 365-371.

Sileo, T.W., & Prater, M.A. (1998). Preparing professionals for partnerships with parents of students with disabilities: Textbook considerations regarding cultural diversity. *Exceptional Children, 64,* 513-528.

Sinclair, E. (1998). Head Start children at risk: Relationship of prenatal drug exposure to iden-tification of special needs and subsequent special education kindergarten placement. *Behavioral Disorders, 23,* 125-133.

Sinclair, M.F., Christenson, S.L., Evelo, D.L., & Hurley, C.M. (1998). Dropout prevention for youth with disabilities: Efficacy of a sustained school engagement procedure. *Exceptional Chilren, 56,* 7-21.

Stainback, W., & Stainback, S. (1989). Common concerns regarding merger. In S. Stainback, W. Stainback, & M. Forest (Eds.), *Educating all students in the mainstream of regular education* (pp. 255-274). Baltimore: Brookes.

Stainback, S., Stainback, W., & Ayres, B. (1996). Schools as inclusive communities. In W. Stainback & S. Stainback (Eds.), *Controversial issues confronting special education: Divergent per-spectives* (2nd ed., pp. 31-43). Boston: Allyn & Bacon.

Steere, D., Gregory, S., Heiny, R., & Butterworth, J. (1995). Lifestyle planning: Considerations for use with people with disabilities. *Rehabilitation Counseling Bulletin, 38*(3), 207-223.

Stevens, J. (1992). *Applied multivariate statistics for the social sciences* (2nd ed.). Hillsdale, NJ: Erlbaum.

Stevens, S. (1946). On the theory of scales of measurement. *Science, 103,* 677-680.

Stevens, S. (1951). Mathematics, measurement, and psychophysics. In S.S. Stevens (Ed.), *Handbook of experimental psychology* (pp. 1-49). New York: Wiley.

Storey, K., & Certo, N. (1996). Natural supports for increasing integration in the workplace for people with disabilities: A review of the literature and guidelines for implementation. *Rehabilitation Counseling Bulletin, 40*(1), 62-77.

Strauss, A., & Corbin, J. (1990). Basics of qualitative research: Grounded theory procedures and techniques. Newbury Park, CA: Sage.

Swanson, H.L., & Hoskyn, M. (1998). Experimental intervention research on students with learning disabilities: A meta-analysis of treatment outcomes. *Review of Educational Research, 68,* 277-321.

Swanson, H.L., Hoskyn, M., & Lee, C. (1999). *Interventions for students with learning disabilities: A meta-analysis of treatment outcomes.* New York: Guilford Press.

Tankersley, M., Kamps, D., Mancina, D., & Weidinger, D. (1996). Social interactions for Head Start children with behavioral risks: Implementation and outcomes. *Journal of Emotional and Behavioral Disorders, 4,* 171-181.

Tarver, S. (1999). *Current practice alerts: Focusing on Direct Instruction.* Reston, VA: CEC-Division for Learning Disabilities and CEC-Division for Research.

Taylor, R. (1999). *Assessment of exceptional children.* Needham Heights, MA: Allyn & Bacon.

Thomas, S., & Rapport, M. (1998). Least restrictive environment: Understanding the direction of the court. *Journal of Special Education, 32*(2), 66-78.

Tracey, T.J. (1991). Counseling research as an applied science. In C. E. Watkins and L. J. Schneider (Eds.), *Research in counseling* (pp. 3-31). Hillsdale, NJ: Lawrence Erlbaum Associates.

U.S. Department of Education (2000). To assure the free appropriate public education of all children with disabilities. *21st annual report to Congress on the implementation of the Individuals with Disabilities Education Act.* Washington, DC: U.S. Government Printing Office.

Vaughn, S., Moody, S.W., & Schumm, J.S. (1998). Broken promises: Reading instruction in the resource room. *Exceptional Children, 64*(2), 211-225.

Villa, R., Thousand, J., Meyers, H., & Nevin, A. (1996). Teacher and administrator perceptions of heterogeneous education. *Exceptional Children, 63,* 29-45.

Walker, M.L. (1993). Participatory action research. Rehabilitation *Counseling Bulletin, 37,* 2-5.

Waller, S.A., Armstrong, K.J., McGrath, A.M., & Sullivan, C.L. (1999). A review of the diag-nostic methods reported in the *Journal of Autism and Developmental Disorders. Journal of Autism and Developmental Disorders, 29,* 485-489.

Wax, R. (1979). Gender and age in fieldwork and fieldwork education: No good thing is done by any man alone. *Social Problems, 26,* 509-523.

Weatherley, R., & Lipsky, M. (1977). Street level bureaucrats and institutional innovation: Implementing special education reform. *Harvard Educational Review, 47,* 171-197.

Wehmeyer, M., & Schwartz, M. (1997). Self-determination and positive adult outcomes: A follow-up study of youth with mental retardation or learning disabilities. *Exceptional Children, 63,* 245-255.

Weiss, R.S. (1994). *Learning from strangers: The art and method of qualitative interviewing.* New York: Free Press.

Wehman, P. (1996). *Life beyond the classroom: Transition strategies for young people with disabilities* (2nd ed.). Baltimore: Brookes.

Wiener, J., & Sunohara, G. (1998). Parents' perceptions of the quality of friendship of their children with learning disabilities. *Learning Disabilities Research and Practice, 13,* 242-257.

Wiersma, W. (2000). *Research methods in education: An introduction (7th ed.).* Boston: Allyn & Bacon.

Will, M. (1986). *Educating students with learning problems: A shared responsibility.* Washington, DC: Office of Special Education and Rehabilitative Services, U. S. Department of Education.

Winston, R.B. (1985). A suggested procedure for determining order of authorship in research publications. *Journal of Counseling and Development, 63,* 5150519.

Wolfensberger, W. (1994). A personal interpretation of the mental retardation scene in light of the "signs of the times." *Mental Retardation, 32,* 19-33.

Wright, B.A. (1983). *Physical disability: A psychosocial approach* (2nd ed.). NY: Harper Collins.

Yin, R.K. (1989). *Case study research: Design and methods.* Newbury Park, CA: Sage.

Zigmond, N., & Baker, J. (1990). Mainstream experiences for learning disabled students (Project MELD): Preliminary report. *Exceptional Children, 57,* 176-185.

Zigmond, N., Jenkins, J., Fuchs, L., Deno, S., Fuchs, D., Baker, J., Jenkins, L., & Couthino, M. (1995). Special education in restructured schools: Findings from three multi-year studies. *Phi Delta Kappan, 76,* 531-540.

INDEX

DATE DUE

GAYLORD

PRINTED IN U.S.A.